Small-Business Ownership for Creative People

Jennifer Lawler

Small-Business Ownership
for Creative People

Jennifer Lawler

ALETHEIA
Publications

Lawler, Jennifer
Small-business ownership for creative people

Library of Congress Catalog Card Number: 99-73599
ISBN: 0-9639260-9-8

Cover design: Bart Solenthaler
Interior design and composition: Guy J. Smith
Copyeditor: Leslie Bernstein

Aletheia Publications, Inc.
46 Bell Hollow Rd.
Putnam Valley, NY 10579

Printed in Canada
10 9 8 7 6 5 4 3 2 1

Contents

The author publishes two newsletters of interest to creative freelancers. *Small Business Ownership* helps creative small-business owners run their businesses more effectively. *Writers at Work* provides information for writers at all experience levels. For a sample copy or subscription information, write to: P. O. Box 3724, Lawrence, Kansas 66046.

Acknowledgments

Many creative friends and acquaintances shared their ideas and tips for making creative business ownership more prosperous. They deserve my gratitude. Special thanks is owed to Susan Lennon, a writer whose hard-nosed business practices make her a model to emulate.

I must also thank my husband, Bret Kay, a small-business owner himself, for kindly shepherding me over the years through the process of understanding small-business basics (although it must be said that he actually enjoys subjects beginning with the word "accounting.")

My parents, Tom and Yvonne Lawler, should be acknowledged as well. Without them, this book would *never* have been finished. Their encouragement over the years has meant a great deal to me, although I probably never mention it.

And to Jessica, who makes everything (even sleepless nights) worthwhile.

Introduction

Small-Business Ownership for Creative People takes a step-by-step approach to starting up and running the kinds of small businesses that creative people—writers, photographers, artists—are most likely to be involved in. Although creative people may think of their work as a profession or a career, making and selling creative work is really a small business. Most often, such businesses have a single owner/proprietor, which means that one person has to do it all. This can seem overwhelming, but creative people can manage it by understanding the principles of business.

This book gives an overview of the general principles small-business owners need to know. It also covers common problems creative people encounter when they run small businesses. It is intended to be a place to start. It will give you the information you need to know so that you can find out more about your particular needs and concerns. It will help you understand and speak to other business professionals you must deal with (attorneys, accountants), but it doesn't replace the guidance of these professionals. Plenty of detailed information and examples from actual small businesses will help you learn how to make your business successful.

How This Book Works

Small-Business Ownership for Creative People provides easy-to-understand business basics, presented in a nonthreatening way. You won't be expected to know the difference between a cash-basis business and an accrual-basis business. You won't even be expected to *want* to know the difference. But the book helps motivate you to see that understanding this (and other business principles) can make you more successful. The book also provides specifics for making the job easier (how to handle working alone, marketing for creative people, what equipment you really need to get started). Even the very beginner will be able to understand and apply these business basics.

The book also serves as a motivational tool for creative people who are thinking of quitting their day jobs to pursue their creative goals. It encourages you to see that considering your work as a business will make it more profitable and will allow you the time and opportunity to pursue low-paying or nonpaying (but still fulfilling) artistic endeavors as well. Many people dream of the day they can work creatively for a living. Here's how to make the dream come true.

Sixteen chapters cover the basics of running a small business. An index, a glossary of business terms, and an appendix listing organizations and publications of interest will also help you develop the know-how to apply business principles to your creative work. Numerous charts and graphs illustrate the main points so that you can see what is being described.

How This Books is Different

A couple of years ago, when I first realized that I was actually running a small business, I turned to the business section of the bookstore for help. There I found hundreds of books on marketing, time management, home offices, and small-business ownership. I even bought quite a few of them. But not one of these books really addressed my needs. A business plan is a fine document for a manufacturer to have, but it wasn't a very useful tool for me (I don't know a single creative person who ever had a business plan).

Like most creative people, I will never be able to afford an assistant, so I'll never need to know how to hire one. What I did need to know was how to be my own assistant and how to organize my work so that I wasn't spending all my time managing my office instead of writing. I also needed to learn how to line up contract help (artists, lawyers) for specific projects.

Instead of complicated budgeting and forecasting, I needed to learn how much it cost to make each sale, how I could make more from each sale, and how to keep overhead down. This included ideas as simple as *not* browsing through the office products store or the computer warehouse (there's way too much temptation in that!) and educating myself on products and services specific to my business.

The book covers everything from determining what to charge to performing excellent customer service—but all slanted toward the creative person with no business background. If you're a creative person already working full-time at your business, or if you're just thinking about becoming a writer or photographer, this book is for you. If you're unsure about making the jump to full-time small-business ownership, the book also addresses the needs of part-time small-business ownership. There's even a chapter on deciding whether you're ready to take the plunge. You can skip around to learn more about special topics of interest, but reading it from front to back will help you avoid the pitfalls that ensnare many creative people, and will give you plenty of ideas and advice on making your business successful.

By taking the time to pick up this book, you've taken an important step toward owning a small business. Welcome to the challenging but rewarding world of making a living from your creativity (with a little help from your brain)!

1

Are You Ready to Make the Move?

IF YOU'RE a creative person—a writer, an artist, a photographer—chances are you dream of the time when you can make a living by your art. If you don't dream of that time, it's probably because you're already making that dream come true. This book can help by providing the information you need about business principles and the specifics you must have to make your creative business successful. If you treat your creativity as if it's a business, you'll be able to make more money, do more of the projects you want to do, and otherwise fulfill your hopes and aspirations.

But if you haven't yet started to make that dream a reality, you're probably wondering how to begin. You might be wondering if you're ready to make the move.

Are you ready?

People know they are ready in different ways. Some people plan their move over months and even years, acquiring clients and building portfolios. Others know they are ready when they quit their day jobs in the middle of the day. As for me, I combined both approaches. I had built up a steady clientele—and then quit my day job in the middle of the day. But the first option, being prepared, is the better one. Before you make plans to abandon your current occupation, you should consider some factors that might influence your decision.

Why Start a Business?

Before committing time, money, and effort to starting your business, you must ask yourself why you want to start your own creative business. Is it because you're tired of working hard? Most self-employed business owners work longer hours than their corporate counterparts. If you're tired of working 50 hours a week, consider that on average full-time freelancers work 60 hours a week—and usually for less pay than if they worked for a traditional employer. However, there is some flexibility. You can work in your pajamas. You can cook breakfast for your kids every morning. You can work at midnight if that's when the urge strikes you. If you want to take a day off and go to the zoo, you can. You just don't get paid to do it.

Most creative people choose to become self-employed because they reach a point where they can no longer stand fitting into a corporate profile that doesn't suit them. They want to be their own boss. They want to explore interesting subjects and turn down projects that don't appeal to them. They want more control over their work lives and more control over how their work and personal lives intersect. They understand the amount of work involved and have prepared for it. If you're interested in becoming self-employed, do it for the right reasons, and don't make an ill-informed decision.

Do You Have Experience?

Before you take the plunge, it is essential to gain proficiency in your field. Do you have any experience in your chosen field? If you dream of being a writer but have never actually written anything, the freelance life is not for you. If you think it might be, make the effort to obtain some assignments before abandoning your day job. When the reality of deadlines and late nights hits, you might find that you prefer your regular occupation.

Are You a Self-Starter?

You also need to ask yourself honestly if you're a self-starter. Can you motivate yourself to begin working day after day even without a boss to motivate you? It may sound like heaven to be free of your inconsiderate boss and unkind coworkers, but they'll be replaced by inconsiderate and unkind clients who rarely pay on time. Are you able to work hard every day even if you're the only one who sees you doing so? Remember that hard work and effort usually pay off when you're in someone else's employ, but they don't necessarily pay off when you're on your own. As an employee at someone else's company, you might work hard on a presentation for a potential client. The client might not hire your company. You'll be disappointed, but you'll probably still get paid. If the same thing happens when you freelance, you *don't* get paid.

Do You Need a Steady Paycheck?

Which leads to the next point to consider. How much do you need the security of a regular paycheck? If the household relies on you to bring home a certain amount of money every week, you'll have to be extremely cautious about freelancing, especially until you have built up a client base. If you don't mind feast one week, famine the next, you're an ideal candidate for owning your own creative business.

Also consider your financial goals for the next few years. Are you planning to buy a house? Self-employed creative people may have trouble getting mortgage and other loans unless they have been in business for at least five years and can show tax returns indicating consistent income. If you're planning on making major purchases in the next few years, either reconsider the purchases themselves or think about staying with your present position until after you've secured the loan or made the purchase.

Do You Have the Support of Your Family?

If there are other family members to consider—a spouse or children—you'll need their help and input as well. You may have to convert them to your cause. Talking about the importance of your dreams is a start. You'll need their full cooperation if you expect them to go along with the feast-or-famine program.

If you're incredibly lucky or incredibly smart (or maybe both) and you're with someone who's supportive, you might ask if that person would be willing to shoulder more of the financial burden (or would be willing to give up some things) so that you can pursue your dream. Some people negotiate a chance to pursue a dream by giving themselves a certain period of time to start contributing steady income to the household. If they can't meet the deadline, they return to their former career. (This works best if you *can* return to your former career. In other words, don't burn your bridges.) The drawback to this approach is that creative businesses require time and persistence to become successful. Make sure you give yourself every opportunity to succeed. Although you must be prepared to fail, you must also be convinced that you won't and that any problems you have at first are temporary. You need to gain the support of your family and significant others, but they should also be aware that you're in it for the long haul.

Is Your Personality Suited to Freelancing?

Assess your personality. If you're a security-oriented person, keeping your day job and working creatively part-time may be the best solution (unless you're trying to break your addiction to security). One talented writer found that she didn't have the stomach for the tension that came with freelancing—getting assignments, meeting deadlines, handling clients. Her significant other wasn't exactly helpful, either. "I do better with a boss," she says, "and I enjoy my writing as a hobby." With the pressure off, her art is a refuge, not another stress-filled activity.

Think about whether you're able to work alone. Can you do it day after day, week after week, month after month without starting an affair with the UPS driver? If you don't have a spouse or other family members who are home at least now and then, you'll need an extensive support group of friends and other creative people. Even if you do have a spouse and family, you'll probably need a support group anyway. You must not only *tolerate* working alone, you must *enjoy* it. If you don't enjoy working alone, you'll be finding excuses to avoid working. You'll be going to lunch with your mother or shopping with friends instead of finishing the project that's due tomorrow.

```
┌─────────────────────────────────────────────────────────────┐
│                          Figure 1                            │
│                       Are You Ready?                         │
│                                                              │
│   Do you have experience in the field?                       │
│                                                              │
│   Are you a self-starter?                                    │
│                                                              │
│   Can you live without a steady paycheck?                    │
│                                                              │
│   Are you able to work alone?                                │
│                                                              │
│   Are you free of financial concerns (e.g., medical insurance,│
│   retirement fund)?                                          │
│                                                              │
└─────────────────────────────────────────────────────────────┘
```

Additional Concerns

Finally, consider these last concerns. Do you have any medical problems that might make it difficult for you to get health or life insurance on your own? If that's the case, you may need to stick with your job for the benefits. Also, if you're near retirement or close to being vested in a retirement program through your employer, you might be wise to wait a few years before you make your move, simply because of the financial considerations.

However, if you meet the criteria—you don't mind uneven income, you're a self-starter, you enjoy working alone, and you're in good health (or covered under a spouse's medical plan)—you'll probably truly enjoy the rewards of running your own creative business.

Committing to a Creative Business

Many creative people begin their businesses part-time. Although this can make it more difficult to get certain clients or assignments, it also takes away much of the risk, fear, and uncertainty. It's a good way to start building the portfolio or gathering the clips you'll need to get the bigger assignments and the better clients.

Holding down a full-time job and working creatively part-time while juggling a family, a social life, and other interests may seem like a lot to ask, but the truth is that people who own creative small businesses usually work at least 60 hours a week. In fact, many full-time freelancers will tell you that they're never not working, it's just that sometimes their hands are doing other things.

As you consider making the transition to pursuing your creative dreams, consider the many demands on your time. Then identify the three things that are most important to you. These might include relationships, such as a spouse or children or good friends. They might include hobbies, such as golf, horseback riding, or woodworking. Consider all the things that are important in your life and choose the top three. If working creatively is not on your top-three list, then keep it as a wonderful part-time hobby, but don't try to make it a business.

You must be passionately committed to your creative business to be successful. But if you *are* passionately committed, you *will* be successful. Sometimes you'll be more successful than at other times, and maybe you'll never bring home six figures, but you'll be able to make a living at it.

Before You Begin

Before you make the transition, give yourself time. Regardless of your personal circumstances, you should set aside enough money in savings to cover those shortfalls that inevitably result when starting a small business. You'll also need to set up your office with essential equipment and supplies. If you're a writer, that includes a good computer with a good letter-quality printer, an e-mail service, and probably a fax machine that can double as a copier. You'll need a desk (as large as you can manage) and plenty of storage for files. You'll also need bookshelves filled with reference books—an unabridged dictionary, a thesaurus, an encyclopedia, and general references in your area(s) of expertise. Then you'll need office supplies: printer paper, printer cartridges, envelopes of all shapes and sizes, pens, address labels, and sundries. That's the minimum (well, the minimum is a typewriter and a ream of white paper, but realistically speaking, the require-ments listed here are the basics).

If you went out and bought all that today, you could easily spend $10,000 in one shopping spree. But if you acquire what you need over time, it won't be long before you have what is necessary without having gone into debt for it (at least not too deeply). Giving yourself time also means you can pick up some good deals you might otherwise have missed if you'd been too rushed, such as your cousin George's antique lawyer's desk or the slightly used computer from your mother's ill-fated attempt to go on-line. Always tell everyone you know what pieces of equipment you're interested in. You'd be surprised what you can purchase cheaply or even get for free this way.

Most important, as you save money and wisely purchase the necessary equipment, you can acquire clients who will form the basis of your business. Then, once you begin running your busi-ness full-time, you'll have a core client list ready and waiting.

Combining Employment with Business Ownership

Some experts recommend that you continue with your day job until your freelance income reaches about half your day job in-come; then, when you make the switch to full-time, you won't suffer an abrupt change in income level (at least theoretically). Instead of switching from a full-time job to a full-time business, another possibility is to go from a full-time day job to a part-time day job once you've begun lining up clients. Such an arrange-ment could go on indefinitely. The only drawback is that it isn't always possible or well-paying enough to be worthwhile. The point of this approach is to free up more time for you to work at your business while guaranteeing a certain, though perhaps small, income each month.

Some people manage combinations of full- and part-time day jobs with full- and part-time creative businesses throughout their lives and enjoy the whole experience, but most creative people want to make a living solely by their creativity. The following chapters will help you do just that. These essentials apply whether you keep your day job or not and whether you work at your business full-time or part-time. Chapter 16 has more information on combining employment and business ownership.

Remember, though, that advance planning is essential. Instead of making an impulsive decision, plan your business and try not to burn any bridges. If you suddenly quit your job and must rely on your freelance income without being prepared, you may find yourself making poor decisions based on fear or uncertainty. Give yourself the best chance possible to become successful.

2

Starting a Creative Small Business

IF YOU decide you want to start making a living from your creativity, you have to know the basics of operating a business. To some optimists, operating a business seems simple and straightforward at first: make money, pay bills. But of course it isn't quite that simple and straightforward.

Most creative people, however, believe business is more complicated than it actually is. Many artistically inclined souls are afraid to strike out on their own because those business details seem overwhelming. Relax. If you're smart enough to create something worthwhile, you're smart enough to master business basics. The problem is that creative people tend to fall asleep when subjects as boring as "macroeconomics" and "contractual liability" come up. Although it is not possible to make those topics interesting, I promise to introduce you to them as painlessly as possible.

If you're contemplating starting a small business, you'll discover—or may already have discovered—that most of what is written about business ownership has absolutely nothing to do with you. Business books and articles spend a lot of time talking about training employees and finding your successor as CEO (that would be chief executive officer). If you're like most freelancers, once you're gone, so is your business. And if you had enough money to hire an employee, you wouldn't be wondering how you're going to pay for your Ford's new alternator. Ergo, most of this stuff is worthless to you. In fact, it's worse than worthless because it makes the entire concept of business ownership seem alien, unattainable, and fraught with danger. But business ownership isn't hard. At least, it isn't hard the way analytical calculus is hard. Business ownership is hard because it requires hard work. But it isn't alien, unattainable, or even very much fraught with danger. You just have to decide that it's worth doing.

The Business Plan

If you ask businesspeople for advice, the first thing they'll tell you is to write a business plan. A business plan is a description of the business you intend to run, how you plan to market it, and how much money you expect to earn. I've written a couple of business plans for people in my life (not that I'm proud of this), and some of these pieces run to 200 pages.

The main point of the business plan is to ensure that everyone in the organization understands what the company does and what direction it is taking. The plan is also used to induce banks and other financial backers to lend the owner(s) money.

I don't know of a single creative person who started a business with a business plan. I know I didn't. Basically, my plan was this: I was going to publish anything I could convince an editor to publish, and I was going to try to earn a living at it.

My significant other, Bret (who makes an occasional appearance in these pages as the guru of small-business ownership), owns a business himself. His business is providing air filtration services for industrial and commercial customers. He has a staff of twelve, a fleet of service vans, and a building in a business park. He has borrowed large sums of money from the bank to buy equipment and land, and he has a number of employees who must all be on the same track. Besides, he has a degree in business. Of course he has a business plan.

I, like most other creative people, work from a spare bedroom furnished with old bookshelves and computer equipment.

A pair of dogs that wander in and out liven up the decor. I have no staff, unless you count the babysitter (and since she is essential to the success of my business, maybe you can). I have never had a formal business plan, nor have I ever seen any particular reason to waste time developing one.

The Informal Business Plan

However, I have always set goals and parameters for my business, and in this way I have always had an informal plan. An informal plan is a good idea for anyone interested in operating a creative business. An informal plan should simply list what you want to accomplish as a freelancer or self-employed creative person and how you can accomplish it.

The most important thing you need to know is what your business will be. This is more difficult than it first appears. In the beginning, I decided I would write anything for anybody. But then I realized I had certain strengths and weaknesses. I am not, for instance, a very good article writer. Oh, I can do it, but not without a lot of agony and frustration, mostly because I am bullheaded and want to do things my way. I also over-research everything, so that I end up with three boxes of information for a single 800-word article. I learned that books were my thing—or "niche," which is the hot new business buzzword. Now I write books, with an occasional technical writing or editing project. I do write articles, but only to promote my books. I simply take a few pages of information from one of my books, revise it, add an introduction and conclusion, call it an excerpt, and I'm set. I know it's my business to write books, and I've gotten pretty good at it since I'm no longer trying to convince myself to become an article writer.

Dena, an artist, wanted time to paint. She knew she wouldn't be able to feed her cats that way, so she considered what she could do as an artist to support her painting habit. She decided that she wanted to use her work experience to design and create vinyl signs for vehicles. This was a surprising choice but a sensible one. (Think of all the businesses that have their names on their delivery vehicles. Someone has to put those names there.)

Instead of thinking she would do whatever people wanted to hire her to do, Dena found the right business focus for her.

Another writer—call her Stacy—has never decided what she wants to do. She just takes whatever comes along. This leaves her with little expertise in any specific subject matter. Since she hasn't defined what she does, her energy is scattered everywhere and she doesn't accomplish much. Needless to say, Stacy's approach is not very proactive. She is dissatisfied because she is not very successful. If Stacy would simply decide what her writing interests were and pursue assignments based on them, she would soon become more successful. As she developed her expertise, she would be able to attract other, better-paying clients and editors. But she is afraid that defining her writing goals will somehow limit her. In fact, it is her inability to define her writing goals that is limiting her, making her expend a lot of energy with little to show for it.

Defining a Market or Audience

Once you know what you plan to do in your business—and this doesn't mean you can never change your plan or take on projects outside your area—you need to identify your market and your audience. If you don't consider your audience/market, you can end up without any clients or buyers. Magazine article writers need to know their editors and the types of people who read the magazines they submit to. Photographers need to consider who would be interested in their area of expertise. A wedding photographer can certainly shoot weddings, but he or she could expand the market by pursuing couples celebrating anniversaries, coworkers planning retirement dinners, or people organizing other ceremonies.

Think of ways to increase your audience or market that won't change the nature of your business. If you paint portraits, increasing your market by also photographing people isn't necessarily the best approach. Instead, think about how the same skills can apply to different groups. You paint portraits of debutantes? Maybe you could also paint portraits of corporate bigwigs, local political leaders, and prominent business owners. You need to consider the potential audience and market for your business as well as for individual projects.

Marketing Your Services

Dena, the artist, determined that many local businesses used vehicles for delivery or transportation of goods and services, and that they might be interested in putting signs on those vehicles. But she had to figure out how to get their attention. This is the third point to consider in your informal plan. How will you market your services? Most writers follow the tried-and-true method of querying editors of likely magazines or publishing houses. But they could also pursue business-related writing or technical writing by contacting nearby businesses. They could write memoirs for families or histories for churches or colleges. If they chose these subjects, they would need to consider the best method for advertising their skills, such as by direct mail, direct phone contact, a display ad in the telephone book, or other methods. The writer also needs to consider ideas beyond the immediate sale to an editor. He or she could have friends write letters to the editor when an article comes out. When a writer's book is released, he or she could tell the local press, arrange book signings, and send postcards to friends and relatives. (Chapter 13 provides additional information on marketing.)

You also need to think about the competition. What can you provide that is special? If you're a photographer, why should a person choose you to shoot their wedding? Do you have tons of experience? Have all your customers been satisfied customers? Do you provide a free eight-by-ten with every order over $100? If you're a writer, what experience or perspective do you bring to an issue? How much have you published? Do you never miss a deadline? Do you always provide a floppy disk or electronic file with your manuscript for the convenience of the editor?

Tracking Expenses

Your informal business plan should also include a method for keeping track of finances. It is essential for small-business owners to

---

Figure 2

Informal Business Plan Essentials

Before you get started, you need to hammer out the basics of your intended business. You don't need to tear your hair out over this. Just sit down with a legal pad and a pen and maybe a good Chardonnay and do a little brainstorming.

What will your business be? Focus, focus, focus!

Who is your market or audience? "Anyone I can rope into it" is not the right answer.

How will you market your product or service? Doing whatever your competitors do is *not* ideal.

How will you keep track of expenses? Relying on the bank to send you overdraft notices is not the most proactive approach.

---

keep expenses under firm control. When you're employed by someone else and you need a new phone or a computer upgrade, you simply request it and sooner or later (if your needs are legitimate) the phone or upgrade magically appears on your desk. This is not the case when you're a small-business owner. You need to think long and hard before spending money on the new phone or the new upgrade. If you absolutely must have the phone—otherwise no one can call and offer you a contract—you need to know your minimum requirements. Yes, you should purchase good-quality equipment, but is there really a $30 difference in quality between two otherwise identical phones? In order to track expenses (and pay taxes correctly), you need to keep financial records, which will be discussed in Chapter 3.

Types of Business Ownership

Once you have a sense of the nature of your business, your intended audience/market, and how you might reach them, you need to know the form of business organization you intend to run. If you are a freelancer with no partners in the business, you run a *sole proprietorship*. There's just you and the cat, and the cat does not materially participate. A sole proprietorship is the least complicated type of business to own, but it has some drawbacks. A business with a single owner is closely linked to the proprietor's (owner's) personal wealth (or lack thereof). If your business gets sued, you get sued. If your business goes bankrupt, guess what? There is no way to protect your personal assets, such as your car or home, should a financial loss occur in connection with your business. (If you have a spouse with assets and earnings, your spouse's assets and earnings are also at risk.) But a sole proprietorship is very easy to handle at tax time. Several special forms are used, but the taxes are simply part of your personal income tax. You don't file separately for your business. (Tax issues are discussed in Chapter 4.) You typically don't have to license or register a small business (with certain exceptions), making start-up a snap.

A *general partnership* is a business with two or more principal partners. (The cat is optional.) The partners, called general partners, agree on each person's financial responsibility, duties, and compensation. A general partnership, like a sole proprietorship, doesn't protect the owners from business-related lawsuits. If one partner gets sued while acting for the business in any capacity, the other partner is equally at risk. Since personal wealth and income are not protected, the spouses of partners can be affected by a lawsuit or bankruptcy.

Partnerships are commonly used when one person has an idea and another has the financial backing for it, but they are sometimes used when two or more creative people with complementary skills decide to go into business together. Some states require partnerships to register and further require the parties to have a written agreement outlining the details of the partnership. States that don't require an agreement assume a 50-50 split of revenue (money earned) and expenses (money spent) unless a written agreement specifies otherwise. Beyond this, a separate bank account in the name of the partnership is required, and a separate income tax statement must be filed with the federal, state, and local governments. Any taxes due are owed by the individuals, however, and appear on each partner's individual income tax returns. This keeps the tax record-keeping simpler than for other business organizations with more than one owner. (Partnerships are discussed in more detail in Chapter 14.)

You can also incorporate your business. This always requires a lawyer (don't let anyone tell you otherwise) and can be expensive and time-consuming. *Corporations* limit or reduce a business owner's liability. The personal wealth of the owner(s) is not at stake, with the exception of anything he or she actually invested in the business. Therefore, if someone sues the company, the company and its profits could be lost, but the owner's personal wealth (e.g., your house) would not be at stake. The corporation itself is recognized as a separate entity, just like a person, in the eyes of the government.

There are two main types of corporations: C corporations and Subchapter S corporations. *C corporations* must file separate income tax statements and pay corporate income taxes. Owners are paid salaries or dividends that are further taxed as their personal income. For this reason, C corporations make profits that are "double taxed." *S corporations* allow the owners to record income on their personal income tax statements and so avoid double taxation. Only large companies or those with complicated ownership issues need to be registered as C corporations. Most creative small-business owners can incorporate as S corporations.

Another type of corporation, called a *limited liability corporation* (sometimes called a *limited liability company*), also limits the owners' potential liability and has many similarities to a partnership. The liability of the partners is limited to whatever they have invested in the business. Like an S corporation, a limited liability corporation (LLC) allows business income to be reported on the owners' personal income tax statements, thus avoiding double taxation. An LLC allows different owners to share in the profits differently, which cannot be done with an S corporation.

All three types of corporations must be registered with the state and federal governments. Also required are a written agreement among the owners, special separate income tax statements,

---

Figure 3
Types of Business Ownership

Sole proprietorship
   simplest type of business ownership
   one owner
   unlimited liability
   simple income taxes (relatively speaking)

Partnership
   simplest type of business ownership with two or more
      owners
   unlimited liability
   slightly more difficult income taxes

C Corporation
   complex type of business ownership
   limited liability
   complicated taxes
   "double taxed" profits

Subchapter S Corporation
   complex type of business ownership
   limited liability
   moderately complex taxes

Limited Liability Corporation
   moderately complicated hybrid of partnership and
      corporation
   limited liability
   moderately complex taxes

---

a separate business bank account, and slightly more complicated record-keeping.

All partnerships and corporations must obtain an employer identification number (called, not very originally, an EIN) from the federal government. This number appears on tax and payroll paperwork. Even if the business has no employees, the number is required. If you run a sole proprietorship and you employ others, you must also request an EIN. (If you run a sole proprietorship and it's just you and the cat, you don't need an EIN.) An EIN can be obtained by using IRS Form SS-4, Application for Employer Identification Number.

Professional Liability

Although the idea of protecting yourself from lawsuits is appealing, corporations are not necessarily the best choice for creative people. Why? Because being the owner of a corporation or LLC does not prevent you from being sued under professional liability laws. Professional liability means that people in certain professions—physicians, lawyers, writers—are personally responsible for the actions and outcomes that occur when they practice their profession, regardless of the form of the business they own and regardless of whom they are employed by.

A writer can be personally sued for plagiarism or copyright infringement regardless of the type of business she runs. If she is found guilty, her business, home, and personal assets can all be lost. A photographer can be personally sued for invasion of privacy even if the act occurred while he was employed by the local newspaper and was acting under the direction of the managing editor (the paper and managing editor can also be sued).

Professional liability can be a serious concern, depending on your business. If you're an investigative reporter, or you write unauthorized biographies, you might get sued—and, however unfairly, lose. You can protect yourself with professional liability insurance, which is discussed in Chapter 6. You should obtain written permission from subjects before taking their photographs or telling their stories. You should familiarize yourself with copyright law so that you don't mistakenly infringe on another person's rights. An attorney with experience in professional liability law can help you decide whether you are at risk.

Incorporating may make sense if your company will employ other people or if it will own land or expensive equipment. If you employ an engineering student to deliver the fruit baskets that you make and that person is involved in an auto accident, your company can be sued. If your company is a corporation, the amount you could lose is limited to your business. Professional liability would not be an issue in a case like this, since having an accident while delivering fruit baskets is not the same as publishing defamatory statements about the shift manager at the hardware store.

If you need a bank loan for your business, you may be required to form a corporation in order to protect the bank's financial liability. One writer who freelances for the health care industry incorporated her business because she found that she got paid faster as a corporation than as an individual. Since writing is the lowest and slowest paid occupation on earth (with the exception of fine art), every little edge helps.

You can change the form of your business as it grows and changes. You may begin as a sole proprietor, then decide to take on a partner and form a partnership. As your profits grow, you might decide to form a corporation for the tax benefits. Or if you begin a partnership and your partner doesn't hold up his or her end of the deal, you can become a sole proprietor. Consult an attorney to learn more about the pros and cons of each type of business ownership.

Your Company Name

You can give your business a name even if you run a sole proprietorship. You don't have to incorporate to use a "doing business as" name (also called a "dba"). All you have to do is register the fictitious name, usually with the state, county, and/or city clerk. This requires a small fee.

If you do use a fictitious name as a sole proprietor, you can't call your company an LLC or a corporation or put "Inc." somewhere in the name. Beyond that, practically anything is acceptable. If your clients will be local, that's probably all you need to worry about doing.

For complete protection of your company name, however, you can file for trademark registration with the federal government. Minions will conduct what amounts to a title search, and

if no other company has the name, you'll be allowed to trademark
it. This means that if someone else uses your company's name, you
can send them mean letters telling them to stop. Applying to trademark your company name prevents you from using a company
name belonging to someone else. That way, you won't receive a
letter six years down the road saying you have to change the name
of your company or prepare to defend a lawsuit. This can happen
even if you used the name first, if you didn't register it first. The
drawback, of course, is that trademark registration takes time and
costs several hundred dollars. (Those minions are expensive.) It
may be worthwhile if you'll have clients from across the country
and it's possible that your company name could become widely
known. You can apply for trademark registration at any time; it
doesn't have to be done the second you open your business.

Special Requirements

You'll need to learn about any special requirements your city and
state has for businesses. Sometimes special licenses are required
(for instance, to practice medicine or to cut hair or to sell real estate). Find out if you need to register with any regulatory agency.
Corporations are overseen by several commissions; financial advisors must register with the Securities Exchange Commission; other
occupations require other registration. You can check with trade
and professional associations for statewide and national licenses and
registration. For rules and regulations regarding your city or county,
the local office of the Small Business Administration (SBA) is as good
a place to start as any. Be forewarned that the SBA maintains a con-
descending attitude toward creative people, apparently as a matter
of policy, but as long as you call or visit with a list of specific questions or concerns, the SBA can point you in the right direction and
provide useful resources. The first thing they always (always!) ask is
whether you have a business plan, regardless of what you want to
know. Tell them you're researching it, which is why you're talking to
them. Much of their information applies to manufacturing or service businesses with employees, so you will have to make them
focus on your particular issues instead of letting them tell you what

you would do if you were going to open a chemical processing plant. The SBA is run mostly by government employees who failed as small-business owners themselves, so don't take them too seriously when they question your ability to run a business, which they will.

Zoning Laws

Most residential areas have zoning laws prohibiting people from operating businesses from their homes. Such laws are intended to prevent neighborhood blight and security problems (garish signs, increased traffic, delivery trucks blocking access, people coming and going at unseemly hours). If you're a writer who conducts most of her business over the phone and through the mail, zoning laws aren't a big deal. If you're a photographer and your clients meet with you at your house, you might have a problem, particularly if a neighbor complains. To address potential problems, always maintain friendly relations with your neighbors and your neighborhood association. Be willing to compromise. Perhaps you could meet some of your clients at a nearby coffee shop or tell them that, as an added service, you will visit them. Know local zoning ordinances because being in violation of them is hard on your wallet and can even put you out of business.

You should also check local ordinances to find out whether you need a business license to operate your type of business. Business licenses are usually readily available for a small fee. Call city hall or the city clerk and ask for guidelines for small-business owners and home-based business owners.

If you sell a product, you'll collect sales tax and turn it over to the appropriate government offices. Professional services, such as writing an article, are exempt from sales tax. As long as you report your income, no problem. But if you're a photographer who sells photo albums as a sideline, or a potter who sells vases, you will need to collect and remit taxes to the city, county, and state. To determine how to do so, contact the city clerk, county clerk, and state treasurer, since each may have different reporting requirements. The SBA also has advice on collecting and remitting sales taxes. Once you obtain a sales tax number, you can purchase your supplies on a tax-exempt basis, which can save you money.

If your community imposes property taxes on personal property such as furniture or computers, your business will owe business taxes on its assets (the things it owns). Check with your local tax assessor to determine what you need to do to pay these taxes. If you don't call the assessor yourself, he or she may not call you for ten years, and by then you'll owe twelve million dollars in back taxes, interest, and penalties, give or take a few bucks.

Renting Space

If you decide to rent space in order to meet zoning regulations or get the office or work area you need, be certain you select an appropriate site. One artist needed space for her ceramics studio, but since she needed a work space, not a retail space, she was able to negotiate an inexpensive rent for the top floor of a downtown restaurant. If you rent retail space, you're going to put more pressure on yourself to make enough money to pay the rent and meet your personal expenses, so consider alternatives. You might join a co-op. These are partnerships of people with similar creative interests who display their products together, taking turns tending the store. Be certain that such an operation is well run before getting involved, and make sure that whoever is responsible for signing the lease is making the rent payments. Co-ops can also be found that supply office space and answering/secretarial services for those who need someone to cover the office when they're gone. These make good alternatives to hiring and training a receptionist or secretary of your own.

Artists can also consider subletting space from an already existing retail operation. A gift shop in a strip mall might rent a corner to an artist. The artist wouldn't need to make all of his or her sales from this corner, but could display sample products, plus business cards and brochures. Some craft and antique malls rent space in small stalls where artists can display their wares. Artists can also consider consignment shops, where they leave their work for a specified period of time. If the item sells, the store owner gets a commission and the artist keeps the rest of the profit. If not, the artist takes the item and goes home. Artists can also sell directly to retail business owners, usually at a discount. The business owner then sells the product to his or her customers at a higher price.

All of these options are worth exploring as alternative—and less expensive—ways to sell your work. Renting your own retail space should be your last resort. After you get started selling your artistic work, if sufficient demand exists, you can consider moving into your own retail space.

Other Considerations

You will need to purchase suitable insurance (Chapter 6) and learn how to set fees (Chapter 13) before you get started. You should also establish a separate bank account for the business, and, if possible, a separate credit line. You may be able to get a personal credit card imprinted with the name of your company so that you can clearly distinguish between personal and business purchases. Not only does it simplify your recordkeeping, but it makes the IRS very happy, which should be one of your goals now that you've become a small-business owner.

Gaining Experience

Before you start up, you need to plan how to gain experience in your field if you don't already have it. Think about what you do, organizations you belong to, and people you know. Then consider how to use these things to increase your experience. If you're an insurance actuary who wants to be a writer, volunteer to write the company newsletter (volunteer to start one if there isn't one already). This will teach you a great deal about the newsletter business and the writing business. Let everyone you know hear about the company newsletter and how you would be interested in writing more newsletters. Tell the owner of your local gym that you'll write a quarterly newsletter in exchange for a discount on your membership fee (you should never do anything for free, but bartering is perfectly acceptable). Remember that discounts or free services or products you receive in exchange for your services count as income in the eyes of the IRS. Therefore, the $20-per-month discount on your gym membership should be included on your tax return. Of course, you can deduct legitimate expenses you had while writing the newsletter for the gym owner.

Making the Most from Experience

When you gain experience in your field, keep the relevant information readily available. If you start writing the company newsletter, save copies of each issue to show to prospective clients. If your photos appear in the newspaper, make copies for your files. Ask for letters of recommendation when appropriate. Get permission to give names of current clients (even if they're just friends or a local business owner you bargained with) to prospective clients.

Keep a Current Résumé or Bio Sheet

Keep a résumé or bio sheet specific to your field. A résumé lists education and employment history in a format designed to highlight dates, job titles, and responsibilities. A bio sheet consists of several descriptive paragraphs about who you are and what you do. The bio sheet can reflect more of your personality, interests, and aspirations, whereas a résumé is a business tool that primarily communicates facts. Depending on your business, one might be more useful than the other, or both may be necessary.

Having an organized, easy-to-understand way to present your experience and completed projects helps attract clients. Some writers enclose a writing résumé that highlights important details of their writing career, along with a clip (a photocopy of a published story or article), when they send query letters to editors. It gives editors an idea of the work the writer has done without bogging them down with unnecessary trivia, such as where the writer went to high school. Although any résumé you give to a prospective client should be a reasonable length—a few paragraphs, a page at most—keeping a more detailed résumé for your own files helps you record and store important information where you can easily reach it. You can then customize different résumés or bio sheets, depending on the client. If your market is broad, create several different bio sheets that target narrower markets.

Keep in Touch

Once you've worked for a client, let the client know you would be delighted to work with him or her again, and follow up occasionally with letters or greeting cards. Ask the client for referrals to other people who could use your particular skills. Getting referrals and repeat business is an important part of successful business ownership, so cultivate the relationships you already have. Never neglect a former or current client in order to satisfy a *potential* client (well, maybe if the potential client is offering thousands of dollars for you to do so...).

Staying Creative

Finally, you will need to preserve your creativity even under strained circumstances. Trying to become inspired when you're racing the clock can induce traumatic stress, but creative business owners have to do it every single day. When your livelihood depends on your ability to write a sentence well, suddenly a sentence is a very scary thing.

Consider the resources you have. Do you have peers or mentors who will help you through the rough spots? Do you have specific rituals that you find soothing and inspiring? Keep these in mind for when you need a creative charge. Remember to set aside time each week for doing the creative work that is important to you. Schedule this work into your calendar just as you would any other project or job. You will find yourself refreshed and energized if you aren't always putting off what you really want to do in order to finish what you have to do.

3

Keeping Financial Records

FINANCIAL RECORD-KEEPING is essential for the freelancer and small-business owner because the most important part of not going broke is knowing where your money is coming from and where it's going. Record-keeping is also necessary for income tax purposes. Regardless of its importance, keeping good financial records can seem difficult to creative people, who aren't necessarily as detail-oriented as their accountant counterparts. Brainstorming for a client presentation is so much more interesting than recording the amount of money you've spent on pens this year. This chapter will guide you through the basics of financial record-keeping in easy-to-understand terms. Understanding financial information means that you can take control of the financial decisions that are a vital part of small-business success.

Many small-business owners think they can just hire an accountant to figure out their financial information and keep the records. But this isn't the most prudent way to manage a business. You know all those millionaire celebrities who die broke? *They* all had accountants. It's up to you to keep control over financial decision-making in your life and in your business. You can't do this if someone else is in charge of the financial information or if you don't understand the financial information.

One writer, Stacy (not her real name), is very uncomfortable with record-keeping and financial decisions. She doesn't have a system for keeping track of expenses, although she tries to save receipts. She just doesn't always remember where she put them. Often, she must spend hours sifting through piles of paper scattered all over the house to find a receipt in order to exchange or return an item. Each year, she uses an accountant to prepare her taxes, but since she can never collect her paperwork on time, she has to keep instructing her accountant to file for extensions. Then, when the extension deadline draws near, she remembers that she needs to get her paperwork together, panics when she can't find any receipts, and tells her accountant not to bother writing off any of her business expenses again this year. Not only does filing for extensions year after year eventually awaken the IRS, but not bothering to deduct business expenses is costly—maybe so costly that someday soon Stacy won't be able to afford to run her own business. Stacy says she just isn't organized, but the truth is she just doesn't care. If she did care, she would at least put all her receipts in a cookie jar in the kitchen, where she could find them at the end of the year. It's not that hard, and it doesn't require any special organizational skill. It simply requires that you care about taking control of your business and your life.

Why You Need to Keep Records

Since it's your creative life and your money that are at stake, you need to care. Understanding the basics of accounting isn't that hard. You simply have to be open to it. Myself, I don't know the first thing about numbers. I understand the concept of zero, one, two, and more than two. Beyond that, I am lost. Nevertheless, I am able to maintain a basic accounting system that I can analyze to see where my money is going, which is essential to the survival of the business. Although you can (and should) consult with an accountant on occasion, unless you make an effort to understand the basics of accounting, you'll never understand what your accountant is telling you or why it's important.

It's impossible to overstate how crucial the financial picture of your business is, even if it seems crass and cold-hearted to spend all that time focusing on money. The purpose of financial record-keeping isn't to remind you that you failed freshman math. It's to help you understand whether you're making a living or not. Although financial records are necessary to satisfy the IRS and convince financial institutions to lend you money if you need it, these financial records are for *you.* If you don't use them, you'll never understand why you're working so hard and still can't afford to buy shoes.

Cash or Accrual?

In order to keep accurate financial records, you must decide whether to operate your business on a cash or accrual basis. A *cash basis* business records revenue when it is received and expenditures when they are paid. (It has nothing to do with whether you accept cash, checks, or credit cards.) If I'm running a cash basis business and on February 4, I purchase a ream of computer paper, six pens, and a dictionary, for a total of $45.38 (tax included), and in the mail, lo and behold, I receive a check for $250 for a magazine article that was published last June (which I immediately deposit in the bank so that the check I wrote to the mortgage lender won't bounce), my expenses for the day will be $45.38 and my income will be $250. That's it. Occasional issues may seem tricky at first, but in reality they're not. Suppose I accept credit cards. Do I count payment received as of the day I take the customer's credit card, which is when the purchase actually took place, or do I wait until the credit card company writes me a check? The answer is simple: after the credit card company writes the check, when the money is actually deposited in the bank. In the same way, when I use a credit card to purchase supplies, I don't record the expense the same day I purchase the items. Instead, I record the expense the day I pay the credit card bill. That way, I never (or rarely) have to make adjustments in my accounting record. I simply record money I spend when I spend it and note money I earn when I receive it. Couldn't be simpler.

Most creative people who own businesses rely on the cash basis accounting system. Their business finances are no more complex than getting money for their work and spending some of it on business needs.

However, sometimes smaller businesses use the *accrual basis* instead of the cash basis system because of the complexity of their financial calculations. The accrual basis system records income and expenses when they are incurred (or accrued), not when they are paid. This gives business owners a better picture of what their financial situation really is, because it records their financial commitments. That is, if they've signed a purchase order or contract to buy a new service van, that expense appears immediately in the records. Because the expense has been committed to, it is recorded. That way, the business owner won't unwisely make other commitments that he or she cannot meet at the same time.

The accrual basis accounting system always requires adjustments. Suppose that on February 4 you bill a client a total of $1,000 and offer a 10 percent discount if the bill is paid within fifteen days. You will immediately record the $1,000 as income or revenue, even though you haven't got the money in your hand. Now, if your client never pays you, at some later date you will record a "bad debt" expense of $1,000 to balance out the fact that you already recorded the $1,000 as revenue. You're still out the $1,000 your client owes you, but the accounting system doesn't care (and neither does the IRS). A cash basis business can't write off bad debt because it never showed that the money was received. Suppose, on the other hand, that the company pays your $1,000 invoice within fifteen days. Because the client paid promptly, the check is for $900, which is 10 percent off the $1,000 bill. To account for this, since you already recorded $1,000 as revenue, you will indicate an expense of $100 as a discount. A cash basis business, on the other hand, would simply show revenue of $900 when the check was received. The accrual basis system provides more information. You could learn that discounting costs your business thousands of dollars each year, so perhaps you should cut back on the number of clients you offer the discount to, reduce the amount of the discount, eliminate it entirely, or raise your prices. With the cash basis system you might never know how much discounting costs you.

If you're a sole proprietor, you should use the cash basis accounting system (in most cases, the IRS will require it). There are some exceptions, such as if you need complex financial documents, or if your business is involved in complex financial arrangements, or if you maintain an inventory, or if you must track depreciation. (*Depreciation* is the loss of value of goods, such as computers and cars, that happens over time. In general, you do not need to track depreciation unless you spend more than $18,000 on equipment in a year.) Many general partnerships can also operate using the cash basis system, as can some corporations.

The only caution is that cash basis accounting does not adhere to Generally Accepted Accounting Principles, which simply means that since anyone can do it, accountants don't like it. Actually, what this really means is that cash basis accounting does not recognize income until the client's check finally lands on your desk, and it doesn't recognize expenses until you get around to paying the bills. The principles of accounting theory say that income is income as soon as it is earned and expenses are expenses as soon as they are committed to.

You must establish your method of accounting before you put your business into operation because once you've decided on an accounting basis, you cannot change it without considerable trial and tribulation, not to mention permission from the IRS.

Assets and Liabilities

In the accounting world, things rarely make sense (except to accountants), so you will need an extra soupçon of patience. In accounting, *assets* (things you own) are called *debits,* while *liabilities* (things you owe) are called *credits*. This can be confusing. If you get a migraine trying to remember which is which, just record things as assets or liabilities and forget which is a credit and which is a debit.

One of the primary activities of accountants consists of balancing numbers. This is extremely important to them, so you must pretend it's important to you. Accountants like to make *balance sheets,* which show the assets and liabilities of a business (that which is owned and that which is owed). Now, you and I would make a list of expenses and total it and then make a list of revenues and total it, and then we would look at the two lists and decide whether something needed to be done. We would be happy with that. And then we would get on with our lives.

Accountants are not so easy to please. They want both lists, assets and liabilities, to total the same amount—that is, to balance. They will go to bizarre and unhealthy ends to make this happen. Here's what you need to know: *Assets* (what you own) always equal *liabilities* (what you owe) plus *capital* (equity or ownership interest). Capital is, in effect, the difference between assets and liabilities. It's put there to make both sides of a balance sheet balance. (Well, it serves another purpose, which is to show whether the business itself has worth. If the capital number is negative, that's a bad thing. It means that you owe more than the business is worth. If the capital number is positive, then you're on the right track. Probably.)

How are these different amounts figured? In the beginning, the business is an idea in your mind. There is nothing tangible to it. Then you take a computer that you've had sitting around the den and designate it the business computer. You add a hundred dollars from your Christmas bonus to buy supplies. Now you have assets of computer plus supplies on one side of the equation, and capital (the amount the computer and supplies are worth) on the other side of the equation. If you then charged fifty dollars worth of bookshelves to your credit card, you would have assets of a computer, supplies, and bookshelves, and liabilities in the amount of the credit card charge. The difference between the worth of the assets and the amount of the liabilities is the *net worth* of your business, or the owner's interest, equity, or capital, which all mean basically the same thing. If your net worth is a positive number, it means that you could sell your assets and pay off your liabilities and still have money left over for pizza. If your net worth is a negative number, it means that if you sell your assets and use the money to pay your liabilities, you would still owe money to creditors after all your assets are gone.

Figure 4
Business Startup Balance Sheet

ASSETS	Debit	Credit
Business computer (worth $1000)	$1,000.00	
Supplies bought with bonus money	100.00	
Bookshelves bought with credit card	50.00	
TOTAL ASSETS	$1,150.00	
LIABILITIES		
Visa credit card		$ 50.00
CAPITAL		
Owner's equity		$1,100.00
TOTAL LIABILITIES and CAPITAL		$1,150.00

Anything that happens on one side of the balance sheet affects the other side. Look at Joe's sample balance sheet. If Joe took the $75 he has in the bank and put it toward the computer store credit card charge, his asset of cash would become zero, but his liability of computer store credit card charge would be reduced by the same amount—$75. Joe would now owe the computer store $1,175 instead of $1,250. And the totals on both sides of the balance sheet would still be equal.

The balance sheet is a helpful financial document because it shows the health of your business. If what you owe is much greater than what you own, your business could be in serious trouble. If the opposite is true, enjoy your three-week Caribbean vacation because you've earned it.

One system of daily record-keeping essentially mimics a balance sheet. Using this method, you keep track of both sides of the balance sheet on a day-to-day basis. This is called double entry book-keeping. Only if you are insane, extremely compulsive, or in a

Figure 5

Joe's Sample Balance Sheet

As of 12/31/00

	Debit	*Credit*
ASSETS		
Cash in the bank	$ 75.00	
Royalty payment sitting on Joe's desk	1,000.00	
Furniture sitting in Joe's office	12.50	
Computer	2,000.00	
TOTAL ASSETS	$3,087.50*	
LIABILITIES		
Computer store credit card		$1,250.00
Copy center account		100.00
CAPITAL		
Owner's equity		$1,737.50**
TOTAL LIABILITIES and CAPITAL		$3,087.50

*The total is underlined to emphasize its importance.

**The owner's equity is also the *net worth*.

complex financial arrangement do you need to bother driving yourself nuts with double entry bookkeeping. Instead, you will simply keep a general ledger using single entry bookkeeping.

The General Ledger

If your business operates on a cash basis, you don't need to worry about recording depreciation and bad debt. You don't need to worry about your balance sheet on a daily basis. Keep it simple. Use a

---

Figure 6
Joe's Sample Balance Sheet
(after making a credit card payment)

As of 1/1/01

	Debit	Credit
ASSETS		
Cash in the bank	$ 0.00	
Royalty payment sitting on Joe's desk	1,000.00	
Furniture sitting in Joe's office	12.50	
Computer	2,000.00	
TOTAL ASSETS	$3,012.50	
LIABILITIES		
Computer store credit card		$1,175.00
Copy center account		100.00
CAPITAL		
Owner's equity		$1,737.50
TOTAL LIABILITIES and CAPITAL		$3,012.50

---

general ledger. Fine, you say, now if only I knew what a general ledger was. A general ledger resembles a checkbook register to an alarming degree. If you have no trouble keeping your checkbook in order, a general ledger will be a snap. But if you and the bank constantly arrive at different opinions concerning how much money you actually have in your checking account, you're going to have to pay extra attention.

In the ledger—which can be kept using a notebook, a computer program, or a sheet of bark—you write the account information for every financial transaction that occurs in your business. An *account* is the name for an entry in the accounting record. The account should show the amount of revenue or expense, the date it was paid, who paid it or was paid, the reason for the income or expense, and the category of revenue or expense. Using

```
┌─────────────────────────────────────────────────────────────────┐
│                          Figure 7                                 │
│                    General Ledger                                 │
│                                                                   │
│  Date    Payee/Payor              Type    Expense    Revenue      │
│                                                                   │
│  5/1/00  Johnny's Supply Depot    SU      $137.52                 │
│          paper, pens                                              │
│                                                                   │
│  5/2/00  National Publisher, Inc. IN                  $127.50     │
│          royalty payment                                          │
│                                                                   │
│  5/2/00  Lemon's Photocopy Shoppe SU       12.50                  │
│                                          ─────────                │
│  SUBTOTALS                               $150.02     $127.50      │
│                                                                   │
└─────────────────────────────────────────────────────────────────┘
```

account categories is just a way to group similar items together. Throughout the year you may buy large quantities of film, photograph paper, developing liquids, and mounting material. These are the supplies you need to create the photographs you sell. You might call all such expenses "supplies." In addition, you might advertise in the telephone book, in the local newspaper, and through a monthly mailing. All these expenses could be lumped together under "advertising." Revenue includes income from clients, plus special income from one-time sales (such as selling a computer you've replaced), as well as interest earned on investments. Using these categories helps you understand where your money comes from and where it goes. You might see that you spend a great deal of money on supplies. You can then find a cheaper supplier, quit being so wasteful, or choose different-quality materials.

Most business owners use account types that match the account categories the IRS uses, such as "advertising expense" and "professional fees." These are listed on the Schedule C form. You can use simple abbreviations for the account names, such as "AD" for "advertising." Recording only business expenses that the IRS allows makes it easier to file taxes. Chapter 4 contains more information about taxes.

Figure 8

Sample IRS Account Categories

You may also find other account categories of use for your
business. See Figure 16.

Expenses   *Revenue*

AD—Advertising   IN—Income
AU—Auto Expense   OT—Other (specify)
ME—Meals and Entertainment
PR—Legal and Professional Fees
SU—Supplies
TR—Travel
UT—Utilities
OT—Other (specify)

Remember that loans are not revenue and loan payments
are not expenses (although interest payments are expenses), at
least not in the business sense. Some business owners make this
mistake, which inflates their income incorrectly and increases
the amount of taxes they have to pay. It also inflates their expenses incorrectly, which can cause tax problems down the road.
The money from a loan is an asset (something you own), while
the repayment obligation for the loan is a liability (something you
owe), but loans and loan payments do not officially belong in a
cash basis general ledger, which only tracks revenue and expenses.
If you have loans and loan payments, record them on a balance
sheet, not the general ledger. If you have large loans, complex
repayment schedules, or other tricky financial situations, you
should consult an accountant to determine how to set up an appropriate accounting system.

The Income Statement

Once you have established a general ledger for your daily revenue and expense information, you can generate helpful reports.

Figure 9

Income Statement

Month ending 12/31/00

	Debits	Credits
INCOME		
Royalties	$1,000.00	
Work for hire	500.00	
	$1,500.00	
EXPENSES		
Computer supplies		$100.00
Utilities, incl. phone		35.00
Color photo development		25.00
		$160.00
NET INCOME (income minus expenses)	$1,340.00	

The *income statement*, also known as the *profit-and-loss statement*, is one of these helpful pieces of information. It can be used to look at financial records over the course of a week, a month, a year—any amount of time you care to use. The general ledger itself provides the information about revenue and expenses for the period of time in which you're interested.

An income statement simply totals your revenue and your expenses. Expenses are subtracted from revenue to determine *net income*. Knowing your net income for a given period of time allows you to see how much money your business actually generates. If your net income is a negative number, watch out! You're operating at a loss, which can cause your business to fail.

Know Your Cost of Sales

If you produce a product, your income statement and income tax records should show the *cost of sales*, or how much it costs for you to produce the product. Writers and photographers, who

Figure 10

Income Statement

Month ending 12/31/00

	Debit	*Credit*
Sales	$600.00	
Cost of sales		
baskets		$25.00
fruit		30.00
packaging and shipping		15.00
		$70.00
Gross profit	$530.00	
(sales less cost of sales)		
Expenses		
utilities		$ 51.00
warehouse rent		210.00
Total expenses		$261.00
NET INCOME	$269.00	
(gross profit less expenses)		

are primarily involved in services, usually do not need to worry about cost of sales for tax or record-keeping purposes. Even though the end product of a writer's work might be a stack of books, this is not the product that the writer produces. The writer produces only the manuscript or words from which the books are made. The same holds true for a photographer shooting a fashion layout for a women's magazine. The act of creating the images is what the photographer sells.

The exception is the photographer who creates wedding albums in which the album itself is a product sold to a client. A

Figure 11

Informal Cost of Sales

Each year, I calculate how much it will cost me to write a typical 75,000-word manuscript. Then I have a basis for determining how profitable a given project will be. I simply adjust for variations, such as photographs or extensive research. *See also Figures 42 and 43.*

Basic Costs:
> four months of time (45 hours per week × 16 weeks = 720 hours)
> three printer cartridges
> paper, pens, sticky notes, and candy bars
> wear and tear on computer
> anti-inflammatories and splints for carpal tunnel syndrome
> utilities and maintenance
> phone calls
> Internet service
> marketing, including mailing costs, supplies, time spent staring at computer

---

potter who creates and sells three different types of planters will also need to determine the cost of sales.

The cost of sales consists of the direct cost of making the products you sell. If you sell fruit baskets, the cost of the basket, the fruit in the basket, and the cellophane you use to keep it all from falling out of the basket are totaled to determine the cost of sales. If you employ a helper to deliver the baskets, his or her wages are also added to the cost of sales. (The term *cost of goods* refers to the cost of producing a product, not including wages.) Cost of sales does not include the cost of running the space heater in your office because your toes are cold, although that is a legitimate business expense. Only expenses directly involved in producing the product are included.

The cost of sales is deducted from the revenue from sales on your income statement. Knowing this number can help you learn whether you're pricing your products appropriately or should find a cheaper supplier or fire the guy who delivers the baskets. Cost of sales is also required for income tax purposes.

Even if you do not need to determine cost of sales for tax or record-keeping purposes, it can be a helpful principle to understand. You can learn which projects are most profitable for you, which ones you should pursue, and whether you should raise your rates. If you're in a service business, the cost of sales is not used for any official purpose. It's simply used to determine whether you're charging enough to cover your costs and whether individual projects are profitable enough to be worth the time and expense.

Accounts Payable and Accounts Receivable

In addition to keeping a daily general ledger and routinely figuring income statements (including cost of sales), many small-business owners need to keep track of *accounts payable* (the money they owe or will owe in the near future) and *accounts receivable* (the money that is owed to them). Because the cash basis accounting system doesn't record income until the check is actually in the bank, and doesn't consider expenses until they are actually paid, the system does not always give an accurate reflection of the health of the business. Using the cash basis system can cause you to overlook signs of trouble. If a number of clients have owed you money for more than ninety days, your business could be in serious trouble because accounts owed beyond ninety days are verging on the uncollectible. If you have a large bill coming due but haven't planned for it, you could be in trouble when your revenues don't provide enough money to cover the expense.

For many creative small-business owners, these problems aren't extreme. They may have relatively few clients. They might receive two or three checks a month for their services. They can easily remember who owes what and when their clients usually pay. By the same token, creative small-business owners tend to make relatively few purchases in a month, and they certainly know when they're planning to upgrade their computer or if they've committed to a large purchase recently. Nonetheless, officially

Figure 12
Accounts Receivable Journal

Invoice No.	Date Due	Payor	Amount Owed	Comments
1035	10/31/00	Joe Bob's Auto Sales	$ 450.00	sent late notice on 11/25/00
1036	11/15/00	Sport & Fitness Mag.	$ 175.00	
1037		N/A		****void****
1038	11/25/00	Omaha Times	$ 65.00	

tracking accounts payable items (called "payables") and accounts receivable items (called "receivables") can free up mental space for more important tasks. Keeping accounts payable and accounts receivable journals helps you plan to pay business expenses and collect from slow-paying customers.

Your accounts receivable journal (for amounts you're owed) should list the date you sent the invoice (if you allow thirty days for payment, the journal should reflect the due date), the name of the client, and the amount owed, plus an invoice number if applicable. You should update the journal each time you send a bill or whenever a royalty or other routine payment comes due. When the money is received, simply mark the entry "paid." Be sure you also note the income on your general ledger when it is paid.

If you don't receive your payment when it is due, send a gentle reminder notice after fifteen days and again after thirty days, and a more strongly worded letter at forty-five days and again at sixty days past due. Be prepared to consult an attorney should a receivable go beyond ninety days. If a client is consistently late in paying, ask if you can change your billing practices to ensure prompt payment. Perhaps your invoices come right at the end of a billing cycle and if you simply sent the bill a few days earlier in the month it would be

Figure 13

Accounts Payable Journal

Date Due	Payee	Amount	Category	Comments
10/31/00	Corner Bookstore	$ 300.00	Education	
10/31/00	Kwik Kopy	$ 75.00	Supplies	
11/5/00	Authors Guild	$ 90.00	Membership	Find out if they'll take installments

paid much sooner. Or perhaps you could offer an incentive such as a discount for prompt payment. If you feel that the client is having financial problems, discontinue working for him or her.

Your accounts payable journal (for amounts you owe) should be updated each time you incur or commit to an expense. The payables journal should list the date the amount is due, to whom it is owed, for what service or supply, the account category (use the account category you use in your general ledger, such as "AD" for "advertising"), and the amount owed. Depending on how uneven your income is, you can project payables as far ahead as you wish. Most businesses try to project payables about six months ahead, which helps them prepare for upcoming expenses. Trying to project more than six months ahead resembles guessing to a large degree.

As soon as you have paid a payable item, mark it "paid" in your accounts payable journal. Also note the expense on your general ledger when it is paid.

Keeping Documents

In order to prepare important financial records, you'll need to keep certain documents, including receipts for expenses, canceled checks, bank and credit card statements, and invoices plus check stubs (or photocopies of the checks themselves) from clients who

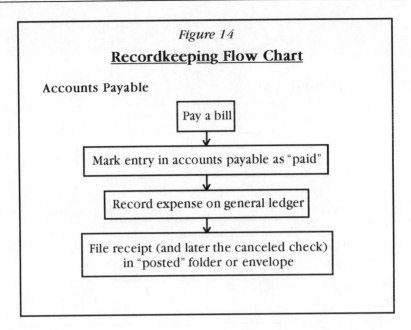

Figure 14
Recordkeeping Flow Chart

Accounts Payable

Pay a bill

↓

Mark entry in accounts payable as "paid"

↓

Record expense on general ledger

↓

File receipt (and later the canceled check) in "posted" folder or envelope

have paid you. Designate a drawer, box, or file folder for records pertaining to financial aspects of your business. Then, each day or once a week, depending on what is appropriate, enter the information in your general ledger. For expenses, attach receipts to canceled checks or credit card statements. For revenue, attach check stubs or photocopies of the check to your copy of the corresponding invoice. File all such documents in an envelope or folder marked "posted." (That's what you're doing when you write the account information on the general ledger—you're posting to the ledger.)

Recording Financial Information

For the general ledger and accounts payable/receivable journals, you can use a spiral notebook, a special ledger/account book or a computer program. Your records can be lists that you type using a word processing program. It doesn't need to be complicated.

You can also use computer accounting programs such as QuickBooks or Peachtree Accounting. The first time you run the program, it will ask you questions about the type of business you own and the kinds of revenues and expenses you have.

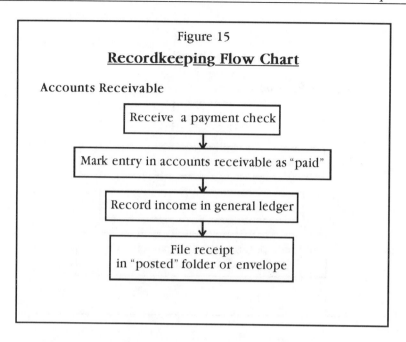

Figure 15

Recordkeeping Flow Chart

Accounts Receivable

Receive a payment check

Mark entry in accounts receivable as "paid"

Record income in general ledger

File receipt
in "posted" folder or envelope

The program tailors the accounting system to fit your needs. Another possibility is to pay an accountant to set up a paper or computerized accounting system to suit your business needs. This is usually the most expensive choice you can make (the professional fees can be written off) but is also the most personalized.

Developing Good Record-keeping Habits

Develop good record-keeping habits right away. Keep all relevant receipts, canceled checks, bank statements, and credit card statements in one place. You don't have to update your financial records every single day of your life, as long as you do so at least once a month. If you always remember to put business receipts in the cookie jar in the kitchen, you'll know where to find the information you need when it's time to update the general ledger.

The IRS expects you to keep itemized receipts for all your purchases. You can't simply guess that you spend $800 a year in postage. You have to have the receipts to back it up. Receipts must include the date, the name of the business from which you purchased the service or supply, a description of what was purchased, and the total amount you paid in order for the IRS to accept the document as a legitimate proof of the expense.

At first, you may find yourself tossing business receipts without realizing it. To counteract this problem, collect every single receipt you receive throughout the course of the day in one central location—your wallet, or an envelope in your purse. Then dump the contents into the cookie jar and sort them out later. By forcing yourself to collect every receipt, you'll soon remember to hang on to business receipts. Use whatever method you need to make certain you keep necessary business records as completely and accurately as possible.

4

You, Taxes, and the IRS

THE IRS hates self-employed people. Just on general principles. Even more than the IRS hates self-employed people, it hates *creative* self-employed people. They don't come equipped with nice W-2 forms, they're always taking those pesky home office deductions, and they make about twelve dollars a year.

In short, the IRS doesn't trust you. Therefore, you must make certain that everything you do in connection with the IRS is aboveboard and can be backed up with documents, signed testimony, and character witnesses. (Well, at least hang on to the documents.)

In Chapter 3, I recommended keeping receipts, bank statements, canceled checks, and credit card statements. These are essential for proving that you did in fact incur the expenses you claim to have incurred. Receipts, canceled checks, and credit card statements all show that you did in fact purchase products or services. Bank statements show deposits and other account information that the IRS may ask for.

That said, there are some handy documents that the IRS provides free of charge to business owners. These may be helpful in planning your tax strategies and preparation. Check out Publication 583, *Starting a Business and Keeping Records;* Publication

334, *Tax Guide for Small Businesses;* and Publication 535, *Business Expenses.*

No Receipt, No Deduction?

What about those occasions when you can't get a receipt to prove that you spent the money? If you buy stamps from a vending machine that doesn't give receipts, hang on to the stamp book cover and note the date and price of the stamps. If you photocopy a few dollars' worth of research materials at the library and can't get a receipt, jot down the amount you spent, what it was for, and the date. You can still deduct small expenses like these. (A computer system for which you do not have a receipt does not qualify as a small expense.) The goal is to have receipts for the overwhelming majority of your expenses.

Saving Income Tax Records

How long should you hang on to tax records, receipts, and related documents? Although the IRS claims that you need only keep tax records for three years after you've filed, the fact remains that if the IRS conducts an audit and has reason to suspect that an earlier return was incorrect or that you underreported your income at some time in the past, they can ask to see documents supporting tax returns you filed when you were 16. What is a legitimate reason for an IRS agent to suspect the veracity of a past return? Psychic intuition is one, as victims of the IRS will tell you. A nasty anonymous tip from a disgruntled ex-husband. A computer error (not yours) that matches your Social Security number with that of a convicted terrorist. It doesn't matter. The IRS doesn't have to prove anything to you; you have to prove things to *it.* Therefore, hang on to all those records. Stick them in a back corner of the basement or under the attic stairs and forget about them, but don't throw them out. If you're ever the target of an audit, you'll be glad you hung on to them. Although there is a statute of limitations (technically speaking), the IRS will go to great lengths to wring tax money out of you if it thinks you owe.

Experts say that state tax returns need only be kept for a year or two, but as long as you're keeping all your federal tax information in a box under the stairs, it doesn't hurt to throw your state and local returns in there as well.

Who Files a Tax Return?

You must file federal, state, and local (if applicable) tax returns for your business each year, whether you made money or not. You must include all the income you received during the year, regardless of whether you claim any business-related expenses or not. This means that even if you don't treat your creative work like a business, you still have to report and pay taxes on any money you make from it.

If you run a sole proprietorship, your income and expenses from the business appear on your personal income tax return. A sole proprietor files a Form 1040 (US Individual Income Tax Return) plus a Schedule C (Profit or Loss from a Business) or Schedule C-EZ (Net Profit from a Business). Schedule SE is necessary for self-employment tax (more on that later). If you run a general partnership, your business expenses are recorded on a special partnership tax return while your share of the business income appears on your personal income tax return. Most partnerships require Form 1065, the US Partnership Return of Income Tax and Schedule K-1, which shows the partners' personal income from the partnership. If you run a corporation, the corporation files a separate tax return listing revenue and expenses. Any income or dividends paid to you by the corporation should be included on your personal tax return. Corporations file Form 1120, US Corporation Income Tax Return. (Corporate taxes are due on March 15, whereas individual and partnership taxes are due on April 15.)

Employees and the IRS

If you have employees, you need an Employer Identification Number, readily available from the IRS. You must calculate and deduct your employees' income tax payments and calculate, deduct, and *match* their Social Security payments. These payroll taxes must be remitted weekly or monthly, depending on the size of your business. Some of these taxes are a deductible business expense. Consult a tax accountant if you employ others on an hourly wage or salary basis.

Income Tax and Self-Employment Tax

If the revenues from your business exceed the expenses from your business, the profit is your personal income (unless you have organized a corporation that pays you a salary and invests the rest of the profits). You owe income tax on this money. If you are a sole proprietor, a member of a general partnership, or an owner of some corporations, you also owe self-employment taxes. The self-employment tax keeps the Social Security system afloat. When you were employed, your employer deducted a share of your wages from each paycheck, matched it, and sent the total to the Social Security Administration. Now that you're a small-business owner, you're responsible for calculating and paying the entire amount owed.

The tax forms describe how to calculate the income tax and self-employment tax you owe. Sole proprietors can deduct a portion of the cost of health insurance (the portion increases each year) from their self-employment taxes. Keep track of this expense so that you can claim it.

Preparing the Return

Each year, at the end of December, make a copy of your general ledger for the year and keep it with all documents that support the ledger entries. Then, when you are ready to prepare your taxes, you will have all the information you need in one place. If your general ledger has been kept up to date, it may be all your accountant needs in order to prepare your taxes for you, if you choose to go that route.

You can prepare your tax return in one of several different ways. You can bring the pertinent information to a tax accountant or tax preparer; you can use a computer software program (updated annually) to walk you through the steps; or you can sit down with a pile of forms and a bunch of informational booklets and do the deed yourself.

Sole proprietors often prepare their own tax returns, especially if they've kept accurate records, have simple income and expenses, understand the explanations given in the tax booklets, and don't mind spending some time with a calculator checking details. This does not include very many creative people.

Tax Software Programs

One year my significant other introduced me to the wonders of tax software—TurboTax, Kiplinger Tax Cut, and similar programs. Never again did I prepare my tax return using a pencil, a calculator, and three pots of coffee (although I do miss the pitcher of margaritas I used to indulge in afterwards). Tax software programs require an investment of forty or fifty dollars, but they're so easy to use that even I can get them to work. You still need to be organized and have all the pertinent financial information in front of you, but you don't have to worry about whether you're putting the right number on the right line. You also don't need to worry about whether you're adding and subtracting correctly, since the program does that for you (a plus for me, since I can't count beyond "more than two").

Tax programs print out the tax forms you need with your numbers neatly typed in place. (No last-minute running to the post office to see if you can find a Form 4562.) You can double-check facts and figures and revise your numbers as often as you want before sending the forms in with your payment check (creative small-business owners never get money back from the government). Most tax software alerts you to tax changes so that you can take advantage of them in the coming year, and warn you if you're about to do something stupid, like claim a home office deduction in excess of your business profit.

Since you're now a small-business owner, you'll need a business version of such software. (Some versions for personal use can handle single proprietorship businesses, sometimes called Schedule C businesses, unless your tax situation is very complex.)

If you use certain accounting software, such as QuickBooks or Microsoft Money, to keep track of your general ledger, some tax software programs will simply import information directly from your accounting system to your tax records, which makes the whole ordeal much easier. Some business owners use tax programs, then ask their accountants to look over the results as a double check. (This is cheaper than getting the accountant to do the whole caboodle to begin with. It's also a solution for those years when you have procrastinated about getting everything to your accountant and now he or she doesn't have time to do your return for you.)

If you own a partnership or corporation, it's wise to consult an experienced tax preparation specialist in order to understand how to file your tax returns properly. Sole proprietors can also benefit from consulting a tax preparer, at least for the first year. Discuss the information your accountant or tax preparer will need ahead of time so you can stick it all in a shoebox and present it to him or her at the appointed time.

Legitimate Business Expenses

Most of the expenses you have in connection with your business are considered legitimate business expenses. Supplies you purchase, equipment you lease, furniture you buy—all these expenses can be deducted from your business income. You can even deduct things such as books and magazines related to business. For writers, that includes practically any reading material; if it is something you use in research or if reading the book itself is research (you want to know how various romance writers write romances so that you can write one), deduct it.

If you have a phone line for your business or for your business computer or fax, the entire cost of the phone service is deductible. If you use one line for both home and business purposes, you cannot deduct the basic service charge. Long distance calls for business reasons are always deductible, however.

You can also deduct advertising costs and professional fees such as accounting, bookkeeping, and legal fees. You can deduct

---

Figure 15

Tax Deductions

Accounting and bookkeeping fees
Advertising
Auto expenses
Bank service charges (including credit card fees for business credit cards)
Education (for developing your work skills or business ownership skills)
Furnishings and equipment
Health insurance (partly deductible)
Insurance (business-related insurance, including professional liability insurance)
Legal and professional fees (including consultants)
Magazines and books (needed for business)
Maintenance and repairs (for business assets such as computer)
Meals and entertainment (50 percent deductible)
Membership dues (for business-related organizations)
Online fees (in proportion to time you spend online for business purposes)
Supplies (including office supplies, postage, and the like)
Telephone expense
Travel expenses (including conferences and meetings)
Utilities
Wages

---

delivery fees; insurance (except health insurance, although you can get a credit for this on your self-employment tax); licenses; equipment repairs and maintenance; continuing education costs, including workshops and seminars; plus wages for employees and temporary help. For large equipment purchases, you can deduct depreciation expenses. For business start-up costs, you need to spread out (amortize) the total amount over sixty months. Most standard business deductions (with the exception of the home office deduction) can be claimed using Schedule C. A special tax form, Form 4562, is needed to calculate and claim depreciation and amortized expenses.

Also keep in mind that since such purchases/expenses are deductions, the sale of certain business assets is considered income. If you've sold equipment, land, or other business-related property, check out the instructions for Form 4797 (Sale of Business Property). You should also consult with a tax advisor regarding deductible business expenses and allowed amounts.

Business Travel, Meals, and Entertainment

If you travel on business, save receipts and documents related to the trip. The cost of lodging and transportation is deductible, as is a portion of meals and entertainment (currently 50 percent). Keep a detailed list of what you did on your trip in order to prove it was taken for a business reason. Legitimate business travel includes attending a conference, meeting with potential clients, promoting your new book, researching your competition, plus others. You can see the sights while traveling on business and no one will care. You just can't take a trip for personal reasons and then try to pass it off as business travel. You can certainly bring a spouse or friend along on a business trip, although you cannot deduct their portion of the expense. What you can do is determine how much it would have cost for you to do everything alone and deduct *that* amount. If a hotel room for one person runs $100 a night, while the same room for two people costs $130, the amount to claim as a business expense is the single rate of $100. Get a rate sheet from the hotel to verify the amount. There is nothing sneaky about this. If you had gone by yourself, you would have paid the full amount. By the same token, if a friend flies free, the air expense is not half the cost of your airline ticket. Remember, you would have had to purchase the ticket whether your friend came along or not. Keep all relevant information, tabulate legitimate expenses, and record them on your general ledger.

You can also deduct part of the cost of business meals and entertainment, whether at home or away from home. Save receipts from restaurants, ticket stubs, and the like. Note the business reason for the meal/entertainment, whom you were with, and the date. Record the details on your general ledger. Then keep this information in your "posted" envelope. Get Publication 463, *Travel, Entertainment, Gift and Car Expenses,* from the IRS for further information.

Automobile Expenses

If you drive for business-related purposes, you can deduct automobile mileage and tolls. Each year, the IRS determines how much you can write off for mileage (such as $0.32 per mile). This amount includes wear and tear, routine maintenance, and gasoline. If you're reimbursed for this expense, you cannot also claim the deduction on your taxes. Above and beyond the standard mileage expense, you can write off tolls you paid while you were driving for business-related reasons. You can ask the toll official for a receipt or, if you prefer not to infuriate all the people in the cars behind you, just note the date, the amount of the toll, and the business reason associated with paying the toll. Record this information on your general ledger and stash the note in your "posted" envelope.

In order to claim the auto mileage expense, you have to keep a mileage log for your vehicle. Although this seems like a lot of busy work (it *is* a lot of busy work), the write-off can add up to a substantial amount of money if you frequently drive to meet with clients, visit job sites, or conduct business. Simply note the date, the mileage at the beginning and end of the trip, the total number of miles, the business reason for the trip, and where you went. Some office supply stores sell preprinted forms for this information. You can make your own form, or you can buy a spiral notebook for sixty-nine cents and use that. It is entirely up to you. All the IRS requires is that you write everything down. (And they mean *everything*.) Get Publication 463, *Travel, Entertainment, Gift and Car Expenses,* for further information.

Home Office Deduction

You can also take a home office deduction, assuming that you work out of a home office. Although taking this write-off does increase your chances of getting audited, you have nothing to

Figure 17
Mileage Log

Date	Start Mileage	End Mileage	Total Miles	Purpose of Trip

fear if the claim is legitimate (well, very little to fear). For the write-off to be legitimate, your home office must be used routinely and solely for the purpose of conducting business. Even if you don't have a spare bedroom that you can convert to an office, you can deduct a home office that takes up a corner of the basement or living room as long as the space is used only for business and as long as it is your primary place of business.

The home office deduction includes a portion of rent or mortgage proportionate to the space, plus an equivalent portion of the cost of utilities, maintenance of the entire structure, insurance, and property taxes. For instance, if you live in a 1,200-square-foot duplex and your office takes up the 10' by 12' back bedroom, the office is 120 square feet, or 10 percent of the whole. You can claim 10 percent of the rent on your duplex plus 10 percent of the utilities. You can also add in the direct costs of the office, such as rewiring an electrical outlet to accommodate your computer system.

You cannot take the home office deduction if you have a loss from the business or if taking it would create a loss for the business. You can claim a *portion* of the home office expense, however. If your business has a profit of $800 and claiming the full home office deduction of $3,000 would create a loss, you cannot do so. You can, however, claim $800 worth of the deduction so that your profit is reduced to zero and your income tax therefore is also reduced to zero.

Always calculate the home office deduction after other expenses, since it cannot exceed the profit you made from your business. Claiming the home office deduction requires you to file Form 8829, Business Use of Home.

For the record, you might photograph the space and draw a layout of the entire house, showing the dimensions of the various rooms. This is especially helpful if you're audited after you move from one location to another.

Independent Contractor Status

The government will agree that you're self-employed (an independent contractor) and entitled to business expense deductions only so long as you meet certain requirements. The IRS believes that many employees call themselves independent contractors, which costs the government money. Employees who claim business expenses when they shouldn't are cheating the government out of tax revenue. Other problems also result. If everyone were an independent contractor, employers wouldn't have to pay benefits, provide leave, pay payroll and unemployment taxes, contribute to workers' compensation programs, Social Security, Medicare, and retirement programs, and supply office space, equipment, and coffee. It would be much cheaper for them. It would also leave many workers unprotected and exploited. (Not everyone wants to be an independent contractor or small-business owner.)

Therefore, the IRS applies certain rules to make sure that an independent contractor is really an independent contractor. An employer can tell an employee when and where to work and how to do a job. An employer cannot do this with an independent contractor. He or she simply specifies the work to be done. Of course, it's not as if this criterion makes it easy to distinguish between an employee and an independent contractor. The fact that you work at home doesn't make a difference (people who telecommute are still considered employees). To avoid being reclassified by the IRS (and possibly having to pay more in taxes), you should work for more than one client (this is simply good business practice anyway). You should maintain control of the project. The client shouldn't tell you whom to hire or how to do

---

Figure 18

Maintaining Independent Contractor Status

Work for more than one or two clients.
Maintain control of the project.
Invoice clients per project, not per hour.
Incorporate your business or use a "doing business as" name.
Maintain your own office.
Pay your own taxes and insurance.
Perform your own marketing.
Keep written contracts.

---

your job or when you should be in the office (except, of course, by appointment). You should be responsible for maintaining your own office, paying your own taxes and insurance, and doing your own marketing. You should also have written agreements with your clients, specifying the job you will do, when you will do it, how much you will be paid, and other details as applicable to your business. Generally, invoicing a client by the job is wiser than invoicing by the hour. If your business is incorporated or has a "dba" ("doing business as") name, you are more likely to be considered an independent contractor.

Most small-business owners do not need to worry about being reclassified as an employee instead of an independent contractor (especially if they follow the above guidelines), but bear in mind that the more you treat the work you do as a business, the more likely your work will be viewed as a business by the IRS.

Form 1099

When you work on a freelance basis, your income may arrive in a variety of forms, such as royalty payments, work-for-hire contracts, and barter. Your clients don't deduct income or self-employment taxes from their payments to you. That's your responsibility. If a client pays you more than $600 in a year (this amount changes from time to time), he or she will probably send a Form 1099 to you and to the federal government at the end of each year. The

1099 lists the amount of money the client paid you. It is similar to the W-2 form you received when you earned wages. However, you cannot rely on receiving 1099s to know how much money you made in a given year.

When you receive a 1099 in the mail, make certain it is correct. It should show your social security number (or Employer Identification Number, if applicable). It should also show your name and address, plus the total amount of money you were paid for the calendar year. All of this information should be checked for accuracy. If the 1099 is incorrect, ask the client to send a corrected 1099 to the government and to you.

The 1099B is used for bartered and brokered goods and services worth more than a specified amount. If you barter extensively in your business, you may need to use or receive these forms. Check the instructions, readily available from the IRS, or consult an experienced tax preparer.

The Nonprofitable Business

Small-business owners often assume that they must make a profit in order to write off business expenses. This is not the case. The IRS doesn't care whether you make money or lose money, as long as you're running a business. It's just that if you lose money year after year, the IRS is inclined to think that you don't have a business so much as you have an expensive hobby. If you don't show a profit in the first year or two of business, the IRS isn't likely to get too upset with you. After that, if you show a profit two of every three years or so, you probably won't alert an examiner.

If the IRS does come calling, you will need to show that you devote a substantial amount of time to your business (that is, you don't work at it on alternate Sundays and on Wednesdays when the moon is full). You will need to show that you run your business like a business. If you have an accounting system set up (even if it's set up in a notebook), that's a plus. Saving documents related to your business efforts is also important. An aspiring writer could save copies of query and rejection letters. Even if the writer doesn't manage to get much into print the first year or two, these letters will prove that significant time and energy was invested in running the business. Photographers or musicians could save any marketing material they have used and keep records of contacts with clients in order to prove that they've been running a business.

Many experts suggest keeping a daily appointment calendar in which you note the number of hours you worked and what you did. This doesn't need to be extensive. "Feb. 4, 4 hours, query letters, research for travel article" will suffice. The notes that you jot down on your calendar, to-do list, or daily planner regarding business-related phone conversations, errands, and appointments will also confirm that you're running a business, not a hobby.

Although you do not have to make a profit to write off business expenses (remember, you can't use the home office deduction unless you *do* turn a profit), it does help make your case if you have *some* revenue or income from your business, whether or not your expenses are greater than this amount. Don't forget the small sums of money that people might pay you for various business-related reasons. Also, don't forget that when bartering, the value of the service or product you receive should be considered income. (Business expenses related to goods or services you provide in a barter are legitimate deductions.) Determine the fair market value of a bartered product or service, which can be easy or difficult, largely depending on your mood. If you write ads for your hair stylist in exchange for a free monthly haircut, all you need to do is find out how much your hair stylist usually charges for a haircut, and multiply that by the number of free cuts you receive in a year. Some products or services may be slightly more difficult to determine. The IRS requires you to use Form 1099B to identify income that resulted from a bartered or brokered exchange. Consult this form and its instructions for information on determining market value for goods and services.

Estimated Tax Payments

The IRS doesn't like to wait for its money, although it will let you cool your heels waiting for your refund. An impatient IRS breeds impatient IRS agents, who get a little upset if they have to wait a whole year to get hold of your money.

When you were an employee, every paycheck was subject to withholding. Your employer estimated your tax liability based on your salary and the number of exemptions you claimed on your W-4 form (you filled this out when you were hired). Then your employer deducted a certain amount of pay for local, state, and federal taxes, as well as for Social Security, and sent this money to the government. When you filed your tax return for that year, you simply adjusted the amount you had already paid to compensate for various factors. Sometimes you might have had to pay a little more, sometimes you might have gotten a bit of a refund. Either way, the IRS liked you because you were gainfully employed and your employer remitted a portion of your earnings on a regular basis.

If you're a small-business owner, this is no longer the case. Your clients will not determine how much of your pay to withhold. They'll send you the whole check and you'll squander it, and then at the end of the year you'll owe the IRS ten grand and...hold on. That's why the IRS wants—indeed, *expects*—you to make estimated tax payments throughout the year. They don't trust you not to squander all that cash. Besides, if you earn money in January and the government doesn't see its share of the money until the next April, why, the entire country could end up in financial ruin. Do you want to be blamed for the collapse of the economy? I thought not.

The idea of figuring tax payments more than once a year can make you run shrieking from the room. It's enough to make you get a job. (That's what the IRS wants you to do.) But it doesn't have to be that hard. Remember, the IRS just wants its money on a regular basis. It also has a legitimate concern that a business could be doing well in January of one year but be bankrupt by April of the next, leaving the IRS without its fair share of the money.

If you don't have a profit of more than $1,000 or $2,000 each year, then for the most part you needn't worry about making estimated tax payments. Your tax liability on $1,000 or $2,000 is not that great, so it isn't as if you're keeping a lot of cash from the government. Of course, if you're only making one or two grand a year, your primary concern should be preventing imminent starvation by attracting more business.

If, on the other hand, you show a profit of $5,000 or $10,000 at the end of the year and you didn't make estimated tax payments, the IRS might sit up and take notice. If they feel that you should have been making estimated tax payments in a year when you did not, they might send you a nasty letter telling you to start. Or they might hit you with some penalties and interest charges. (They aren't going to prosecute you and throw you in jail as long as you don't file *fraudulent* tax statements or try to hide income or something devious like that. They'll just torture you a little.)

Normally, a small-business owner in a creative profession can simply file quarterly estimated tax statements that show income and expenses to date. This requires Form 1040ES. Along with the tax statement, you'll send a check for an appropriate amount of federal tax and self-employment tax (which the IRS sends to the Social Security Administration). Of course, if you're making estimated federal tax payments you may need to make them for state and local taxes as well. Check with your local and state governments for their policies.

There are some ways around paying estimated taxes, such as not making a profit, although that may not strike you as a very positive plan. If you have a wage job, even a part-time job, ask your employer to increase your withholding by whatever dollar amount you determine is necessary to meet your tax liability. (The government doesn't care where your tax money comes from as long as it comes.) Then, at the end of the year, when you file your tax statement you will already have paid your share (or close to it) of the tax bill. If you have an employed spouse and you normally file jointly, you can have your spouse increase his or her withholding to cover the amount of tax liability your business will have in the upcoming year. This method works for sole proprietorships and general partnerships, whose income is reported on your personal income tax statement.

Hold on, you say. I have no idea how much money I'm going to earn in a given year, so how am I going to determine a withholding amount or know when to make estimated tax payments? You have a couple of choices. If you're just starting your business and have no idea what your income is going to be, then relax. Total your general ledger once a month. As soon as you have made five or six thousand dollars after deducting expenses, file an estimated tax statement and then keep them coming. (If you're a creative person, it may take years for you to earn five or six thousand dollars after expenses, so maybe you'll never have to worry about this.) Once you start filing estimated tax statements, however, you're going to have to keep them up if you don't want to wake the slumbering beast (i.e., the IRS). The alternative, of course, is to increase withholding at your job or your spouse's job as soon as you begin making money, but not before (if you don't have a wage job or a spouse, welcome to the world of estimated tax payments).

Keep in mind that the IRS, for all its sins, doesn't expect you to be able to predict the future. Therefore, pay attention to the past. If this is the first year of your business, and you don't make estimated tax payments but you do pay the IRS in April, you probably aren't going to get into trouble, particularly if you haven't made tons of money. However, the IRS will expect you to learn from experience. If you earned $10,000 in your first year of business, they believe you can assume you'll make $10,000 in your next year of business. If you make estimated tax payments based on that premise, and you happen to make more than $10,000 in a year, they aren't going to arrest you. If, on the other hand, you make $10,000 in your first year but don't bother changing the withholding amount at your wage job or sending estimated tax payments in your next year, the IRS will get a little testy.

A note of caution: The main point is that the IRS doesn't expect you to make guesses (well, okay, it is called an *estimated* tax payment), but they do expect you to pay taxes in a timely manner. It's just that we get accustomed to filing tax returns once a year, so we think we pay taxes once a year when this is not the case. If you're a wage employee, you pay taxes all year long; you just don't have to think about it.

The estimated tax payment paperwork required of small-business owners is not that difficult or time-consuming. Discuss estimated tax payments with an accountant who can help you get started.

Another note of caution: If, at any point in the year, you score big and land a six-figure advance or sign a contract worth fifty grand, you should consult a tax accountant right away. A tax accountant (or tax attorney) can help you reduce the tax bite as much as possible. You will also need to let the IRS know within a reasonable time frame of your newfound wealth, in order to share it with them. Trust me when I say the IRS knows how to sniff out money. They have agents who keep track of lottery winners and who follow business and industry news just to make sure people aren't trying to underreport the amount of money they make.

You've Made a Mistake

Let's assume that you honestly meant to include that $100,000 advance check you got for your newest romance novel on your income tax return, but it completely slipped your mind, what with signing the six-figure deal with Steven Spielberg and interviewing Sharon Stone (who wants to play you in the story of your life). Now what?

The answer is simple: The 1040X. Although the "X" seems sinister, it's not. It stands for the Amended US Income Tax Return form, which is a brief, two-page document that simply asks you to admit the error of your ways and submit the requisite check to make up for your erring. (Although creative business owners rarely get refund checks from the government, if for some reason you forgot to deduct that new computer system you purchased, you can claim it as an expense on the same form—the 1040X—and tell the government why you think you're entitled to the refund. "Because I have to pay the orthodontist" is not the correct answer.) You may have to amend your state and local tax returns as well.

Avoiding an Audit

Most people with regular jobs have about a 1 percent chance of being audited. You, on the other hand, have about a 10 percent chance of being audited. This is because it is easier for self-employed people to hide money than it is for people with normal wage-earning jobs. Self-employed business owners can hide

---

Figure 19

Top 7 Red Flags

Taking a loss on your business year after year.
Expenses that equal more than 60 percent of revenue.
1099s that don't match up with reported income.
Income that varies widely from one year to the next.
The home office deduction.
Incorrectly prepared forms.
Unsigned forms.

Audit Avoidance Strategies

Try to turn the occasional profit.
Keep costs under control.
Make sure 1099s are accurate and that you've reported all
    income.
Hold off paying expenses until the following year.
You can choose not to take the home office deduction, or
    you can make sure you can back it up.
Double-check each form.
Sign everything.

---

money by accepting payments in cash and not reporting the income, by inflating expenses, and by reporting personal expenses as business expenses. Auditing the self-employed is also a cost-effectiveness issue. Turning up discrepancies in the tax return of a small-business owner is likely to yield greater tax revenues than squeezing a working-class family of four for a couple of extra nickels because they don't have the documents to back up a charitable deduction of $100.

The IRS randomly audits business owners (they also randomly audit regular people, just not as often). Although the main reason for this is to see who's stealing (the government considers it stealing if you don't pay your fair share of taxes), two other important reasons include discovering where business owners are making mistakes (in order to educate them) and discovering where business owners find loopholes (in order to close them).

As you learn more about business ownership and tax issues, you'll discover that there are red flags that the IRS looks for. When they see these flags, they're more likely to audit a business owner. ("More likely to" isn't the same thing as "will.") If you continually show a loss from your business, year after year, the IRS might get curious. If your business expenses are more than 60 percent of your income or revenues from business, that can be a red flag. The IRS also matches up those 1099 forms with your tax statement to make certain you aren't misrepresenting the amount of income you make. The IRS likes consistency, so if your income tax statements vary widely from one year to the next, they might investigate. This is especially true if you make tons of money one year and none the next and the explanation isn't immediately apparent (i.e., you abandoned your job to start a creative business). The IRS doesn't mind if you increase your income as long as you increase your tax payments too. They just hate it when you start making less money than you used to. Taking the home office deduction can sometimes trigger an audit, especially if it's in connection with another red flag, such as a sudden decrease in income. Incorrectly prepared forms can cause an audit. Even if you simply forgot to sign your return, you might find an IRS agent on your front porch. That's no way to start the day.

Audits take different forms. Sometimes the IRS will simply send a letter asking for clarification on a certain question. If your answer satisfies them, you're off the hook. If not, they may pursue the investigation, perhaps by asking you to send materials to back up your statements or prove your deductions. (Remember to always, *always* make copies of everything you send so that you can send the documents again after the IRS loses them.) Occasionally you may be notified that you miscalculated your tax payment, and you'll simply send a check to cover the difference (with interest and penalties if the IRS is feeling especially snippy). This is simply to say that not every audit is a full-scale field investigation in which special agents come knocking on your door to take a look at your home office. If you do find yourself on the wrong end of an audit, and it isn't something simple like you can't add and you owe $219 instead of $210, retain an accountant or tax attorney who has experience with audits. Such professionals will often be able to resolve the situation without extensive trauma to you. Since they're neutral, they aren't likely to volunteer more information than is needed or answer questions about your lifestyle. (The IRS loves to ask questions about your lifestyle to see if you're living large and reporting small; they also love to sit there quietly waiting for you to break under the pressure of their cold gray stares and tell them where the unreported stash is located.)

As long as you keep accurate records and document the activities of your business with care, you should survive an audit at least reasonably intact. Although the IRS may disallow some deductions or otherwise find a way to make you pay for the audit, if you can show that you did not hide income or misrepresent expenses and that you acted in good faith, in a businesslike manner, you may have to pay additional taxes, penalties, and interest, but you won't lose your business or go to jail with all the other criminals who did claim personal expenses as business deductions.

What is the main problem IRS auditors discover when they tackle small-business owners? Laziness. Yep. You work like a maniac all week and the IRS accuses you of laziness. What they're referring to is laziness in record-keeping. You know exactly what I mean, because you can't imagine anything more boring than keeping track of little pieces of paper and adding together rows of numbers. If you're not able to discipline yourself to keep track of such things, don't quit your day job. Don't even *think* of starting a business or taking pay for your creative work, because you'll just get into trouble. It's not as if record-keeping is horrendously difficult to do. You just have to convince yourself that it's important (it is). Now get to it.

5

Finding Capital and Managing Debt

WHEN YOU start a small business, you soon learn that you need more stuff than you could have believed possible. You need office or work space, equipment, possibly a computer system, and supplies. You may need to consult with accountants and attorneys, depending on how complex your business arrangements are likely to be. All this costs money. So how are you going to afford it?

Well, you could put it on your VISA, but then what happens if you don't have a client for six months? Although many small-business owners finance their businesses this way, especially during difficult times, it isn't the best way to achieve success. The problem for creative people is that while loans for small businesses are available through banks and organizations like the Small Business Administration, they're difficult for creative people to obtain, since creative people often lack business savvy and their professions are notoriously unreliable. This is further complicated by the fact that, realistically, creative people's businesses can't grow much beyond what they themselves can do in a given day. The exception is the creative person who makes gift baskets or something similar; with training, paid employees could do the job and someone else could own the company. But, for the most part, a photographer can photograph only so many weddings in a given day and in a given year. With an assistant, he or she might become more efficient and therefore more profitable, but again, growth is necessarily limited. An interior designer can design only so many interiors, although she could also hook up with other interior designers and employ assistants to create a more profitable business. Therefore, it is hard for banks and other investors to value (determine the worth of) such a business. If something happens to the owner, the business disappears. There's nothing left over except maybe a computer and some books. There's no business to sell. (There might be copyrights and other intangibles of value, but the worth of these is limited unless you're Stephen King.) These drawbacks make investing in creative businesses quite risky.

Funding the First Few Years

One way to fund a business start-up is with personal income. Your goal may be to become a freelance photographer. Although you may have some equipment, you may need more. You'll also need savings to fall back on, as well as working capital—money for supplies and marketing until your business starts producing revenue. You can purchase the necessary equipment over time, using funds from your day job. If you do part-time photography while still employed, you can use the money you earn to invest in equipment and working capital. (This will also help you drum up business for when you take that final step.) The only drawback to such an arrangement is that you may need such expensive equipment that you'll never be able to purchase it using your day job income.

However, it may be easier to get a business loan while you're still employed, although you'll need to be able to show how you'll get the business going while holding down your present position.

Cash Flow

I discovered in my second year of full-time writing that *cash flow*— the amount of money that's immediately available for use—is an extremely important business principle. I had signed a number of book contracts, several of them requiring many photographs.

The cost of purchasing film and developing it was about $1,000 per project. Each project also required an investment in other supplies. Then my computer monitor died. I knew that within six or eight months I would have income in the form of royalties from some earlier projects, and I knew that within a year or two the current projects would pay off. In the meantime I didn't have any business income to pay my business expenses. I ended up using personal credit cards to finance the projects. Nevertheless, I took this as critical learning experience. (You'll have plenty if you become a small-business owner.) I learned to diversify my sources of income so that some projects paid off within a few weeks, while others paid off after longer periods.

Developing such strategies is essential to surviving the first few years in business. If you encounter cash flow problems (not having enough business income to pay business expenses, even if your business is profitable), reconsider how you conduct your business. If you're a photographer who needs to purchase supplies, ask your clients for a deposit when they sign an agreement with you. Charge a cancelation fee so that you don't take too great a loss if all your June weddings are called off. Make certain that you bill clients in a timely fashion. Have a system for handling collections (besides just sending another letter to the client's accounts payable department). Put off paying bills as long as possible (without incurring late fees, which just worsen your cash flow problem). Lease equipment instead of investing all your spare cash in purchases.

Plan for future expenditures. If you know your photograph enlarger is on its last legs, start pricing new ones now. Or keep an eye out for a used one in reasonable condition. (Plenty of people buy equipment like this, figuring that they're going to become a photographer only to discover after a week that they're better suited to being a secretary.) Figure out what you need and how much it's going to cost. Start setting aside income for this purpose. Instead of spending that $10 rebate check on caramel corn, put it toward the equipment purchase. Then, when you are able to find the equipment you want for a good price, purchase it. This beats having the enlarger fall apart halfway through a project that's due in two days. If you don't plan ahead, you'll end up buying the wrong piece of equipment for 20 percent more than you should have paid and you'll put it on your credit card and be forced to curse your stupidity for at least six months.

Personal Credit Cards

If you decide to use a personal credit card to finance business-related purchases, keep some guidelines in mind. The more you use personal credit cards to fund your business, the harder it is for banks and other potential lenders to see how the business is really doing. (It also makes it hard for *you* to see how the business is doing.) Apply for a business credit card to prevent this problem and to simplify your accounting. Especially if you're strapped for cash, you may not be eligible for a business credit card, at least from major card companies such as Visa and MasterCard, but what about a credit card or credit line from the suppliers you use most? If you use office supplies, Staples, Quill, and other suppliers offer credit cards or credit accounts for business use. You may be able to meet their criteria. If you're purchasing a computer system, you may be able to establish a line of credit or apply for a credit card with the computer store or even the computer manufacturer.

If you must make business-related purchases and you have no other means of obtaining the money, you'll have to turn to your personal credit cards. But keep in mind how high the interest rate is (often more than 18 percent). If the purchase is substantial, or if you make many smaller purchases that add up, the interest charges can be steep. Use personal credit cards as a short-term solution only, such as when you know you have money coming in but you must have a new printer today. Pay off the credit card balance immediately. If you find yourself always relying on personal credit cards to get you through financial crunches in your business, you need to reassess your business and gain better control over your expenses and cash flow. Perhaps you're not taking your business as seriously as you should. Consider how to increase profits on the projects you do while cutting costs. (Chapter 13 discusses this in greater detail.)

Obtaining Bank Loans

If you need working capital, don't dismiss applying for a bank loan just because you think you won't qualify. Although obtaining bank loans for creative small businesses is tricky, there are some things you can do to increase your chances. You'll need to write that pesky business plan before you even approach the bank, so get started.

If you have collateral, the likelihood of obtaining a loan is much greater, regardless of the type of business you're in. You might own a classic Corvette that you would never sell, but that might serve as collateral for a $5,000 loan. If you have equity in your home, a banker might be willing to make a business loan with that as collateral. If you'll be using the loan proceeds to purchase equipment and can show the bank that you're a reliable, serious businessperson, you'll be more likely to get the loan than if you need operating capital to buy supplies and hire an office assistant. (The bank can always seize the equipment if you default, but the office assistant would probably resist being confiscated.) The better the loan officer and the bank know you, the greater the likelihood of your obtaining a loan, so check out your neighborhood bank before going across town to a huge, impersonal financial institution. Bank loans are also easier to obtain if you have people willing to go out on a limb for you (that is, if you have co-signers, such as parents who are themselves well-established). If you show that you're willing to invest in the business yourself, or can show that you *have* invested in the business yourself, the bank is more likely to view you as a serious prospect. Also, if your personal financial history is unblemished, that helps. If you have a bankruptcy or a lot of slow pays, you'll have more trouble. Address such problems before you start your own business.

Before filling out the loan application, talk with a loan officer to determine the likelihood of your receiving a loan. Most lenders are happy to let you know their guidelines for different types of loans. Have a clear, precise idea of how much money you need, what you need it for, why you think your business would be

---

Figure 20
Steps to Obtaining Loans

Write a formal business plan.
Know the financial situation of your business.
Put up collateral or equity if possible.
Plan to use the loan for equipment or other material purchases.
Get to know the bank and the loan officer.
Find co-signers, such as parents.
Show willingness to invest in your business yourself.
Clean up your personal credit history.
Learn loan guidelines before applying.

---

a good risk, and any extenuating circumstances, such as willing co-signers or a Corvette in the garage. Talk with the loan officer in person, not over the phone—it's too easy to give you the brushoff that way. The point is that it's best not to apply for a loan unless there's a reasonably good chance that you'll get it; having been turned down for a loan in the past may make it more difficult for you to get a loan in the future.

The Small Business Administration guarantees certain types of loans so that banks can relax some of their requirements. Limited government funding is also available, especially for women and minorities. Contact the local branch of the SBA for information on these programs.

Unlike your mortgage or car loan, business loans come with reporting requirements. This way, if your business seems to be running into trouble, the bank can catch it right away (before you go bankrupt) and take steps to remedy the situation. The bank might insist that you install a manager or organize a board of directors to help you run the business. You'll need to keep good records (which you're already doing, right?) and report on a monthly or quarterly basis. If you qualify for SBA- or government-backed loans, the reporting requirements will be extensive. The government may interfere just the tiniest bit in the way you run your business. If you're an eccentric genius, this will drive you quite mad. If you only need a little bit of money—a thousand dollars—it isn't worth applying for an SBA loan, even though they handle micro loans. (Micro loans are tiny loans for people who don't need a lot of money.) Pawn your mother's antique engagement ring instead.

Nonbank Investors

If you don't qualify for a bank loan, you may be able to find a non-bank investor. Most venture capitalists (people with a lot of money looking for investment opportunities) won't be interested because of the type of business you own (the profit potential for outside investors isn't large, since you probably won't become a billion-dollar corporation). Still, there are people who might be interested in investing. If you have friends or colleagues with spare cash lying about, you might consider going into partnership with them. In this type of partnership, the friends provide the money while you provide the talent. The revenue is split among the partners. Such deals are structured in various ways. Sometimes the investing partner has to get all of his or her investment back before the proceeds are split. Sometimes the investment is simply the cost of becoming a partner (each person brings something of equal value, such as money or talent). You'll need an attorney experienced in partnership agreements to negotiate this type of investment.

Or maybe your parents have some money set aside that they don't know what to do with. Or, if they're more creditworthy than you, you might even be able to convince them to take out a loan to invest in your business. Such investments also have reporting requirements (such as your mother calling you up and saying, "So how much money did you make this week, dear?"), but it might be worth it, depending on your level of desperation.

Still no luck? You have a terrible credit history, no collateral (all you own is your socks), you've already quit your job, you have no friends, and your family laughs when you mention borrowing money. There is some hope (not a lot, but some). There is always the tried-and-true method of getting a part-time job, although this has the drawback of generally being poorly paid. You

---

Figure 21

Sources of Financing

Fund the business start-up before leaving your full-time job.
Lease instead of purchase.
Personal credit cards.
Business credit cards or line of credit.
Bank or credit union loan.
SBA-backed loan.
Parents, friends, colleagues.
Form a partnership with an investor.
Use home equity or other collateral.
Obtain a part-time job.
Emphasize cost-cutting measures, prompt payment, and
        quick cash sales.
Hold a garage sale.
Pawn your valuables.

---

can generate some quick cash sales or induce clients to pay faster by offering discounts for prompt payment. You can hold a garage sale to finance that new printer. You can also control costs.

Cost-Cutting Strategies

To control cash flow, you can cut costs. Begin by keeping accurate records of expenses and revenue. If you're not claiming legitimate write-offs, you're costing yourself money. Accurate records also show where your money goes so that you can make intelligent financial decisions.

Comparison shop for everything. Never accept the first price you see. Shop through catalogs as well as at regular retail outlets. Learn prices by visiting retailers' and suppliers' web sites so that you don't have to drive from one place to another. Enlist the help of others. If your sister loves to shop, send her with a list of supplies that you routinely need and ask her to search for the best prices. Usually one office supply company sells printer cartridges cheapest while another sells paper cheapest. Instead of doing all your purchasing in one place, buy each product where it's cheapest. Of course, if you waste six hours in search of a twelve-cent discount on printer paper, you're not exactly cutting costs. Driving around town picking up supplies at eight different stores is time-consuming and wasteful. Instead, keep a notebook in which you list the supplies you regularly use. Then, as you learn prices, record them in the notebook. When it's time to get printer cartridges, simply flip through the notebook to find the cheapest source. Arrange your errands so that you can drop by the office supply store when you're already in the area, instead of making a special trip. As soon as you know you'll need to make a major purchase, such as a new fax machine, record it in the notebook. When it's time to make the purchase, you'll know where to do so.

Keep control of office supply costs. Don't allow family members to use your business supplies. They don't need to use your expensive letterhead to write down directions to a friend's house. Reuse paper by printing rough drafts on the back of used sheets, or turn used sheets into scratch pads. Question every expenditure you make for supplies.

Negotiate purchase prices whenever possible. If you're buying a fax machine, ask for a discount on the discontinued floor model. Extended service plans rarely repay the cost, so don't bother with them. If you're going to need a fax and a copy machine, find one that offers both functions. Or find a printer that also faxes and copies. Purchasing combination equipment is less expensive than purchasing two or three separate pieces of equipment. However, make sure combination equipment does each function with the quality you need. Most people don't have to worry about excellent copy quality—they just need copies. But if quality copies are essential, then invest in a stand-alone copier.

Don't overestimate your needs. Do you really need a scanner? Can it wait? If you do need a scanner, determine your bare minimum requirements for it. Although quality counts, is the difference in the quality of two similar scanners worth $150? We have a tendency to equate price with quality even though the two aren't necessarily connected. The best value is *not* the best price for the best piece of equipment. It's the best price for the piece of equipment that best suits your needs.

Consider leasing equipment instead of buying it, particularly for equipment that frequently needs to be replaced or upgraded, such as computers. If you have to invest in a lot of expensive equipment, leasing can be a good alternative to taking out an enormous bank loan to buy the equipment. No matter what type of equipment you need, there's a company that rents it out.

Control utility use. Keep long-distance calls brief. Use e-mail instead, if you can. Remember that long-distance faxes cost you the same as long-distance phone calls, so if you can send an e-mail instead of a fax, you can save money. Turn lights off when you aren't using them, keep the thermostat slightly higher or lower (depending on the season) than usual, and turn off equipment at the end of the day.

If mailing costs contribute to your expenses, find the cheapest shipping service. For regular mail, the post office is your best bet. If you do a lot of bulk mailing, you can get special discounts on your postage. Stop in at the nearest branch to find out how to apply for a bulk mailing permit. For regular packages, UPS is usually cheapest. If you ship books or manuscripts, you can send them through the post office at book rate, which is even cheaper than fourth-class mail. The drawback is that book rate packages travel *very* slowly.

Compare the rate sheets of different shipping companies. Rates vary, depending on the weight of packages and where you're shipping them. You may find that it's cheaper to use one company to ship packages to California and a different company to ship packages to Colorado.

Drop off packages when you can to save on the cost of pickups. Try never to ship overnight or second day. If you must use an express delivery service, the post office has a two- or three-day option that is much less expensive than other such services. If someone wants immediate delivery, see if you can fax it, e-mail it, or deliver it yourself (but only if delivering it won't interrupt your work schedule).

Make sure you and your business are adequately insured but not overinsured. Once a year, compare prices of different insurance companies. Sometimes an insurance company will lower

```
┌─────────────────────────────────────────────────────────┐
│                                                           │
│                       Figure 22                           │
│                    Cutting Costs                          │
│                    ‾‾‾‾‾‾‾‾‾‾‾‾                           │
│                                                           │
│   Remember, the best value is the best price for the      │
│   product that best suits your needs!                     │
│                                                           │
│   Comparison shop, keeping a notebook with price lists.   │
│   Don't let others use office supplies for personal       │
│     purposes.                                             │
│   Negotiate purchase prices.                              │
│   Forgo extended service plans and add-on warranties.     │
│   Purchase multiple-function office equipment.            │
│   Don't overestimate equipment and supply needs.          │
│   Lease instead of purchase.                              │
│   Control utility use.                                    │
│   Minimize long-distance phone calls, especially during   │
│     peak rate times.                                      │
│   Use different shippers for different types of letters    │
│     and packages.                                         │
│   Rely on e-mail and faxes instead of overnight shipping. │
│   Keep your business adequately insured but not           │
│     overinsured.                                          │
│   Make payment terms clear to clients and follow up       │
│     with collections.                                     │
│   Pay bills when they're due, not before.                 │
│   Reduce marketing costs by generating inexpensive        │
│     publicity.                                            │
│                                                           │
└─────────────────────────────────────────────────────────┘
```

rates to become competitive in a certain area or when they have fewer claims than expected. Instead of just dropping one insurance company in favor of another, let your insurance company know that you're planning to do so. In order to retain your business, they may be willing to lower your rates or offer you additional discounts.

When you purchase new pieces of equipment, such as a computer system, be sure that your business insurance will cover it. Some types of equipment or supplies may require special policies.

Make your payment terms clear to your clients. Note the payment due date on the invoice. If a client misses a payment, immediately follow up with a polite letter and a copy of the invoice. If necessary, follow with more strongly worded letters. Immediately discontinue working for clients who owe payments sixty or more days past due. Some business owners stop working for clients who owe payments thirty days past due, but don't alienate your clients by being too ruthless. At the same time, don't let clients take advantage of you. You've provided a service; you're owed money. Period.

Don't pay your own bills until they're due. This keeps your money in your hands as long as possible. Some people pay bills as soon as they receive them, reasoning that they should send the money while they have it. This is not a businesslike approach. Keeping your own money gives you the opportunity to earn interest on it or use it should an emergency crop up.

Control marketing costs by creating press kits instead of placing ads. Give lectures that generate interest in what you do, and network with others. Attending trade shows and conferences in your professional field or in your potential clients' fields can also boost your business. (More information on low-cost marketing can be found in Chapter 13.) Just remember that you don't have to invest in expensive print, direct mail, or telemarketing campaigns in order to increase awareness of your product or service.

Cutting costs does not mean being miserly. If your marketing materials need to be on good-quality paper to stand out from the crowd, make that investment. But do you need to pay a designer to create a logo? Probably not. Be wise with your dollars and make good spending decisions. If you have to run out to the copy shop twice a day to make copies and pick up faxes, it's probably time to invest in your own fax/copy machine. But just because you scan a photograph into the computer once a month doesn't mean you need to buy a scanner. (Copy centers can scan anything onto disk for a nominal fee.) When you're printing your Great American Novel in order to send it to the editor at Random House, use the good-quality 20-pound paper. But rough drafts of an article can be printed on the back of an old manuscript.

Your Personal Financial Future

Your personal financial future is intimately connected with your business. If your business is successful, you will be able to save money, put the kids through college, and retire before you're 82. But this will happen only if you prepare for it. It won't happen by accident or because the rights to your first novel sold for six figures.

Many small-business owners make the mistake of investing all their time and effort in their business without taking care of their own financial future. In fact, they often jeopardize their financial future by using personal credit cards for the business or investing all their savings in it. They reason that if the business is successful enough, it will pay for their needs. Or maybe they hope that at some point they'll sell the business and retire on the profits.

This isn't going to work for you. (Or at least probably not.) As a creative person, you *are* your business. Once you're gone, there is no business. The exception might be if you have a child or partner who could take over, or if your business produces a product that someone could continue to make after you're gone. But for the most part you're not going to be able to sell your business when you're 65 and retire on the proceeds.

Personal financial problems also affect your business. If you don't have enough personal savings to cover the cost of a new furnace in your home, you may have to sell business assets in order to buy it. Or you may find yourself abandoning your business to become a paid employee because you need the steady paycheck to purchase a new house.

Therefore, you need to plan for the future. I know, I know, planning for the present takes up enough time as it is. But the future has an alarming way of becoming the present when you least expect it. At least once a year you should consider what your future needs will be and reassess any plans and goals that you've already set. You may have children you want to put through college. You may want to retire while you're still young enough to travel. Along with your goals, you need to consider what you'll do if things don't work out the way you planned— for instance, if you become disabled. Once you've identified personal financial concerns, you need to consider how you'll meet your needs. (Chapter 6 discusses insurance, including life and disability insurance.)

Personal Savings

As your business becomes profitable, you must set aside a certain amount for savings because the unexpected invariably happens just when you're having trouble getting your clients to pay.
Most financial planners recommend having readily accessible
savings (money under the mattress) equivalent to two months'
income. For small-business owners, readily accessible savings
should include business operating expenses as well as personal
living expenses. Small-business owners need to save more than
two months' income, since it can take time to restart a business
you've had to shut down while recuperating from the malaria
you contracted photographing giraffes on safari in Africa.

Beyond emergency savings, you should set aside additional
money toward retirement. Since you don't have an employer
anymore, you won't have an employer-funded retirement program to take care of you. Especially in light of current concerns
about the viability of the Social Security system, it's probably not
a good idea to rely on it in your old age. If you're younger, you
can invest some of your retirement savings in riskier investments,
such as high-tech stocks. The closer you are to retirement, the
safer your investment strategies should be.

Although you may want to help your kids pay for college,
most experts recommend that you take care of your retirement
first. Many retirement funds (such as individual retirement accounts, or IRAs) can be used to pay for education if needed. Or
you can pay some college expenses out of your income when
the time comes. Your kids can help pay for college by taking jobs
during the summer or working part-time during the school year.
Government grants (which you don't have to pay back) and student loans (which you do have to pay back) are also available. A
combination of these different funds can be used to put your
child through college. But if you haven't looked after yourself,
you'll still be working when you're 82. Although there are student loans for students, there's no such thing as a retirement loan
for retirees. Essentially, then, take care of yourself first because
no one else will.

Investment Tools

Depending on how quickly you need access to your money, you can invest in a variety of ways. For immediate access, you can invest in a regular savings account at your local bank or credit union. This alternative prevents your money from being stolen from under your mattress, but it doesn't offer a very good interest rate. However, it gives you almost immediate access to your savings, so when the furnace explodes and you realize it's time for a new one, you have the cash on hand (well, almost on hand) to purchase it.

Another safe investment is a *certificate of deposit* (CD). When you invest in a CD, you are guaranteed a specified interest rate if you leave your money in the bank for a set period, which you decide on in advance. Usually, the longer the period, the higher the interest rate. The interest rate on a CD is better than that on a regular savings account but less than what you can find elsewhere. You can invest in thirty-day, sixty-day, or five-year CDs, and others. During the agreed-upon time, the bank uses your money to speculate wildly or to invest soundly, depending. At the end of the set period of time, the *maturity date* arrives, meaning that you can withdraw your money and the interest it has earned, or you can reinvest the money and interest in another CD or some other investment. If you need your money before the maturity date, for instance to pay the mortgage, you can withdraw it, but you have to pay a penalty and probably won't see any of the interest you had been promised.

These types of savings programs are perfectly safe. (They're insured by the FDIC, up to $100,000 per depositor. If you have more than that in your savings account, you don't need me to advise you on your financial future.) The regular savings account is a good choice for stashing emergency funds. CDs are a good choice for people planning to use their investments over the long term, rather than the next few years, but not right away. These are also good tools for people nearing retirement age. Also, by investing in CDs with different maturity dates, you can use the invested money plus interest for living expenses as each comes due.

Many investors choose *mutual funds*, or groups of stocks. Your investment is spread throughout a number of companies, so that if one loses money or goes bankrupt, you don't lose your entire investment. Investing in mutual funds is very popular because it's often safer than purchasing individual stocks and bonds. Mutual funds may not return as much money as one winning stock, but then, what are the chances of picking one right stock, anyway? Mutual funds can be started for as little as $50 or $100 a month.

Investing in individual *stocks* with the help of a broker or investment service is an option for some. If you're interested in this type of approach, you'll need to understand how to monitor stocks and bonds and how to purchase them. You usually need a large initial investment for this approach to make sense. Although you could purchase one share of stock for $100 (more or less, depending on the company), by the time you pay the broker's commission, the stock would have to triple in value in three months to be a worthwhile investment. On the other hand, if you have $5,000 under the mattress (and if you can lose it without going bankrupt), this is certainly an investment strategy worth looking into.

Individual retirement accounts (IRAs) are another popular investment tool. Depending on your circumstances, you can deposit a certain amount of before-tax dollars into an IRA. You don't pay taxes on the money or the interest it earns until you retire. The theory is that when you retire, you'll be in a lower tax bracket so you'll pay less in taxes. IRAs can be linked to mutual funds or to specific stocks.

Financial Advisors

A financial advisor can help you prepare for the future. This is not the same as a stockbroker, who buys and sells stock on your behalf. A financial advisor tells you what types of investments are most appropriate for you and can help you calculate how much money you'll need to meet your various needs for retirement, education, and other circumstances.

Don't hire an advisor who works on commission (your first clue that an advisor works on commission is when he or she offers to work for you for free), who will try to steer you to investments that provide the biggest commission and are not necessarily right for you. Hire a financial advisor whom you pay by the hour or for the service as a whole. Remember that in most cases people can call themselves a financial advisor without any specific education, experience, or licensing. Get referrals and don't follow an advisor's recommendations blindly. Do some research and investigation on your own.

Last Will and Testament

All business owners should write a will. Although there may not be a business after you're gone, there may be copyrights to protect, royalties to distribute, and the like. A simple will can save your survivors plenty of headaches. You can make your own will if you want. Most states recognize holograph wills (wills written in the deceased's handwriting) as long as they have the signatures of two or three witnesses. The witnesses don't have to read the will; they just acknowledge that the signature is yours.

Consulting with a lawyer can prevent you from making mistakes. This is especially important if you have minor children or many assets. You'll need to appoint a guardian for your children and an executor for the will. This is the person who arranges for your final wishes to be met. As a creative person, you can designate a literary or artistic executor whom you trust to handle creative matters. This special executor should be someone with experience in the relevant area, such as rights and royalties, which the general executor might not understand.

The Benefits of Planning

By planning your own financial future, you'll be able to enjoy the rewards of your work. Every now and then (at least once a year), step back from your business and look at your personal situation. If you haven't already, take the time now to determine savings and investment goals and devise a realistic plan for achieving them. Then, as your business grows and becomes more profitable, review your plans regularly and make any necessary changes.

6

Understanding Insurance Needs

ONE OF the principles of small-business ownership is that if you don't have insurance to cover it, it will break. If you do have insurance to cover it, it will outlast you. When you're a creative person establishing a small business, you have two sets of insurance concerns: those that are business-related and those that are personal. Both types will be discussed in this chapter.

Some of the risks of running your own business cannot be covered with insurance, or the insurance costs would be prohibitively expensive, or the risk factor is so small that it wouldn't be worth paying for coverage. This chapter will help you make sound decisions regarding your insurance needs.

Sources estimate that more than half of small-business owners, especially home-based business owners, have inadequate insurance or believe they're covered for certain problems when actually they are not. Be certain to check with your insurance agent (and read the policy, asking for help and explanation as needed) regarding the exact coverage you have.

What types of insurance do you need for your business? It depends, of course, on what type of business you have. A writer working from home has different needs than a ceramicist who operates a studio open to the public. By understanding the purpose of different types of insurance, you can decide which types apply to your business.

Business Owner's Coverage

A business owner's policy is a package of different types of insurance. Similar to homeowner's or renter's insurance, it covers theft and property damage to a business. It can also cover other basic business insurance needs, such as liability insurance. If you work from home, you'll need a rider or special amendment to your homeowner's or renter's insurance. *Incidental business riders*, as these are called, can be tailored to fit your needs. A business owner's policy can also cover at-home businesses, although it's more expensive than an incidental business rider. Some insurance companies offer special in-home business insurance plans that provide liability coverage (which protects you in the event of being sued), replacement of income (which provides income if something happens that makes it impossible for you to run your business), and regular property coverage for theft or property damage.

General Liability Coverage

Liability coverage is important if you rent or own business or commercial property. It's also necessary if clients or employees visit your home for business-related reasons. If you're a photographer who meets people in your living room and one winter day a potential customer slips on your sidewalk and breaks her ankle, she could sue you. If you have a homeowner's policy, you may think that's enough (after all, the UPS driver could sue you, too, if he slipped on the ice while delivering a package, but no one seems to worry about that). However, some homeowner's policies won't pay if the liability is the result of using the home as a place of business.

Before making a decision, consider both your clients' requirements and your own. Depending on the type of business you run and the businesses you serve, your clients may ask you to have general liability insurance. This is common if you (or your employees, if any) will be working on or with the client's property. (If you have employees, clients may also ask for proof of workers' compensation and unemployment insurance.)

Property Coverage

Property coverage protects your business in the event of theft and natural disasters. For your business-related property, you may wish to consider *replacement-value* policies. Ordinarily your property is insured for what it's worth. A three-year-old television might be worth fifty bucks. A two-year-old computer might be worth one hundred bucks. That's what the policy would reimburse you should the television or computer be stolen. If your family television is stolen and you get a fifty bucks from the insurance company for it, you aren't going to be able to run out and buy a brand-new television. This is not such an important consideration when it's just the television you're talking about. But if it's your business computer that's stolen, it's not as if you can wait around to see what kind of deal you can get on discontinued models in six months. You're going to have to replace that computer right away, and chances are it's going to cost you more than the computer you lost was worth. That's why you probably need replacement-value coverage, at least on some of the big-ticket items. This will cover the actual cost of replacing the property that was lost with similar property. (That is, if you lose a nineteen-inch television, the insurance company isn't going to reimburse you for a big-screen television. It will reimburse you for another nineteen-inch television.)

Property Risk Reduction

In addition to insuring your property, you can further protect it by reducing the risks associated with it. To reduce the risk of theft, install good strong locks and exterior security lighting. Invest in an alarm or security system, especially if you have expensive equipment, if you've invested in expensive inventory, if you live in an area with a high crime rate, or if other factors place you at great risk for theft.

Natural disasters such as fire and flood can destroy your property. Be certain to guard yourself against these risks as much as possible. For fire risk, install smoke detectors. Keep important documents and computer disks in a safety deposit box at the bank or at least in a fireproof box in the basement. Know where your fire extinguisher is (you do have one, don't you?) For flood risk, keep that fireproof box in the attic, not the basement. As soon as the river starts rising, put a flood plan into action by locating and safely storing materials essential to the survival of your business. Your insurance agent can give you specific pointers for protecting your business from loss, and may arrange for a discount on your insurance premium for the risk-reduction steps you take.

Be sure to clearly think through all the property issues related to your business before deciding that you've done all you can to reduce risk. Losing a computer to a thief isn't just a matter of losing a valuable piece of equipment. It also means that you lose records and data. What can you do to keep the loss of data from shutting down your business? Be sure to back up computer files often so they can be reconstructed later. Keep these disks in a separate place, such as a fireproof box in the attic. Once a month, back up the entire computer system and store the disks off-site. (Off-site can be your mother's basement. The point is to spread the risk. The chances of your mother's house going up in flames at the exact same moment yours does is so unlikely that we'll have to consider arson if it happens.) By the same token, you should keep a copy of business phone numbers and addresses that are vital to your operations in a separate place. The more time and thought you devote to risk reduction, the more likely you are to prevent property loss or at least reduce its impact on your business.

Valuing Insured Property

To prevent a loss from destroying your business, you'll need to value your business property adequately. You can hire an appraiser if you need help with this. Your insurance agent can also offer guidelines for valuing business property.

In addition to inventory and equipment, there may be less obvious but still essential business property that you need to cover. For instance, I have an extensive reference collection that has taken years to put together. It would probably cost me several thousand dollars to replace all those books if they went up in flames, yet I rarely think about that expense. Without my reference materials, I can't do much work. Your business may have similar property that you haven't considered covering but that would be difficult or expensive to replace. Also, determine the cost of the supplies and other miscellaneous items that you typically keep on hand. Losing these materials in a flood or fire could cost you hundreds of dollars, but it isn't something most people consider when they purchase insurance for their business property. Try to think of all aspects of your business and determine what is most at risk and most worth insuring. Inventory may require a commercial policy instead of a regular property policy.

What about your clients' property? Is it adequately protected? Do you ever keep clients' materials in your office? What would happen if they were stolen or destroyed? Even if you don't think you need business coverage for your property, you may need it for your clients.

What about taking your own property off-site? Some insurance policies cover as little as 10 percent (or even none) of the value of property that you take away from your home or place of business. The laptop computer you bring everywhere might be insured when it's sitting in your living room, but not insured (or underinsured) when it's sitting on a client's desk. What other property do you take off-site with you? Is it worth insuring? If so, you may need to purchase *off-premises coverage.* This can be a rider or an additional insurance policy. If most of your work is done off-site (as with a photographer who specializes in weddings), off-premises coverage may not be enough. You probably need a commercial policy.

Business Interruption Insurance

Business owner's insurance packages sometimes offer business interruption insurance. If a tornado levels your home office and you not only have five years' worth of business records to reconstruct but can't fill your clients' needs because you can't work in the bare lot that was once your house, you have a problem. Business interruption insurance kicks in with payments to help you make ends meet while you get your business up and running again. If you take care to store records off-site and to record all your computer information on disks, which you also store off-site, and you're certain that no matter what, you can get your business up and running right away, you may not need this coverage. Otherwise, it can be a good value.

Professional Liability Coverage

General liability insurance protects you if a client breaks her ankle on your front step, but it won't help you if you get sued by a local politician who is unhappy with your profile of him that was published in last week's paper. Although incorporating your business protects your personal wealth from some liability concerns, it doesn't protect you from professional liability. If you could be sued over your professional practice, you should look into professional liability coverage. Sure, you don't ever plan to defame people, but what happens if you don't think you have and they beg to differ? Or what happens when for some reason you are unable to fulfill your services as contracted? This coverage will pay the costs of defending a lawsuit (the insurer may require that their lawyers form part of the defense) plus a specified amount of damages awarded should you lose such a case. Although professional liability coverage can be important, don't advertise the fact that you have it (in other words, don't print it on your business cards). This is merely spreading the word that your pockets are deeper than they appear, and could invite nuisance suits.

Insurance for Employees

If you employ others, you should consider commercial policies that combine general liability insurance (for the client who breaks her ankle) with *worker's compensation coverage* (in case your assistant develops carpal tunnel syndrome trying to keep up with the amount of paperwork you generate) and *unemployment insurance* (for when you fire the fruit basket delivery person). If you have employees, clients will expect you to have this type of insurance coverage. (So will your employees and the government.) Be sure to get a certificate of insurance that you can copy and for-ward to clients.

You may also want to provide health insurance or other benefits to your employees. Insurance agents with experience in employee insurance plans can help you with this. If you do employ others, check local, state, and federal laws for employment practices and guidelines you should know.

Business Automobile Insurance

Even though you have insurance on your vehicle, you may discover that you'll need an additional rider or a different policy if you use your personal vehicle for business reasons. Be sure to check with your insurance agent.

Umbrella Policies

Umbrella policies cover costs in excess of those covered by your underlying policies. Say, for instance, that your general liability insurance covers up to $200,000 in claims. But someone is injured on your property and incurs $300,000 in medical expenses. (Okay, so a meteor would have to fall on him. These things happen.) The umbrella policy picks up the $100,000 difference between your liability insurance cap and the medical bills. Umbrella policies are cheap because someone else is responsible for the initial liability. Only under the most extreme conditions will these policies kick in. Worth thinking about, especially if you run a business with substantial risk factors, such as dangerous equipment.

Credit Insurance

You may have been offered credit insurance when you signed up for a credit card or other type of loan in the past. Credit insurance provides limited coverage in the event of disability or death. The coverage is limited to a specific loan, such as an auto loan or credit card, and pays monthly installment payments on the loan should you become disabled either temporarily or permanently.

These policies also pay off the loan entirely should you die during the loan term. For the most part, credit insurance is expensive and provides little value for the cost. You would be better off purchasing a general disability plan that would help pay *all* your bills, plus a separate life insurance policy (or leave an estate with enough assets to cover your debts). The exception to this no-credit-insurance rule concerns some mortgage loans, where the lender requires credit insurance (called private mortgage insurance) in order to approve the loan. In this case, and *only* in this case, you should consider credit insurance. If you can show that you have other disability and life insurance, you may be able to talk your lender into letting you take the mortgage without the additional insurance. You may need to provide proof of continuing coverage whenever your lender asks.

Personal Insurance

For peace of mind, you may need three additional types of insurance: disability, life, and health. Often these benefits are provided by employers, but now you are your own employer. Sometimes lack of insurance coverage can prevent people from striking out on their own. You don't need to go to that extreme. Coverage is available to individuals, even to those with serious risk factors. You may have to pay more than when you worked for another company, but the cost shouldn't be prohibitive. Here's what you need to know.

Disability Insurance

Disability insurance comes in two forms, short-term and long-term. It pays a certain percentage of your average income while you're unable to work (due to injury or illness). Usually, people who purchase disability insurance should purchase both short- and long-term policies. Short-term policies cover you soon after the onset of a disability, such as the first day of an accident and the second week of an illness. These policies may continue providing income replacement for six months or so. Then, if your disability lasts more than six months, your long-term disability insurance will start. Long-term disability insurance may continue paying for years. You should coordinate the plans so that the long-term starts as soon as the short-term ends.

Short-term disability insurance is more expensive than long-term because you are more likely to break your leg and lose three weeks of work than to succumb to a serious illness that puts you out of commission for a year and a half. These policies usually coordinate with Social Security and other benefits you may receive (such as worker's compensation).

If you have adequate savings to cover several months' worth of personal and business expenses, you may not need short-term disability insurance. In this case, you would coordinate the long-term disability plan to coincide with the amount of savings you have.

Whether you need disability insurance depends on many factors, including your personal feeling of risk. As a creative small-business owner, if something happens to you, very likely your business will fold. Without you, the business is nothing. This being the case, disability insurance starts to look pretty good. You might consider your assets—savings, a car, a house that's almost paid off—and how long you could keep afloat without income. (Sure, the government might give you a hand, but that could take months.) If you have a gainfully employed spouse, this may reduce your perceived risk. Of course, your gainfully employed spouse could be involved in the same auto accident that disables you, so that's no guarantee. If you're in a partnership or corporation with other owners, you may decide that everyone should be covered by disability insurance so that the disability of one person doesn't destroy the entire business and, with it, the livelihood of the others. Check costs for different levels of disability coverage to help you decide what to do.

The amount of coverage you purchase is usually a percentage of your monthly income. Because your monthly income may be erratic, this can be hard to calculate. You also need to cover any business expenses that might occur while you are disabled. If you purchased a new computer system for your business using a business line of credit and then broke both arms in a freak rollerblading accident, your business would still have to pay for the computer although you would be unable to work. What would you do then? You may need to invest in a combination of disability insurance and readily accessible savings.

Life Insurance

Life insurance pays your survivors after your death. It replaces your income, at least for a period, and provides cash to pay expenses such as your burial costs, debts, and taxes. There are two main types, term and whole life insurance. *Whole life* insurance, sometimes called *cash-value* insurance, works something like a savings account. You pay more than the premium amount, and the extra investment becomes available to you on retirement. These plans are rarely a good choice. If you need the invested money before retirement, you'll pay big penalties. The return on your investment may not be very good. You should purchase life insurance as life insurance. Invest for your retirement in a different way.

Term life insurance requires you to pay a set premium for a set period of time (a term). If you die during the covered period, the policy pays a specified benefit amount. The premium should be guaranteed over the life of the term. It comes in various lengths, such as five, ten, or even thirty years. You can also purchase life insurance that is renewable annually. This starts out less expensive than longer-term plans, but as you renew the plan each year, it becomes more and more expensive. Such coverage works as a stopgap measure but shouldn't be part of a long-range plan. Check with different companies to determine their prices for different terms. You may qualify for special premiums if you're young, in good health, and have both parents living. If you're in a partnership or a corporation with other owners, you may wish to have all owners insured so that the death of one member does not destroy the business. If you have adequate savings and your survivors, if any, will be provided for out of your estate (e.g., if you own your own home, have investments, etc.), you may not need life insurance.

Figure 23

Insurance Options

Business Owner's Policy. Package of insurance that
        provides property coverage and liability coverage
Incidental Business Rider. Provides coverage for home-
        based businesses
General Liability Coverage. Provides coverage should an
        employee or client be injured while on your
        property for business-related reasons
Property Coverage. Provides coverage for equipment and
        supplies in the event of theft or natural disaster.
        Choose *replacement value* policies for big-ticket
        items such as computers.
Business Interruption Insurance. Provides replacement
        income should you be unable to operate your
        business owing to a covered loss
Professional Liability Coverage. Provides coverage
        should you be sued for damages arising from the
        practice of your profession
Worker's Compensation and Unemployment Insurance.
        Required coverage if you employ others
Umbrella Policies. Provides coverage in the event that
        damages or claims are in excess of the underly-
        ing coverage amount
Credit Insurance. Pays monthly payment on a specific
        loan should you become disabled, either short-
        term or long-term; pays off entire note in the
        event of death. Expensive, with little value.
        Purchase disability and life insurance instead.
Disability Insurance. Pays a percentage of your monthly
        income should you be disabled owing to injury or
        illness. Short- and long-term policies are available.
Life Insurance. Provides survivors with a specified
        benefit in the event of your death. Choose term
        life instead of whole life or cash-value policies.

Health Insurance

The greatest concern of the self-employed is obtaining and paying
for adequate health insurance. Often people aren't sure where to
get it and how they can afford it, especially if they have health

problems. There are several types of health insurance, each with its own costs, guidelines, and reimbursement policies.

Health Maintenance Organizations. Health maintenance organizations, or HMOs, consist of networks of physicians, hospitals, and other healthcare workers and organizations under contract. These contracting providers agree to accept set fees for their services.

HMOs hold down healthcare costs by requiring patients to use contracting providers (otherwise coverage can be denied) and by limiting access to specialists. You must have the permission of your primary physician in order to visit a specialist, and primary physicians in these plans may be discouraged from making referrals. HMOs also require patients to seek preapproval before undergoing outpatient procedures or for hospitalizations for anything other than an immediately life-threatening injury or disease. Routine blood work, x-rays, and other tests may also require the HMO's permission.

Legislative efforts are under way to help control some problems associated with HMOs, such as disallowing coverage for necessary care. If you're generally healthy and can find a participating doctor you're comfortable with, such a plan could be right for you. HMOs have varying co-payments (the amount the patient owes for a covered service). They're usually less expensive than any other type of health insurance coverage.

Participating Provider Organizations. These plans, called PPOs, work like HMOs, except for a few features. The insurer contracts with physicians, hospitals, and other healthcare providers and organizations, and these contracting providers agree to accept a set fee from the insurance company. Patients who use these contracting providers get the most coverage. But patients can also see out-of-network providers, in which case they pay the difference between the insurer's set fee and the healthcare provider's charge. Patients are not prevented from visiting specialists, nor in most cases do they need to seek permission for routine tests, outpatient procedures, or most hospitalizations. Because there is more flexibility with these plans, the coverage is more expensive. The insurance company holds down costs by paying only a set fee for services and by requiring the patient to pay an annual deductible and a specified co-payment amount.

The deductible and co-payment amounts can vary, which will increase or decrease the cost of coverage. For individuals with complicated health issues, PPOs are a better choice than HMOs, even though they may be more expensive.

Traditional Medical Plans. These increasingly rare insurance plans, called indemnity plans, cover almost any medical service a patient chooses to have (exceptions usually include plastic surgery and other elective procedures, chiropractic services, and experimental treatments). The exclusions are stated on the policy. Everything else is covered. Such plans pay a percentage of the cost of each medical service, typically 80 percent. The patient is responsible for paying the remaining 20 percent, up to a specified amount each year. Once the patient has paid the annual out-of-pocket expense, the insurance plan pays 100 percent of all medical costs until the new year begins. The patient does not seek permission for services, tests, procedures, or hospitalizations. These plans are usually the most expensive, since the insurer can do little to control costs. A variation of the traditional indemnity plan is the *major medical plan*, which covers certain outpatient tests and procedures as well as necessary hospitalizations but does not cover office visits or routine blood work and x-rays. If you're in good health and don't anticipate seeing your physician more than once a year, a major medical plan makes a lot of sense, especially if you don't want to enroll in an HMO. Costs are similar to those for a PPO.

Hospitalization Plans. Hospitalization plans that cover a specified percentage of hospital costs are also available. If a hospitalization plan will be your only coverage, you need to be in excellent health. You should also set aside a certain amount of money each month to cover routine medical expenses, since the treatment for most injuries and illnesses does not require hospitalization. These are the least expensive health plans of all.

Where to Find Health Insurance

You can obtain health insurance from a variety of sources. If you're employed full-time, your employer may provide a plan. Some companies provide part-time workers with benefits (although they have to pay a larger share of the premium than full-time workers). If

Figure 24

Health Insurance Coverage

Health maintenance organizations (HMOs). Many services are covered, but only if member uses contracting providers. Usually the least expensive type of comprehensive health insurance coverage available. Members are not covered if they use noncontracting providers. Visits to specialists must be approved. Most inpatient and outpatient procedures must be preapproved.

Preferred provider organizations (PPOs). PPOs pay a set fee for covered services. If member uses contracting providers, once the deductible or co-payment amount is met, no further expenses result. More expensive than HMO coverage. Some tests and procedures may require preapproval. Members may visit specialists at will and can use noncontracting providers (they pay the difference between the PPO's set fee and the healthcare provider's charge.)

Traditional medical plans (indemnity plans). Traditional plans cover most healthcare services. Once a deductible is met, the member has no further out-of-pocket expenses. Usually the most expensive type of healthcare coverage. Exclusions are stated on the policy; all other healthcare services are covered.

Major medical plans. Major medical plans cover certain outpatient tests and procedures as well as inpatient stays. Similar to HMOs in cost. Routine office visits, blood work, and x-rays aren't covered.

Hospitalization plans. Hospitalization plans cover members during inpatient hospital stays. The least expensive type of coverage. No routine healthcare services are covered, nor are outpatient tests and procedures.

you're not employed by another company and you can join a spouse's plan, that is generally the best choice.

If you're still employed, sign up for COBRA insurance as soon as you quit to go out on your own. COBRA, the acronym for the budget act of 1985, requires businesses with more than twenty employees to give full-time employees the option of continuing their medical insurance for eighteen months after they leave the company. You have to pay the full price for coverage, plus an administrative fee of 2 percent of the cost of the premium. After the eighteen-month period, you'll need an alternate medical insurer. You should line this up before your eighteen months have come and gone and maybe even before you quit your job, depending on how difficult you believe it will be to find appropriate coverage at a reasonable cost.

You can also purchase an individual policy through an insurance agent. You will need to consider how large a deductible you are willing to settle for, how much total out-of-pocket expense you can reasonably handle, and what specific needs you have, such as dental or vision insurance. Many large insurers, including Blue Cross and Aetna, are now insuring individuals. Some, like State Farm, offer only major medical or hospitalization coverage. Most plans have a waiting period before they will cover preexisting conditions. If you have a condition that may apply, be sure to ask about it and check on the length of the waiting period. If you have preexisting conditions that make it difficult for you to be insured under an individual policy, you may be able to purchase health insurance through a group. An industry association may provide cheaper health insurance than what you could arrange as an individual. Check trade and professional organizations (such as the National Writers Union). Some small-business and home-based business groups also offer group insurance plans. Check with the local chamber of commerce. Although you'll have to join the association to get the insurance, it might be worth the extra expense.

Some states also have a high-risk insurance pool. These allow people who are unable to purchase individual health insurance to participate in a state-sponsored health insurance program, in which premiums may be tied to income. Check with your state insurance commissioner to find out more about this option.

All types of insurance—business and personal—are available through independent and affiliated agents, but make sure you have the right agent. The agent who handles your life insurance policy may not be knowledgeable about business insurance. Your business insurance agent should be familiar with small-business needs. If he or she often works with home-based business owners, that's a definite plus. If you purchase several plans (such as business owners' and life insurance) from one company, you will often be eligible for a discount on rates. Nevertheless, shop around and compare rates to get the best coverage possible at the most reasonable cost.

7

Contracts, Agreements, and Other Legal Documents

I<small>F YOU'VE</small> freelanced for more than a week, you know that contracts are a way of life. Businesspeople come up with contracts, agreements, and legal documents for every action they undertake. Sometimes you have to wonder whether you really need them. Often you don't. But most businesspeople aren't sure when they do and don't need legal documents, so they spend more time with their lawyers than with their loved ones.

Typical Contracts

When you're starting a business, you may sign legal documents for loans, leases, and the like. These are necessary evils, so you should be prepared to read legal documents thoroughly even if you don't understand half the words. If you have questions about a document, ask, or obtain a copy of the document to review with your lawyer *before* you sign it. If you do ask a lawyer for advice, make sure you consult one who has worked with small-business owners and is familiar with contract law.

Two writing partners once hired a highly recommended lawyer to draw up a partnership agreement, which they both signed. Only later did they realize that the issue of how to terminate the partnership, sometimes called the buy-sell clause (an essential part of a partnership agreement), was not even *mentioned* in the agreement. Fortunately, the two were reasonable people. When they decided to terminate the partnership, it was a mutual decision with no repercussions. But if they'd had a disagreement regarding how to split the proceeds of the partnership, they would have had a difficult time trying to settle the problem with such a poorly prepared contract. Just because a lawyer is involved is no guarantee that a contract says what you wanted it to say. For this reason, familiarize yourself with the types of contracts you're most likely to use or be asked to sign. If you're thinking about entering a partnership, learn about partnership contracts. If you're interested in publishing, learn about author-publisher agreements. Ask the SBA in your area for resources. Check the library for books that show sample contracts. Make certain the basic points of any negotiation are covered in the agreement.

I once entered into an auto lease believing that I had covered every possible loophole. I learned later that an acquisition fee of almost $1,000 was tacked onto the lease cost. The salesman defended himself by saying, "You didn't ask." Of course, I will never do business with that sleazy auto dealer again; nevertheless, he has my thousand bucks and the car cost me a lot more than I was planning to spend. Another Learning Experience. What I learned was to read, read, read! Don't let people rush you into signing anything. Also, ask plenty of questions. If I had asked the salesperson, "Is there an acquisition fee?" and if he had lied, I would have had a better case against the dealer. (Regardless of what salespeople believe, oral representations are legally binding, though hard to prove in court.)

It's obvious to most people that auto dealers will try to take advantage of you. It's less obvious that other people, such as your clients, will also try to take advantage of you. But you must enter every agreement and read every contract assuming that someone is trying to take advantage of you. Your goal is to find out just how, and whether you should let them. Cultivate cynicism when confronted with legal documents.

Client Contracts

Your clients may ask you to sign legal documents when you work with them. In addition to specifying the work to be done, they may ask that you agree to confidentiality clauses, which is perfectly legitimate. If you're going to be privy to their business secrets, they need to have recourse should you go blabbing everything you know to their strongest competitor. The problem with some of these agreements is the broad and general terms in which they're written. Specify that sensitive information must be marked "confidential." The confidentiality agreement shouldn't include information you learned from a third party or from public knowledge. The confidentiality clause should have a time limit.

One variation of this clause asks you not to reveal work you've done for a company. Ghostwriters routinely agree to this. But if you can't claim a client as a client, how are potential clients going to believe that you know what you're doing? How can you show that you have relevant experience when you're not allowed to tell anyone whom you've worked for? Don't sign one of these unless you no longer need recommendations to get work, or you don't need to advertise the additional experience, or you're getting paid really, really well.

Clients may also ask you to sign noncompete agreements. A noncompete agreement, as the name implies, says that you will not conduct business that competes with the client's business. There isn't a single reason why you should sign. If it's the only way to get the client to hire you, you'd be better off finding a new client. You have every right to earn a living from your work, and no one should try to control that, certainly not a client. Walk away from noncompete agreements or you may regret it.

Some clients want the right of first refusal on creative work. You write a book and you promise to let the publisher consider publishing your next book before you show it to another publisher. As long as you're satisfied with the financial arrangements you have with this client, granting the right of first refusal may work to everyone's advantage. You don't have to shop your manuscript to every publisher in New York, and your publisher gets an exclusive look at your new work.

If you grant the right of first refusal, set specific response times. Otherwise, the publisher could take three years to reject your second book, by which time you've starved to death. Also, be sure you know what you're granting the client the right to look at. Many ask to see a completely finished manuscript. But like many nonfiction writers, you might work from proposals. I certainly do. If no one likes a proposed idea, I drop the idea knowing that at least I haven't wasted too much of my life. I don't want to have to write an entire manuscript before finding out that the client with the right of first refusal doesn't want to publish the book.

The right of first refusal can work to your disadvantage if the company isn't paying you well, since generally if they accept your next work, they do so at the same contract terms.

Assigning Rights

If you're a creative person, you must understand how copyrights work in order to use them to your advantage. Copyright law protects the works you create from the moment you create them. No special registration is required, although you can register for a copyright with the Library of Congress. It requires an application and a fee. This registration simply proves that the Library of Congress had a copy of your work on file at the time that you registered it, which could be helpful in a lawsuit. For copyrights created since 1978, copyright protection extends for fifty years beyond the death of the creator, so remember to assign copyright ownership in your will.

The more of your rights you keep, the more you can earn from your work. In any agreement between a creative person and another company, the agreement should specify that all rights return to the creator if the company goes bankrupt or doesn't use the rights within a specified time period, and for whatever other reasons you deem important. Otherwise, your publisher could go bankrupt and sell your rights to some guy in Canada you never heard of, and good luck getting any money you earned.

There are five kinds of rights to a creative work, including reproduction, adaptation, distribution, performance, and display,

---

Figure 25

The Five Kinds of Rights to a Creative Work

1. Reproduction
2. Adaptation
3. Distribution
4. Performance
5. Display

---

all of which apply to different kinds of works in different ways and some of which overlap. For a photographer, the right to reproduce and to display work is more important than the right to perform it. A writer is more concerned about reproduction and performance than about display. These five rights are further divided into categories based on the type of use. These include first rights, one-time rights, second serial rights, all rights, and subsidiary rights.

Selling *first rights*, also called first serial rights, grants the exclusive right to publish the work for the first time. These rights are sometimes qualified by region, such as "first North American serial rights." The "serial" means that the work can be broken into segments and published that way. (Think of a magazine printing a novel in six installments.) Selling *one-time rights* grants the nonexclusive right to publish a work. These rights are usually granted to two or more noncompeting markets that are interested in the same piece of work. You can sell as many one-time rights to a piece as you've got buyers for. Selling *second rights* or second serial rights grants the right to reprint a work after it has already appeared elsewhere (think of *Reader's Digest*). Work can be reprinted as often as you can find buyers for it. Selling *all rights*, just as it sounds, grants the use of all rights to a work. The writer can never use the work again in any form (more on this later). For the most part, you should never sell all rights to a piece of work. *Subsidiary rights* include adaptation, translation, and dramatic rights, which allow your work to be adapted and presented on stage or screen.

Artists and writers are often asked to grant all rights to a client. Often these are called *work-for-hire* agreements. Anything you write or create for the client becomes theirs to keep and to use permanently and irrevocably. Creative people should never sell all rights unless it's for a project they know they'll never have a use for, such as a company's annual report. In that case, assigning all rights is acceptable. But if you were to create an entire article or book, it would be unwise to assign all rights to the client, unless it was for something like a company history. Even in that case, you must be well paid for your work in order to compensate for the loss of copyright.

More and more traditional publishers are asking for all rights to a work in order to profit from using your work on the Internet and in other ways. Unless you're very well compensated for giving up all your rights, refuse such demands. Don't let an editor or publisher intimidate you into assigning valuable copyrights without fair recompense.

Exchanging Rights for Payment

To be considered legally binding, the assignment of rights, including copyrights, usually must be accompanied by a payment of some kind. A writer might agree to assign rights to an article in exchange for a payment of $200. Or she might assign rights in exchange for royalty payments. But the writer couldn't agree to assign rights without the other party offering something in exchange. You will need to consider this when you ask for or grant rights. The payment doesn't necessarily have to be money. It could be copies of the magazine containing your article. The payment could also be a token amount, like one dollar.

Your Business Contracts

In addition to signing contracts required by clients, you may wish to use agreements of your own. You can consult with an attorney to discuss creating a standard agreement if you do much of the same type of work, such as consulting. Or you can do what many people are beginning to prefer: Write a memo of understanding. This is a letter that outlines the agreement between the client and you. In this case, the less legalese, the better. State the work you will perform, how the work will be evaluated (i.e., how it will be determined that you've done your job), when the work will be performed, and your fee. You can also note cancelation fees and any specific points that apply to your business. If your client disagrees with anything in the memo, you can either revise it or hold your ground.

A written memo of understanding (or any agreement) isn't going to make much difference if a client decides not to pay up. You're still going to have to decide if it's worth hiring an attorney to sue, but such agreements can be helpful at the start, to make sure both parties understand what has been arranged. That's why memos of understanding should be clear and concise. The more complicated the arrangement, however, and the greater the length of the project, the more you should consider asking a lawyer to draft a contract. But for basic work (such as writing the company's annual report) a memo of understanding should suffice. You don't need a lawyer to look it over if you feel that it covers the key issues, but it doesn't hurt.

The memo of understanding should be signed by both parties to make it legally binding. Even if you don't think you need to be so formal, you should at least send a letter of confirmation to your client upon taking on a project. This is simply a business letter, signed by you, that outlines the work you will do, the date by which it is due, and the amount you will be paid. Although such a letter is not a contract, it makes your intentions and expectations clear. If the client disagrees, he or she can respond appropriately. Writing expectations down so that all parties can see them is more important than the exact form of the agreement.

You may also need legal documents for other purposes. If you're a photographer, the people who appear in your photos may need to sign model releases that allow you to publish the photographs. This issue is of particular importance if you photograph minors. When you use a model release, keep it simple. Specify the day the photos were taken and have the model agree that you can use the photos in a publication at your discretion.

Figure 26
Copyright Categories

First (serial) rights—grants the exclusive right to publish a
   work for the first time.
One time rights—grants the nonexclusive right to publish
   a work.
Second (serial) rights—grants the right to reprint a work
   after it has first appeared.
All rights—grants the right to use the work forever for any
   reason.
Subsidiary rights—grants the right to adapt, translate, or
   stage the work.

The model should certify that he or she is an adult. If the model
is a minor, a parent or guardian, specifically identified as such,
should sign the release.

Contract Essentials

Once, an editor gave me a model release drafted by her company's
lawyers. The release was two pages long and densely packed with
legalese. One phrase struck me: "For material consideration received, the undersigned agrees...." To me, that phrase meant that
either the publisher or I had paid the model for her permission to
use the photos, which was not the case. I called the editor and
explained that no one had paid the model or had any intention of
doing so. The model was getting her picture in a national publication; what more did she want? The editor said, "Oh, that phrase
doesn't mean you have to pay her." I asked what it did mean. She
said, "It's just boilerplate." I concluded that the editor had no idea
what the phrase meant. But boilerplate is legally binding, so I
asked if we couldn't use my standard release instead. The editor
refused. In the end, I bought the model dinner, reasoning that
that qualified as "material consideration."

The story illustrates two points. One: Don't trust clients
when they tell you that something in a contract doesn't matter. If

Figure 27

Memo of Understanding

Date: July 3, 2000
Re: Seminar in Business Writing Skills

Joe Smith, of Creative Communications Company, and May Anderson, of Computer Solutions, agree that Joe Smith will lead a four-hour business writing seminar for twelve Computer Solutions employees on Saturday, August 15, from 8 A.M. until noon. The seminar will cover the basics of writing business letters and memos as described in the course outline (attached). Changes made to the seminar arrangements (number of employees, course outline) must be submitted in writing to Joe Smith before August 1; afterwards, a $75 scheduling fee will apply.

The seminar will be deemed a success if seven or more employees (60 percent) produce business letters during the seminar that meet the following criteria:

> The letter includes a clearly stated point.
> Evidence or information supporting the point is supplied.
> Fewer than five grammar and spelling errors (combined).

At the conclusion of a successful seminar, Computer Solutions will pay Joe Smith the amount of $500. If ten or more (85 percent) employees produce letters meeting the criteria, a bonus of $100 will be given.

Signed,

x_____   x_____

Joe Smith   May Anderson
Creative Communications   Computer Solutions

it didn't matter, it wouldn't be in there. If you ever have any questions about the terms of a contract, do not sign it. Ask for a

(continued on p. 110)

Figure 28

Letter of Confirmation

Creative Communications Company
11133 Farmington Road
Toledo, Ohio 12345-0012

May Anderson
Computer Solutions
1212 Perriman Drive
Toledo, Ohio 12333-0033

July 3, 2000

Dear Ms. Anderson:

Thanks for your interest in my business-writing seminar. I'm certain Creative Communications Company will be able to help your employees develop the necessary skills to communicate effectively in the business world.

This letter is just to confirm the details of our phone conversation on July 1. I plan to lead a four-hour business writing seminar for twelve Computer Solutions employees on Saturday, August 15, from 8 A.M. until noon. The seminar will cover the basics of writing business letters and memos as described in the course outline (attached).

The seminar will be deemed a success if seven or more employees (60 percent) produce business letters during the seminar that meet the following criteria:

The letter includes a clearly stated point.
Evidence or information supporting the point is supplied.
Fewer than five grammar and spelling errors (combined).

My usual fee for a successful four-hour seminar is $600, but since you wanted assurance that the seminar would help even the less skilled employees, I am willing to accept a $500 fee with a $100 bonus should ten or more (85 percent) employees meet the criteria.

Please let me know if you would like to make any changes before August 1; afterwards, I'm afraid I'll have to charge a scheduling fee of $75.

Thank you for choosing Creative Communications.

Sincerely,

Joe Smith

few hours or a day or two to double-check it. If you lose the client, it's not a relationship worth having anyway. The other point: People love their own contracts. I tried to convince this editor to use my short, simple release form, but she wouldn't. It wasn't worth losing the fee over, so I went along with her. However, since I was not familiar with the contract, I had to make sure it was something I would be willing to ask my models (who double as my friends) to sign. Always check with an attorney about legal documents you do not understand.

Of course, it's easy to say "check with your attorney." What if you don't know a good attorney? How do you know that an attorney understands what your business requires? Professional organizations can help. The Authors Guild maintains a legal department staffed by lawyers experienced in contract law, especially publishing contracts. Members can send a contract to Guild attorneys and they will look it over, explain what it means, and suggest changes that would be in the writer's best interest. This service is free. Other professional organizations offer similar assistance to members.

You will also find software programs, such as Legal Pro, Legal Advisor, and Small Business Attorney, that will help you address basic issues, such as collecting past due accounts and writing simple agreements. The more complicated the agreement and the more money at stake, the greater the chance that you should consult an attorney, but these programs ($30 to $50) are well worth the cost.

It isn't feasible to have an attorney look over every single agreement you come up with in your business life. But keep in mind that simple agreements that outline a project, when it is to be completed, and how much it will cost can be written by anyone using clear, precise language. An agreement that doesn't cover every contingency or misses an important point or two is still better than nothing. It makes both parties think about what they're agreeing to, and it gives an indication of the intentions of both parties.

Don't let fear of legal documents stop you. Educate yourself. Look up sample contracts in the library and read them with a dictionary at your elbow. (The library should have a legal dictionary to explain the jargon.) Just as it's unwise to leave your accounting to your accountant (remember all those bankrupt celebrities?), it's dangerous to leave your legal agreements to lawyers. Determine what you need in a contract, hammer it out with the client, and only then—once everything is settled and only when necessary—should you bring in the attorneys.

Written contracts protect you from misunderstandings, prove that an agreement was indeed made, and remain a necessary evil in the business world. Learning about contracts doesn't have to be deadly dull. Understanding contracts and how they work teaches you a great deal about your business and about how to be a better business owner.

8

Setting Up Your Home Office

IF YOU plan to take your creative work seriously, you need a designated place to perform business activities. The kitchen table is not that place. Even if space is tight, you can squeeze out the extra room if you think imaginatively. Although many people put home offices in the spare bedroom, they can be tucked in the basement or attic, on a sun porch, in a corner of the master bedroom, in a loft, or anywhere else you can carve out a bit of space specifically for business. You can invest in a screen and partition off part of the living room for your office. You can purchase a convertible armoire that opens to expose a desk, computer terminal, and printer. You can install a desk with bookshelves in the breakfast nook. You can even add a prefabricated room to the back of the house. The key is creating a space dedicated to business use. If you have to move your computer in order to fold the laundry, you need to find a better place for the computer (or the laundry).

Office Furniture

Once you have determined where to put your office, you'll have to consider your needs. If you use your office simply for sending out bills and calling clients, you can get by with a smaller amount of space and fewer furnishings. If you're a writer, you may need more space with room for plenty of bookshelves. Make a list of the essentials, but don't be circumscribed by traditional thinking. A desk may be an office essential, but what kind of desk do you need? The standard office issue with a center drawer and file drawers on each side? Or would a long table do? You can buy a six-foot folding conference table for $30 or $40. You can't find an office desk for that price. Make sure your desk (or table) is big enough to house your computer monitor, hard drive, printer, and other equipment plus your phone and supplies. No room left over to work? Some people put two desks together in an "L" shape or parallel to each other. The computer equipment goes on one desk; the other is reserved for non-computer work.

You'll also need a good, comfortable office chair so that you don't murder your back while running your business. You may also need bookshelves within easy reach of the desk, and a file cabinet for holding records and correspondence. You should have a good-quality phone (not the one with the static in the background). If you spend much of the day on the phone, you may want to invest in a headset.

Beyond that, you may need certain specific furnishings to run your business adequately, but it is best to start out with just the essentials. As your business grows, you'll become better acquainted with what you really need. Stick to the basics at first and add later.

You can purchase used furniture through office furniture stores, leasing stores, flea markets, and thrift shops. Whenever you're ready to purchase a piece of furniture or office equipment, let friends and family know. Businesses constantly replace office furniture and upgrade equipment. You can often pick up used furniture for a fraction of the cost of new. Although you don't want to spend money on poor-quality purchases that will have to be replaced in three months, there's no reason everything has to be brand new and top of the line. Save those treats for when you've landed a big contract (but wait until after you've been paid). Think of the nonessentials as your reward for working hard, not as an entitlement for going into business.

Office Equipment

For office equipment, again, stick to the essentials. Most businesses require a computer system. That's where most of your investment should go. (Chapter 9 discusses computer technology in more depth.) You will also need an e-mail service if you're a writer or if your clients are online. Some e-mail providers (such as Juno) give consumers the service for free; advertising pays the cost. The only drawback is that everyone knows Juno is free and it might send the wrong message to your clients. (On the other hand, it might send the right message: They may think that if you're watching your money you'll be careful with theirs.) If you'll be doing research online, you should subscribe to an Internet service provider. Most people use phone lines to access the Internet, and most areas have service providers with local phone numbers (no long distance charges). Flat-rate plans charge $20 or $30 a month for unlimited access. You can also go online using WebTV equipment, by using digital satellite systems (those mini-satellite dishes you see stuck on people's houses) or with a cable modem. (The advantages of other types of Internet access are discussed in Chapter 9.)

You may also need a fax machine. Invest in a plain-paper fax that can double as a copier and/or scanner (unless you specialize in blueprints or graphic design and must produce high-quality copies). You may need an additional phone line for your computer modem and fax machine.

A business phone line is important if you field many business calls throughout the day, if you share your house with others (especially those under three feet tall), or if your business might come across as unprofessional should the babysitter answer the home phone when you're not there. A less expensive alternative is the personalized ring service from your local phone company. You're assigned a second number, which you use for business. The phone rings differently when the second number is dialed, so that you can clearly distinguish between business and personal calls without having to install and pay for a second phone line. You can train your spouse and kids not to answer the phone when it gives the business ring.

An answering machine for business calls is essential, but it doesn't have to be expensive. Make sure the message quality is good. I've heard digital answering machines that made their owners sound as if they were on drugs. This is not the image you want to convey. Find a machine with remote message retrieval so that you can call home from anywhere, enter a code, and hear your messages. You might prefer voice mail, which is also available through your local phone company for a small monthly fee. Purchasing an answering machine is a one-time investment, whereas a voice mail service is an ongoing expense, but some people prefer the reliability of voice mail.

Your outgoing message should include your full name and should be short and businesslike. If the answering machine is used by other members of the household, you can include their names on the tape, but keep it simple. One writer has a silly message in which she and her adolescent daughter speak in high-pitched, breathless voices and squeak like hamsters to indicate the sound of the tone. It isn't amusing even to her friends. How many potential clients have decided against using her services because of the amateurish, unprofessional image that message projects?

A cellular phone may seem important, but unless you're away from your office most of the time it can become just a very expensive and unnecessary toy. Pagers, though less expensive, can be the same—annoying and not very useful. Do people really need to be able to reach you every second of the day? Or does it just make you feel important that they can? If you do get dozens of phone calls throughout the day and you can't afford to miss them, then by all means do your homework and invest in a cell phone. Be sure to sign up for the service plan that suits your needs, not the service plan that offers the fanciest free phone. Cellular phones come in analog and digital versions. Each has different coverage areas and sound quality. Make sure you get the coverage area you need and the sound quality your clients deserve. Keep in mind that you'll be using peak-time minutes when you sign the service plan. You can usually get a gazillion off-peak minutes for free, which is fine if you want to talk to your mom in Pittsburgh on Sunday night, but it doesn't help when you need to cancel a two o'clock business appointment across town. Calculate how much time you'll need, too. A hundred minutes a month is five minutes per business day. Unless you keep your conversations quite short, you'll have to purchase more minutes than that. The cell phone, pager, and other communication tools can probably wait until your business is established and you know exactly what your needs are.

Beyond this, equipment essentials will be dictated by your business. A photographer needs camera and lighting equipment, but rather than installing a professional (and expensive) darkroom, find a professional photo developing shop (not K-mart). If the one nearest you doesn't meet your needs, try a mail-order developer. Especially in the short term, this may be the best way to start a photography business. One photographer who intended to set up a darkroom once she made a profit has been in business for more than ten years without ever getting around to it. Instead of spending all her time developing film, she is acquiring clients and photographing events.

Certain graphic artists might need expensive computer equipment, especially if they're designers who create blueprints, schematics, or diagrams. There are alternatives to purchasing such equipment outright, including leasing and leasing-to-own arrangements. (See Chapter 9.)

A creative person who works as a consultant and gives presentations and speeches will need audiovisual equipment. Although some people still use slide and overhead projectors, these are being replaced more and more by computer presentation systems that allow the user to store interesting text and graphics on the computer and then present them on a screen (much like the old slide show, only much more expensive). Be sure you understand your needs and the technology before you invest in it.

Keep your equipment purchases to a minimum at first. You don't have all the money in the world to invest in equipment, and money you use on equipment can't be used elsewhere. And once you start doing business on a regular basis, you may find that your needs change. A few years ago I needed a fax machine almost as much as I needed my computer. Now I need my e-mail account almost as much as I need my computer (and I don't need my fax machine at all). E-mail and online capabilities have become so important to my business that I switched to a cable modem to allow for faster speed and immediate access to my mail (no dial-up or busy signals on a cable modem). But should my fax machine quit working, I wouldn't bother replacing it.

Instead of buying a fax machine, find a nearby copy or mailing center where you can send and receive faxes, and keep that number handy. (Let your clients know that they're faxing to a place other than your spare bedroom; otherwise they may not include enough identifying information on the fax cover sheet.) Instead of purchasing a scanner, find the copy center nearest you that can scan images or documents to disk.

Although you need to keep equipment purchases to a minimum, you should also respond to the needs of your clients, even if that requires additional investment in equipment. Stacy has yet to step into the computer age. Paralyzed by the thought of using a computer, she can barely type a manuscript using a word-processing program. Needless to say, she cannot e-mail documents to clients. She has steadfastly refused to invest in a fax machine, although one newspaper editor specifically said she must in order to continue receiving his assignments (he gave her a choice of e-mail or fax). The thought of that technology was too overwhelming, so she didn't bother. Needless to say, the editor has found a different freelance writer. And Stacy still doesn't understand what the big deal was.

Being in a creative business is tough enough. Don't make it harder on yourself by refusing to meet the reasonable needs of your clients. If you're uncomfortable using office technology, you can always take classes, either at a nearby community college or at a business-vocational school, or hire a tutor (many communities have businesses that send technology experts to your home to help you understand specific machines). You can also purchase videos and books to help you understand how technology functions.

By carefully selecting equipment and furnishings, you can set up your office for a reasonable investment. By sticking to the minimum necessary purchases, you will be able to respond to your actual business needs, not just indulge in what you want to have. If you're still employed at an outside job, you can make acquisitions over time, but you should designate your office space immediately so that you can begin working creatively right away.

9

Computers, the Internet, and Small Businesses

COMPUTER TECHNOLOGY is vitally important to most small businesses, but many creative people are reluctant to tangle with technology. This chapter is designed to help you understand your computer needs and how a good computer system can enhance your business.

Almost anyone running a small business will find that computer technology helps get work done. Keeping accounts using a computer is so easy that all you have to know is how to turn on the machine. (Well, almost that easy.) Writers must have computers, although they're probably optional for musicians and photographers. Many artists, especially those in graphic design, also need computers for their work. The needs of different business owners vary. If you have special computer needs, you should spend time researching what owners in similar businesses use and what will work best for you.

The Basic Computer System

The basic computer system consists of several components, the main one being the CPU (central processing unit). This is essentially the brain of the computer. The CPU contains the mother board, where many hardware elements are located. Its case usually houses floppy disk and CD or DVD drives (DVD stands for digital video disk, something like a super-CD, and the wave of the future, according to this year's predictions). The basic system also requires a monitor, keyboard, and printer. The components can be purchased separately or together in one package. Purchasing the components separately from a specialty computer store usually gives you the advantage of upgrading easily. This means that when you need more memory, a faster CPU, or a better CD drive, you can simply bring the case to the computer store and explain what you need; they'll tuck it in there for you. If you buy an integrated, all-in-one unit (such as you find at office warehouse stores and discount electronic chains), it's more difficult to upgrade. Integrated units may be less expensive, and they are certainly very simple to install and use.

People who use their computers to give presentations or design layouts and other artwork need good graphics and sound. They will probably want to invest in an easily upgradeable system. They should purchase a computer with a fast processor, the maximum memory, and high-quality sound and graphics cards. Other small-business owners will usually do fine with a standard computer package, which they will simply replace every few years as their needs change and as computer technology improves.

Types of Computers

There are two main types of computers: PCs (personal computers), also called IBM-compatibles, and Macintosh computers (made by Apple). Each uses a different type of operating system, so a computer program that works on one won't necessarily work on the other. PC users despise Mac users, and vice versa, so if you have a preference, go with it. Mac users swear that their machines are easier to use and friendlier to computer-phobics, but in actuality there is little difference between the two types. PCs make up a much larger segment of the market, and most software is developed for PCs. If you'll be sending e-mail or disk documents to your clients (and you probably will), your work should be accessible on their computer systems, and in most cases they will have PCs. Some schools use Mac computers, so if that is pertinent, plan accordingly. Artists and designers often use Mac computers, but graphic art is one of only a handful of industries that prefer Macs.

Purchasing a Computer

Many factors weigh in the decision to purchase a specific computer, such as processor speed (how fast the computer thinks), amount of memory, and which disk drives it includes. Obscure and esoteric facts like refresh rate may also be important. Check current computer buyer's guides to help you make a decision. Once you understand what's out there, you can more easily determine what will best suit your needs. You can also talk to computer salespeople, but keep in mind that people working in discount and electronics stores may know less about computers than you do. Visit computer specialty stores instead and chat with the staff; then make a decision. Here are some basic guidelines for purchasing a computer for general business use.

Processor Speed

Find out the fastest processor speed on the market (just ask a computer salesperson, "Say, what's the fastest computer on the market?") and then purchase the computer that's just a step below. The processor speed is expressed in megahertz (MHz) and might be 400 or 450 or higher. There are different brand names (Pentium being the best known), but the brand doesn't matter as much as the speed.

Although some experts recommend that you buy the fastest computer possible so it will last longer before becoming obsolete, you'll pay a premium for this. The difference in performance between the highest-speed computer and the one next in line won't be that noticeable, but the price difference will be. Usually, the computer with the second-fastest processor speed is going to be the best value.

Disk Drives

Computers have several different kinds of drives. Information is stored on and retrieved from drives, so it's important to have the appropriate ones. The hard drive accesses the main memory of the computer (see the section on memory). Disk drives read information from various types of disks and also record information to disks. These can then be sent to someone or stored in a safe place. Options include compact disk drives (CD), digital video disk drives (DVD), floppy disk drives, and other removable disk storage drives (such as the Zip drive). CD and DVD drives are not always recordable—you can't use them to store information. Having a fast CD drive may be helpful for playing computer games but may not make a lot of difference in your day-to-day activities. However, if you constantly use research materials stored on CDs, the speed of the drive *will* matter. The speed is expressed as a number plus an "×" for multiplication. A 32× CD drive is 32 times as fast as the original CD drives. Most software programs come on CD, so you will need a CD drive on whatever computer you select. If you routinely access CDs, get at least a 32×; otherwise take what comes with your computer.

Many new computers come with a DVD (digital video disk) drive, which many experts consider the future of disk drives. Some DVD drives will also read CDs. However, not much software is written for the DVD yet, so it's not a necessary investment.

You will also need a removable disk storage system, such as a floppy disk drive, which is standard. You can also get a so-called "removable media drive," which is like a floppy disk drive, only it can hold much more information on one disk. A floppy can hold about 1½ megabytes while a "removable media disk" can hold 250 megabites. The best known of these drives is the Zip, by Iomega. Many computers now come with a Zip drive as standard equipment. A floppy drive is necessary if you will be sending documents to clients by disk; a Zip drive is helpful for backing up the contents of your computer on a regular basis. It is also essential for graphic and design work.

Memory

Like you, your computer can't work without memory. Also like you, computers have two types of memory: long-term and short-term. A third type of memory (optional) can increase the speed of the computer's thought process.

Long-term memory is stationed on the hard drive. When people say, "My hard drive crashed," look sympathetic. It's the computer equivalent of having amnesia. The size of this memory can be extremely large. When people brag, "I've got an eight-gig hard drive," they mean that their computer has the capacity to store eight gigabytes (GB) of information in its hard-drive memory. That's equivalent to 12,000 books, give or take a couple of pages, and seems like a lot until you consider that computer programs, which store instructions on the hard drive, are so complex that they take up a lot of space. When it comes to long-term memory, the more the merrier. Long-term memory is cheap, so get as much as you can.

Short-term computer memory, called RAM or random-access memory, is what the computer uses to display and manipulate the file you're currently working on and the program you're currently using. When you're done with the file, you save it, which takes it out of short-term (RAM) memory and puts it into long-term memory. This works just like you do. Most software programs use a lot of RAM memory, especially if they have graphics and sound. The more complex the program, the more memory is needed. If you're working with large files, such as book-length manuscripts, the more short-term memory your computer has, the easier it is to manipulate the document. RAM memory is measured in megabytes (MB). Like long-term memory, it's cheap, so stuff as much in there as you can. (Get 48 MB if possible, 32 if you can't possibly spend another dime.) Remember, if you plan to add RAM memory later (make sure you can), there are several different types and not all are compatible, so you'll need to know what you already have in order to match it.

The third type of memory is optional. Called an L2 cache and measured in kilobytes (KB), it is standard on some computers and can be added to some others. It works like a second memory to back up the first. Get a big chunk if you can, like 512 KB. It's not absolutely critical, so if you must choose between an L2 cache and a faster processor, get the faster processor.

Sound and Graphics Cards

Most computers come with sound and graphics cards installed, and, logically, they produce sound and images on your computer. For most business purposes, whatever is installed on your system is probably fine. Sound cards are important only if you use computer-based presentations with sound. (They're also important if you play computer games.) If you need a good sound card, get one with wavetable synthesis (you don't need to know what this means, just memorize the term). You'll also need a good set of speakers that have a built-in amplifier and a sub-woofer.

If your graphics card is of poor quality, it will slow down the speed of your computer. If you use graphics in your presentations or designs, get a card with as much RAM as you can (yes, graphics cards have short-term memory). Also, make sure the card has 3D acceleration for best effect.

Monitor

You have to see what you're doing, so you're going to have to invest in a good monitor. Monitors vary in quality and size. You can buy 19-inch monitors for a few hundred dollars; not long ago they didn't even exist. The smaller the screen, the less expensive the monitor, but don't purchase anything smaller than a 15-inch screen even if you can find it. Too hard on your eyes, and the price break isn't worth it. Spend *a lot* of time looking at monitors, especially if you'll be using your computer for more than fifteen minutes a day. If the screen flickers a lot, you'll be half-blind at the end of the day. Although contrast and resolution can be adjusted, if the color or appearance of the screen doesn't strike you as comfortable, don't purchase the monitor. Look at the monitor with both text and graphics on it; sometimes images will be presented well while text will be hard to read. Make sure the edges of the screen don't show distortion.

Get a monitor with the smallest dot pitch you can (this is the space between the little points of light on the screen). Dot pitch is measured in fractions of millimeters. The smaller the fraction, the better. Don't consider a dot pitch above 0.28 mm. The images on the screen are made up of pixels, or little groups of dots (yes, that's the technical explanation). The more pixels, the higher the resolution and the better the picture quality. The number of pixels you look for will depend on the size of the monitor you're considering. The minimum for a 15-inch screen is 800 × 600. The bigger the numbers, the better. Also consider the refresh rate, or the number of times the monitor redraws the image per second. This is measured in hertz (Hz) and should be in the neighborhood of 85.

Newer monitors are becoming flatter and lighter, but these can get pretty expensive for small-business owners, especially when you consider what you get for the cost. Sure, a thin monitor takes up less desk space, but you could add a room to the house for what it costs to buy one.

Printer

Invest in a decent letter-quality printer. Although some people think laser printers produce the best-quality work, inkjet printers produce documents of almost the same appearance and cost considerably less. If you frequently switch between color and black-and-white printing, purchase a printer that doesn't require you to change cartridges every time you want to go from one to the other. Check out the documents printed by various printers, comparing image and text quality. If you will be printing graphics and photographs, be sure the printer can reproduce them with as little distortion as possible.

In addition to comparing costs for printers, compare printer cartridge costs. This is where the real expense of owning a printer comes in. If two models produce documents of similar quality, choose the one with the less expensive printer cartridge.

Additional Hardware

You may also need additional computer equipment (called hardware), such as a scanner or an electronic stylus and pad (for design programs or handwriting recognition systems), if your business requires it.

Figure 29

The Basic Computer System

Central processing unit (CPU)	Get the second-fastest processor available.
Disk drives	Floppy and CD drives essential; Zip drive if you back up information all the time.
Memory	Three types: Long-term, RAM, and L2 cache. Get as much as you can stuff into the machine.
Sound card	Does your computer make sounds you can hear? Good enough.
Graphics card	Buy a decent-quality graphics card so that you don't slow down the speed of your computer. For designers and people who make presentations, get a card with as much RAM as possible.
Monitor	No smaller than 15 inches, 0.28 mm maximum dot pitch, highest resolution you can find; refresh rate around 85.
Printer	Inkjet suits most purposes; check quality of printer for both text and images.

Digital cameras, which store pictures that can be transferred to your computer, are becoming more and more popular. Some of these are compatible with floppy disks. You just snap your pictures, pull the floppy out, and stick it into your computer. Others require a slightly more complicated method of downloading, requiring a cable to connect the camera to the computer. Digital cameras have some advantages over traditional cameras. You can see the picture right away, since the cameras have built-in viewers. If you don't like the photo, you can delete it and try again. No waste. You can store a large number of photos on disk or on special memory cards without having to purchase film over and over. Once transferred to your computer, the images can be manipulated. Of course, regular photographs can be scanned in and manipulated, but digital images are captured specifically for computer processing. Such photos can then be placed in slide presentations or documents and printed out on special paper with a color printer. The disadvantage is that even the very top-of-the-line models produce photos that are clearly digital (you can see the pixels or dots). Professional photographers probably won't find digital cameras useful for their work, but people who create presentations may find them indispensable.

For the most part, additional hardware purchases can be deferred until you are comfortable with your setup and know your clients' needs.

Do You Need a Laptop?

If you travel frequently or spend most of the business day out of the office, you may consider investing in a laptop computer. Depending on your needs, you can use the laptop as your main computer and simply hook it up to your printer as needed, or you can use it to back up your desktop computer. Assess your needs carefully before committing to a laptop computer, as they can be quite expensive. If your laptop is going to be your main computer or if it's going to be used to give presentations, make sure it has the processor speed, memory, and accessories you need, such as CD and/or DVD drives and a modem to connect with the Internet. You can use a less powerful model if your laptop will only be used to look up files or type reports while you're on the road. Always look for a good, clear screen, a keyboard that is easy for you to use, and decent sound and graphics.

Electronic Organizers

Small-business owners who are always on the go may want to invest in an electronic organizer. The best-known of these small, hand-held devices is the PalmPilot, but there are others. These organizers allow users to keep "to do" lists, contact names, and calendars. They can be used to record information and to calculate a tip. PalmPilot has a handwriting recognition system so that you can write directly on the screen (using a special stylus). Special computer programs (that won't work in your desktop computer) allow such organizers to create spreadsheets and expense records, and even fax documents. An external (add-on) modem allows you to send e-mail from the organizer, although you can't surf the Internet on it. Some less expensive organizers have fewer bells and whistles. Some don't recognize handwriting, forcing you to type using a little bitty keyboard; others don't allow you to load software programs. Some of the inexpensive electronic organizers allow you to access information, such as addresses, but to input information you have to connect the organizer to your desktop computer and download data. PocketMate and Rex PC Companion are two of the less expensive versions.

Mini-PCs, a hybrid, aren't exactly hand-held computers, but they're smaller than laptop computers. Most have touch-screen displays, but the keyboards are very small, making it difficult to do much typing. Programs for these computers allow them to do word processing, spreadsheets, and even presentations. Most of these systems use a type of Windows operating system, and the files they create are compatible with those you create on your desktop; this means that an article you wrote on Microsoft Word can be easily edited on your hand-held computer. You can also add a modem and additional memory cards to the hand-held computer. Some of these computers are compatible with both Macs and PCs.

Electronic organizers and hand-held computers—like a lot of gadgets—seem fascinating but aren't practical for most small-business owners. Most of us can make do with a daily planner and an address book when we're on the road. But if you're often out of your office and must keep track of many appointments and documents, then one of these might be for you. Otherwise, put it on your wish list and forget about it.

Purchasing Computers

Computers—desktop and laptop—and much of their hardware can be purchased used or reconditioned from many suppliers. Although you can purchase computer equipment at garage sales, this isn't the best way to go for a small-business owner. You won't know what you're getting, and if you don't have the manuals for the computer you could end up unable to operate the thing efficiently. Instead, consider shops that sell used computers (most cities have them). Mail order outfits also sell reconditioned computers. And even their new computer systems cost less than those you will find at retail stores. Some of the big computer suppliers, such as Gateway, also sell used and reconditioned computers.

Software Programs

In order to use your computer most effectively in your business, you'll need to install pertinent software programs. Although most computers come with certain programs installed, these programs may not be what you need. Invest in the software necessary to run your business most efficiently.

Financial Software

Most business owners elect to keep their records on computer. To do so, it helps to have a financial management program. This can be as simple as Microsoft Money, which is basically a checkbook register that can be used as a general ledger to keep track of revenues and expenses. Such programs are easy to use, can sort financial information into categories, and do automatic calculations so that you can always see where you are. If you need to set up an invoicing system or keep track of accounts payable and accounts receivable, you might invest in a small-business accounting program, such as QuickBooks or Peachtree Accounting. These programs ask you a series of questions and then conform the accounting system to your needs. They can also set up integrated invoicing, accounts payable and accounts receivable systems so that you can easily make changes in all your records at one time. Many of these programs also allow you to set up and calculate a budget.

If you're interested in generating many different financial reports, want to do budget forecasting, and can't wait to perform other noncreative applications, you might wish to invest in a spreadsheet program such as Microsoft Excel. Spreadsheets can be programmed to calculate whatever financial information you want, such as how the interest rate on a loan affects the total cost of the loan or the amount of the monthly payments. They can also be programmed to perform as general ledgers. Spreadsheet programs aren't necessary unless you enjoy working with your computer and want to perform complicated financial forecasts.

Word-Processing Software

Most business owners need a word-processing program to send letters and invoices and produce marketing materials. For the most part, the one that came with the computer will probably serve your needs. Or you can invest in a small-business office bundle that includes spreadsheet, database, and word-processing programs. Both Microsoft (makers of Word) and Corel (makers of WordPerfect) offer such packages for less than you would spend buying the programs separately. However, make sure you need the programs in the package. Otherwise you'll wind up spending a lot more than necessary.

If you're a writer, you don't need a software program; you need the *right* software program. After all, you'll spend most of your time working with it. You may have your favorite program already (I'm a WordPerfect person myself), but if not, try out different programs before purchasing one. Make sure you purchase one of the major word-processing programs. There are probably people out there who are still using WordStar, but none of them are editors or publishers. Most editors ask for a floppy disk or electronic document version of the manuscript you submit, and they want the file to be compatible with their system. Both

Word and WordPerfect are widely used; Word is more popular since Microsoft has infiltrated every aspect of the business world. Word and WordPerfect can convert files to each other's format, so this is not a big deal. If you like Word and your editor prefers WordPerfect, compose the thing in Word, then convert it to WordPerfect and send it along.

Desktop Publishing Software

If you create newsletters or brochures on a regular basis, you'll need a desktop publishing program. These provide templates so that you don't have to spend a lot of time formatting to make your newsletter look like a newsletter or to get a brochure to look like a brochure. Instead, you simply input the text and graphics, then print the document. (Well, maybe it's not *quite* that simple.) Many of these programs come with clip art designs and images that you can insert into your materials. You can also purchase clip art programs separately, although be forewarned that, while these pieces of art are copyright-free, they are really intended for limited private use, not business use. (That's why a digital camera comes in handy. Take a photo of what you need and insert it in the document.) User-friendly desktop publishing programs include Microsoft Publisher and PrintMaster.

Graphics Software

If you need to create or manipulate images on your computer, you will need a good graphics program. Be sure the program you choose suits your business needs. You may even need more than one program. For instance, if you manipulate photos, you will want to use a program such as PhotoShop. If you also draw your own designs, you will need a program such as Corel Draw. Some of these programs are complicated to use. If you need them, learn how to use them from an expert. Many computer stores offer inexpensive training programs, as do community colleges and continuing education programs.

Some graphics programs are designed for the small-business owner who doesn't have a lot of computer experience. One of these programs may actually be a wise investment to start with;

then, when you are ready to move on to more complex projects, you can purchase more complex software. Corel Print House Magic lets you manipulate photos and also works as a desktop publishing program. Another program, Jasc Paint Shop Pro, allows for slightly more sophisticated image editing. Other possibilities include PhotoImpact and Windows Draw.

Database Software

If you have to keep track of a mountain of information in a particular format, such as the names and addresses of hundreds of potential clients, then you need a database program. These allow you to create records by establishing a field for each piece of information. Then the information can be accessed using any field. For instance, suppose you want to keep track of potential customers. You'll create a template that shows a field for the customer's last name (Field A, for example), a field for their first name (Field B), a field for their company's name (Field C), and so on. You can then pull up everyone in the same ZIP code or the same state or who works for the same company. You can add fields that show whatever you need to know about the potential customer. For writers who might submit dozens (if not hundreds) of query letters in a year, a database program could be used to record the editor's name, the magazine or publishing company, and its address and telephone number, as well as each editor's areas of interest. When you're ready to write an article on parenting, you sort through your database to pull up the names of magazine editors interested in parenting issues. (As a matter of fact, some database programs designed specifically with writers in mind, such as Ink Link, help you keep track of submissions.) Microsoft Access works for many small-business owners. If you need a database program for a Mac, try FileMaker Pro (it comes in a PC version, too). Less complicated database needs can be addressed with Approach.

Contact Manager Software

Like databases, contact manager programs store important records that you access routinely. A contact manager, however, is designed to help you keep track of your *interactions* with people. That's the main difference. Suppose you're working on several projects at once. Joe Smith calls up and wants to talk to you about making some changes in the presentation you're giving to his business group next month. You're in the middle of finishing the Acme Company's annual report and don't recall the details of the presentation. You open the contact manager, pull up Joe Smith's file, and see when you last talked to him, what you discussed, and other pertinent information. As Joe makes his recommendations, you can make a note of the relevant details. When you start to work on the presentation, all you have to do is check the contact manager to see what the plan is. A contact manager can list everything from addresess and phone numbers to birth dates and the client's project specifications or ordering information. The most widely used contact manager is ACT!, but there are others, including GoldMine, Maximizer, and Outlook.

Other Software Programs

In addition to programs that help you do your work, you may wish to invest in programs that provide basic reference and research materials. Most computers come with a dictionary and thesaurus program installed, although it's almost always easier just to look a word up in the printed dictionary. Most word-processing programs also come with dictionary and thesaurus features so that you can look up a word while you're typing a document. If you need basic reference information such as you might find in an encyclopedia, check out the one installed on your computer. You can also purchase references such as Grolier Multimedia Encyclopedia, Microsoft Encarta, and Britannica CD.

If you need specialized or in-depth reference material, browse through the software section of your favorite computer store. You may find titles of interest, especially in the health care and history fields. Of course, none of this beats a good reference library of books.

You can also invest in software programs that allow you to use voice commands to run your computer. You train the software to understand your voice. Then you simply dictate documents and the computer automatically types them. Or you can tell the computer to open a file or send a fax. Some of these programs come

---

Figure 30

Computer Programs

Tax software	Guides you through your income tax return. For complicated businesses, doesn't replace a tax accountant. Get the business version.
Financial software	Makes recordkeeping a snap.
Word-processing software	Produces letters, invoices, etc. Get Microsoft Word or Corel WordPerfect if you send electronic files or floppies to clients.
Desktop publishing software	Provides templates for newsletters, marketing materials. Modify the design, add information, and presto! Unnecessary unless you're in the business of making newsletters and marketing materials.
Graphics software	Allows you to manipulate images on your computer, including those

(continued on next page)

---

with special microphone/headsets to speak into, which improves the accuracy of the program. The best ones—Dragon's Naturally Speaking and IBM's ViaVoice—are about 90 percent accurate. They can be trained to learn your typical vocabulary so as to improve their accuracy. If you have horrendous carpal tunnel problems from all those years at the computer, you may find that voice-activated software saves your hands. They're best used for typical business documents, not specialized manuscripts. The programs can take quite a while to train, and even then you will spend time going through the document and fixing errors (no program can distinguish among *too, to,* and *two,* although they sometimes

	you scan in, download, or actually create with the program. Necessary for designers; usually too complex for most other needs.
Database software	Essential for organizing mounds of information, such as the names and addresses of 3,000 potential clients.
Contact manager software	Stores records and tracks your interactions with clients. Can remind you of appointments, "to do" items, and follow-ups. Worthwhile if you have a lot of clients calling you up all the time, expecting you to automatically know what they're talking about. You must like computers to use these programs.
Other programs	Reference materials, voice-activated software, and plenty of other ways to spend your money can be found in your favorite computer store. Enjoy the browse, but leave your wallet at home.

try to go by context). If you do tons of writing and have difficulty typing for any reason, one of these programs is certainly a worthwhile investment, but don't expect to put away your keyboard.

You can also purchase faxing software so that your computer can send and receive faxes. You'll need a modem and access to a phone line. Some people find that such programs replace a stand-alone fax, but if you have a document that didn't originate in your computer, you can't fax it. If your attorney develops a contract that you'd like a client to look over and all you have is a hard copy of the document, what are you going to do? Type the whole thing into the computer, then fax it? You can scan it in, but most scanners still aren't very good at duplicating text exactly. And besides, if you're going to put a scanner on your desk, why not invest instead in a combination fax/copier/scanner? Then you don't have to waste time scanning the document in, proofing it for scanning errors, and then sending it. If you need fax capabilities for your business, you probably need a fax machine.

Going Online

While the joys of the Internet may be overstated, most business owners agree that there are definite benefits to going online. Online access provides e-mail capabilities, which are becoming more and more crucial, and the ability to visit sites on the World Wide Web, where information of all sorts can be found. You can buy practically anything over the Internet, arrange travel, or consult with your computer manufacturer to find out why your system keeps crashing. Also, one possibility that many small-business owners overlook is creating your own web site so that computer users can find out about you and patronize your business.

To go online, you need hardware, such as a computer with a modem. (You can also use special television equipment, such as WebTV.) You also need access to the Internet, which requires a physical link and a server. The physical link is the phone or cable line that physically connects your computer to the server. Your computer will need a modem that works with either the phone or the cable line. You will also need a server, or Internet service provider. Sound complicated? It's not that bad. If you plan to go online for business reasons, you'll need to use your computer (you can't print files from the Internet on WebTV). Then you'll need to decide whether you want phone line access or cable access. You can also use digital satellite systems by using a mini-satellite dish (DirecPC is an example), but such systems actually use phone lines to communicate your requests to the server. For most small-business owners, Internet access will require a computer plus cable or phone line access.

Cable access is much faster than phone line access, no matter how fast your phone line modem is. It takes just moments to jump to web sites and download information. There's no wait to dial up (you're always connected to the Internet, you're just not

Figure 31

Internet Access

Access Type	Benefits	Drawbacks
WebTV	Easy access	Can't print information. So far, not a good choice for businesses.
Digital satellite system	Can be faster than phone access.	Requires special equipment installation and fees. So far, not a good choice for businesses.
Cable access	Immediate access 24 hours a day (no dial-up); fast download speed.	Can't access e-mail or Internet away from your desktop computer.
Phone access	Usually reliable access, depending on service provider. Can access Internet and e-mail from all over the world.	Must dial up to get online, slow download speed, can be frustrating and time-consuming.

always looking at the Internet connection). You can set up an e-mail account that works like regular e-mail, including password-protection so that someone walking by your desk can't browse through the letters you received this week. The main disadvantage is that you can't access your e-mail when you're away from your desk, so for people who travel a lot or are out of the office for much of the day this is probably not the best choice. Other possibilities, such as ISDN and T1 connections, are not widely available and are quite expensive. As the technology and availability improves, the price should drop.

If you want the speed of cable access to the Internet for research but need to read your e-mail from the road, you can set up a phone line access e-mail account in addition to cable access

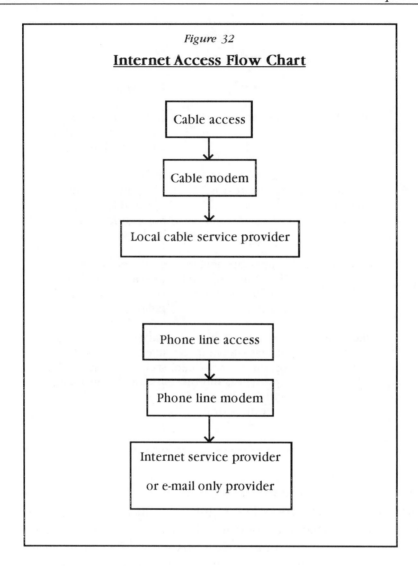

Figure 32
Internet Access Flow Chart

to the Internet. If you don't need access to the Internet (you're not going to visit web sites for any reason) but you do need e-mail, you can sign up for e-mail with Juno, as mentioned above, or Yahoo, MailBank, or many others, and skip the Internet service provider entirely.

If you choose cable access, your service provider will be the local cable company, so it's important that they have trained technicians who can answer questions or help you with any glitches. The cable-compatible modem is usually supplied by the cable company (they'll require a deposit). The cable access alternative is not available in all areas.

If you go the traditional phone line route, you'll have to choose a service provider. Some of the most popular providers, such as AmericaOnline, are national (or international) companies known for their ease of use. You simply slip a disk provided by the company into your computer, answer a couple of questions, and you're set up. You can access your e-mail and hop onto the Internet from almost any computer in the country. But because these providers have thousands of customers, you may get busy signals when you try to dial up, which can be disastrous if you need to respond to a particular e-mail message or look up a web site right away. The traffic can also create slow download times and other problems, especially in smaller cities.

Local and regional service providers can give you more reliable access to the Internet, although they're a little harder to set up. You will need to do some configuration on your computer, so if the term "configuration" makes you break into a cold sweat, call up AmericaOnline and ask for further information. Also, a local provider is not a good idea if you're on the road half the time, because you'll have trouble accessing the Internet outside the local provider's area. If you do plan to use a local provider, don't go with the first one you come across or the one with the cheapest rates. You want technical support, easy access, and few busy signals. Ask if you can have a free trial period before you sign up.

For the most part, Internet service providers charge a flat monthly fee for access. They should provide a local dial-up number so that you don't incur long-distance charges when you surf the web. Also, if you're thinking of establishing a web page, check with your service provider. Many of them will give you a little bit of server space for free or for an inexpensive rent.

If you use phone line Internet access, you'll need a fast modem. Most computers have internal modems; older ones have 28.8K speed while newer ones have 56K speed. This simply indicates the number of kilobits per second that the modem can transfer from the phone line to your computer. (You don't need to

---

Figure 33

Choosing an Internet Service Provider

National and international ISPs, such as AmericaOnline, are easy to use but have unreliable access (busy signals, slow download times). Can access e-mail and the Internet from any computer in the country.

Local and regional providers require some configuration, but once in place they are easy to use. Access is generally very reliable, depending on the provider's equipment. More difficult to access e-mail and Internet outside the provider's area.

---

remember that, just remember that bigger is better, or at least faster.) Phone lines have limited capacity for downloading information off the Internet, so even the fastest modem may be slow for downloading, depending on factors such as line noise. The modem of choice is a 56K that meets the V.90 standard. (Just remember "V.90.") If your computer is older, it may have one of two different types of 56K modems (either X2 or Flex), which are not compatible with each other. If you have one of these modems and your service provider can't support it, you're out of luck, so ask before you sign up. If you use the V.90 modem, however, you will not have compatibility problems.

Creating Web Pages

One of the reasons businesses go online is to create a web page that customers can visit. Not only can a web page (done right) attract customers from all over the country (even the world), it can also be used as a resource for your current customers. You can list frequently asked questions (FAQs, as they are known in computer lingo), provide contact information in case your best customer loses your phone number, and offer other useful services.

Creating and maintaining a web site requires a commitment of time (and a certain amount of cash). Attracting attention to your web site requires effort and care (there are literally millions and millions of web sites on the Internet). Consider your business. If you're a photographer who does local weddings, it isn't going to matter much if someone in Wyoming sees your web site (unless of course you live in Wyoming). If, however, you sell your prints, you can put samples of your work on your web site. Then when that guy from Wyoming sees your work and wants to buy it, you're set. If you're a writer, you may not attract much attention from editors with your own web site—but you might attract readers. It's a matter of balancing the investment of time and money with the possible interest you might generate.

Most Internet service providers offer instructions for creating web pages and allow customers to post them without charge or for a nominal fee. Because a web page takes up space on the provider's server, the ISP will limit the amount of space you can use. Your web page will have to be a plain package if you go this route. You can purchase more server space for a monthly fee, which varies depending on the provider.

If you have the funds, you can hire someone to design your web site. Such designers are called Webmasters. You can find one whose work you admire by visiting various sites on the Internet. At the bottom of the page, the Webmaster's name is usually listed, along with information on how to contact him or her. The simpler the site you have in mind, the less expensive the design. Fees can range from several hundred to several thousand dollars. Be sure the Webmaster gives you the information you need to update the site from time to time.

You can also buy software, such as Corel's Webmaster, My Internet Business Page, PageMill (Adobe), or others, that allows you to build your own site. Some word-processing programs even allow you to design simple web pages. Your Internet service provider probably has a web page template that you can use to design your own site. You can also find web page creator programs on the Internet, which means you don't have to purchase software. The computer language used to create web pages is called HTML, or hypertext markup language, but you don't need to know the language to create a web page.

The Home Page

The most important part of your design is your home page. This is where visitors go first. Make sure your name (or your company's name) is prominent. Then include important facts about your business. If you're a writer, show a copy of the cover of your most recent book or the title page of a magazine article. If you're a photographer or an artist, put some of your most interesting work on the page. Don't overdo the graphics, however, since they take a long time to download. Keep text short as well. Most people don't want to read page after page of text on a computer screen. By using links (called hypertext links or hot buttons), users can go from your home page to another part of your web site. For instance, you might want to show reviews of your book. You could have a "Reviews" link. On the "Reviews" page, you would quote what people said about your book. You could have an "About the Artist" link if you think you might attract clients. You should have a link to contact information, so someone wanting to hire you or buy your work can easily find you. If you don't want to post your street address on the Internet (and I don't blame you), at least include an e-mail address and phone number. You might consider renting a post office box to list on your web page. (Post office boxes can cost as little as $40 or $50 a year.) On your web site, you can create order forms and post rate sheets. You can also publish links to Internet vendors where customers can purchase your work. Writers can create a link to Amazon.com, the online bookseller, so that an interested person can go directly to Amazon.com and have the ordering information readily available.

Be sure all the links in your home page work so that people aren't given error messages when they try to find you.

Posting the Web Site

After creating your web site, you'll need to post it—that is, send it or upload it to a host server. Your web site will take up space on the host server. Depending on how big your site is, you might be able to get this space for free. For bigger sites, costs start at about

$50 a month. Most web software programs have the necessary file transfer abilities to upload your web page.

You should list the site in a variety of places so that Internet users will know about it. People use search engines to help them find web sites of interest. You can add the address and description of your site to these search engines. You can do this yourself, making sure to add it to all the major search engines (Yahoo, Lycos, Excite, HotBot, Infoseek, Northern Light, and AltaVista, for starters), or you can pay a service to do it for you. Some inexpensive software programs also can do this for you. You want your site to be one of the first on the list when a user submits a search, so to avoid being site 4362 of 5000, consider registering your own domain name instead of using your Internet provider's domain name. Otherwise, your address will read something like this: *www.internetservice-provider.com/ nameofyourcompany*. Automated search engines have difficulty indexing this type of address, so they'll skip your web site. If you register your own domain name, your address will look like this: *www.nameofyourcompany.com*, which is much easier for a search engine to index and pull up. Pick a good domain name if your company name is too long or is already taken. Register your domain name right away.

Make sure your pages have descriptive titles so that a search engine can pick up on them. Since some search engines use the first line of text in your web page as the description of your web page, make it count. Also be sure to put keywords in the text of your pages. Every now and then, use several different search engines to access your site. If you're at the top of the list, congratulations; if not, your site needs more work.

You can also arrange to have your address listed at other web sites. Some professional and business organizations have web sites that provide links to the web sites of members. Or you can add your page to Yahoo! Store, Internet Mall, or Virtual Spin for a monthly fee related to the number of products you advertise. You can also connect with other people in similar or complementary businesses and put links to each other's web sites in your own web pages. Or you can join already organized "rings" on the Internet. If you follow these procedures, people will learn about your web site.

You should include your web site address in all your advertising and correspondence. Keep in mind that your site will have to be continually updated to keep it attractive to potential customers. Aim for an update once a month. If you can't commit to this, reconsider using a web site.

By familiarizing yourself with computers, other technology, and their applications to business, you can create a more successful business, accomplish your work more quickly, and attend to your clients' needs more fully.

10

Managing Your Office Without an Assistant

IF YOU'RE the one doing all the work (including all the office work) while the cat grooms himself, the pile of paper on your desk can become your mortal enemy. You spend the entire morning filing correspondence and sending invoices, only to spend the entire afternoon searching for the notes on a phone conversation you had last month. And you still have a stack of your real work waiting for your attention.

What to do? You need to organize your routine so that everything runs as smoothly as possible. And you need to develop good office management skills so that you don't waste time on mundane, unimportant tasks. Did you notice that I didn't mention hiring an assistant? That's because most creative business owners can't afford to—and don't really need to. They just need to know how to manage without an assistant. (If you do decide you can't get along without an assistant, refer to Chapter 14 for more information.)

Although creative people sometimes have trouble tending to details, you'll discover that, with a little effort, you can conquer the mundane without sacrificing your important work. By applying principles of time management and organization to your work, you will be able to get it done with less stress than ever before. The more organized you are, the more time you have, and the more time you have, the more work you get done and the more leisure you can enjoy. It's estimated that most business-people spend six or more hours a week just trying to find things. That's almost an entire workday. Just think what you could do with an entire day!

Managing your work will make you more successful. In the words of interior designer Christopher Lowell, "Being unorganized is a loser mentality." This is not to say that you must go against your nature and enforce a rigid routine or punch a time clock. It simply means that you need to find a way to sort the important from the unimportant and to get your work done when it needs to be done. Wasting your time—which is valuable—is like wasting money. This doesn't mean that you can never pen a lengthy letter to a dear friend rather than send a quick e-mail. It does mean, though, that you should decide what's important. You should be in control.

Arranging Work Space

To improve your organization and efficiency, arrange your workspace carefully. You may have to rearrange it as your needs change and your business evolves, but you should begin with a logical arrangement and then make adjustments accordingly. You should have plenty of workspace. If you use a computer, be sure to make room for both the computer and clear workspace. Your phone and frequently used supplies should be within arm's reach. Reference books that you use often should be within a few feet of your desk. Keep one file cabinet near your desk for active projects. Farther away, store whatever you do not use every day, such as infrequently consulted reference books and extra supplies.

You may have an additional workspace, such as a studio, that needs organization. If you're a photographer with a darkroom, it should be organized so that everything is within reach when you need it. You should have a way of tracking when you need to reorder supplies. Artists need to conquer these same tasks. Supplies and materials should be well organized and within easy reach. You should have a place to keep works in progress so that you don't have to stick everything in the linen closet when the kids get home from school. You should clean your tools and put them away when you're not using them.

Purchasing Organizers

Once you organize your workspace so that the items you use most often are within easy reach, you'll discover that you have a stack of items on or near your desk that you use frequently (paper clips, water gun). Now you need to organize this stuff so that you can find it when you need it and it doesn't clutter up your desk when you don't.

Before you run to your nearest discount office supply shop to find a pen-and-pencil organizer guaranteed to cut your work hours in half, stop and think about what you really need. You need a place to dump your pencils and a place to stick your paper clips. I use a favorite old mug to hold all my pens and pencils. It's much nicer than some black plastic thing and a lot less expensive than an executive wood pencil cup with engraving. A beautiful flat fabric box that once held a wedding gift contains extra calendar pages and notepads. A brochure holder that takes up only a few inches of desk space (it works vertically, not horizontally) holds sticky pads, scratch paper, and plain business envelopes. These things work perfectly well and didn't cost me anything. Keep your eye out for unusual containers that can work in your office. Search your closets, the attic, and the basement for containers. Only after you've exhausted your personal resources should you consider purchasing organizers.

Plan an exploration trip or two before making any purchases. Leave your money and credit cards at home when you do this or you'll spend a hundred dollars. Make a list of everything that needs to be organized on and around your desk, plus any ideas you have for containing the clutter. For example, your list might read "pens and pencils—a cup or mug. Blank forms that I use every day—stackable trays? Active files that I need on my desk—???" Then visit a discount department store such as Target or Wal-Mart. Take a look at their housewares aisles and other sections that carry containers. You may find great ideas. Write down what you see and how much it costs. Then visit an office supply store and see what they have. Explore all the aisles, writing down things of interest. Once I found a set of magnetic bins that attach to the front of a filing cabinet (or another metal surface). Since I have two filing cabinets right next to my desk, I attached the bins and put address labels and stamps in them. Now my mailing supplies are within easy reach of my desk. I would never have known about these items, which were perfect for what I needed, if I hadn't done some exploring. Don't forget your vow not to spend money and splurge on all sorts of unnecessary items. Don't pull out the credit cards until you've made a final decision on what you should purchase.

Another way to preshop is to request a catalog (or two) from Spiegel or another department store (Penney's, Sears) and a catalog (or two) from a big office retailer (such as Quill or Staples). Look through them and note anything that might help in your quest to organize your office. Don't forget to look at sizes. Some things appear much larger than they are, while others appear taller, deeper, or smaller. If you don't want to keep whipping your tape measure out, remember that an index card is 3 by 5 inches, a regular Rolodex card is about 2 by 4 inches, and a sheet of notebook or printer paper is 8 ½ by 11 inches.

Once you've done your research, flip through your notes to determine what will work best. Take price into account. If two similar items would work about equally well, go with the less expensive one. Then make a note of the purchases that you think will satisfy your needs, and buy them when you have the opportunity. Don't worry about whether your desk accessories match. Use what works. The more personal items you can convert to business use, the more you'll like your office. But if everything on your desk is clear plexiglass or hideous pink plastic, who cares? As long as it works, get to it.

Organizing Paperwork

Once your workspace is effectively organized, you need to organize your paperwork. Just as with arranging your office, you may find that you have to reorganize your paperwork periodically in order to suit your needs. The following guidelines will help you gain the upper hand whenever your paperwork rebels against you.

The first step is to categorize everything according to general classifications (and I mean everything from those three-year-old magazines you keep meaning to read to the letter you just got from the IRS). You should have a few main categories, such as *to do, clients,* and *potential projects.* Ruthlessly discard anything that does not have direct bearing on your business (unless it has a direct bearing on your personal life, in which case you should stick it in a *personal life* pile). Divide your file cabinets (or cardboard boxes) into these broad categories and label them. The categories you will use most often should be in the cabinet(s) nearest your desk. Next, sort each category more narrowly. For example, the client category should be further divided by client name. Provide folders for each of the narrower categories, and file any related paperwork in them. Then, whenever you generate or receive paperwork, you'll put it or a copy in the folder where it belongs. If the paperwork you generate or receive requires you to do something first, put it in your "to do" box or pile, then stick it in its folder after the work is complete.

If you have a lot of materials relating to a project and you don't want to add them all to your "to do" box, make sure to put the project on your list of things to do, then store the materials in an appropriate place. (*Not* the upstairs linen closet. Someplace within two feet of your desk is ideal.) When I first began writing books, I used expandable file folders to hold materials related to each project, but that soon became annoying. The folders ripped, fell over, or didn't hold enough. Now the closet in my office is lined with plastic sweater boxes, each one marked with the name of a book project in the works. Whenever I come across material that ties in with one of the projects, I drop it in the corresponding box. It doesn't need to get more organized than that. When it's time for me to work on a project, I drag the box out of the closet, sort through it, and get started. The box stays near my desk while I complete the project so that I have access to all the relevant information and can add to it as needed. When I'm done with the project, I move the materials in the box to a file cabinet in the basement and return the empty box to the office closet, where it awaits a new book project.

You can develop your own system for organizing project-related materials. Experiment with different approaches until you find the right one.

Classifying Your Work

As you divide your paperwork into piles, you will have many questions regarding classification, classification being an inexact science. Does the contract from a publisher go in the client file for the publisher or in the contract file? There is no wrong answer. My advice is to keep it simple. The fewer files you have, the more likely you are to file things in them and then find them again when you need them. Keep client files, since these are essential. Something called a contract file may seem like a good idea, but you're not likely to need all your contracts at one time in one place. You're more likely to need all the material relating to one client at one time. Organize your files so that those you use most are in the front of the file cabinet and those you use least are in the back. Some people suggest alphabetizing your files, but that's not how my brain works. If that's how *your* brain works, then do it.

Keep personal and business paperwork separate, but not so separate that they're in different rooms. Although some people try to keep their work and personal lives completely separate, that usually isn't efficient for the creative small-business owner. If you're going to place five phone calls on Tuesday afternoon, placing a sixth (personal) call isn't going to make that much difference in your day, and you'll be able to attend to some of your personal needs as well. If you have personal errands that need to be done, divide them into two categories: those that can be done outside of working hours (the laundry, grocery shopping) and those that can't (making—and keeping—doctor appointments). Try to keep errands during working hours to a minimum, and delegate as many of them as possible. Spouses and kids are usually more accommodating than we expect if we just ask them to be.

Group the chores that must be done during business hours with related business chores. If you're writing business letters and you need to submit an insurance claim for yourself, do it at the same time. If you're making phone calls to set up appointments with clients, make your personal phone calls, too. Just remember to keep control of personal errands, because they can take as much or more time than business errands. When you put them on your calendar or "to do" list, make sure they're marked "personal." This serves as a reminder to keep your priorities where they belong.

Some people keep a separate desk or work area for personal material, but this can actually make you more disorganized and inefficient. (Your insurance agent calls up to answer a question about a claim, and you have to put the agent on hold while you root through the personal desk in the kitchen, find the information you need, then trudge back to the office and give him or her the policy number.)

Setting Priorities

Once you've classified your paperwork and consigned it to the appropriate folders, there's one pile that's left on your desk. This is your "to do" pile, made up of magazines to be read, projects to be completed, and bills to be paid. Divide the "to do" pile into three parts. The first pile should be for the work that makes money (or is dear to your heart, like the poetry chapbook you're finishing). The second pile should be for the work that supports the work that makes money, such as the invoices that need to go out. (This pile also includes the work that supports projects dear to your heart, such as sending query letters to editors about your new romance novel.) The third pile should be for the work that is none of the above (the magazines that need to be read). Within each pile, sort by order of importance. The work that makes money should be sorted by due date or project length or some combination thereof. The work that supports the work that makes money should be organized by the amount of money and the nearness to money that it involves. An invoice for $1,000 should be first on your priority list, whereas a letter asking a bankrupt

---

Figure 34

Setting Work Priorities

Your "to do" list should classify tasks into one of three categories:

1. Work that makes money or creative work that you find fulfilling. This category includes projects or assignments for which you will be paid, plus creative work like the novel you're writing or the painting you're finishing. Set priorities based on deadlines and project length.

2. Work that supports the work that makes money or that you find fulfilling. This category includes administrative tasks such as sending out invoices for paid work or trying to find an agent to represent your photography. Set priorities based on the amount of money or success involved.

3. Work that is neither. Set priorities based on importance, but spend very little time on this type of work.

---

magazine publisher to please pay the $25 she owes you is less important. The work that is none of the above should be organized in order of importance to you. Discard as much of this pile as possible. Newspapers and magazines that are more than a few weeks old can be tossed without much thought. A letter from an aspiring photographer who wants advice on how to be like you is less important than a letter from a client asking you to recommend a good photographer in Cincinnati. (Answering the letter from the client ensures that you remain in his or her good graces and could result in referrals or additional sales.)

Administrative Tasks

Determine how much time it takes to do the tasks that support your income-producing work. Think about the time it takes to write letters, make phone calls, send bills, update ledgers, and create marketing materials. Then consider how much time it takes to do your real work, the work that pays the bills or nourishes your soul. If you're not spending more time on the work that pays the bills (or nourishes your soul), then you've got to rearrange your priorities. The only exception is at the very beginning when you have few clients and even fewer projects, and most of your work consists of trying to find work.

Because like most people I absolutely despise paperwork, I try to ignore it, and then when it doesn't go away I get annoyed. I finally found an approach that works for me and for many other creative people. I set aside a certain amount of time each week for paperwork. This includes catching up my general ledger, responding to letters, sending out bills, creating queries, and marketing my services. I make phone calls, order supplies, and run errands. Usually I do all this on Monday morning, which helps me get ready for the week ahead. If some of the work overlaps into Monday afternoon, that's okay. But once Monday is over, I do not do any more administrative tasks, even if I still have some left over (I do the most important work first, so what's left over usually is not that important). I just throw everything I receive during the following week into my paperwork box and ignore it until the following Monday. As people request things throughout the week, I make note of what they want (a reviewer wants a copy of a book, an editor wants to see clips), then forget about it until Monday. Occasionally someone will ask me to send a copy of a letter or an invoice (a paperwork-related request), which they need immediately. I'll oblige, since I'm in business to attract clients. But I usually try to ascertain the urgency of the request because if it can wait until Monday it should. This has turned into the most time-saving habit I have ever had. Instead of interrupting my important work every hour to do something unimportant, I am able to take long uninterrupted stretches of time to complete projects.

If you can't do paperwork just one day a week, how about allowing one hour every afternoon for it? Pick a time when you're not at your most alert and creative best. When you *are* at your most alert and creative best, you should be working on projects, not writing "Dear Client" letters. If someone wants something from you, make a note and do it during your paperwork time that day. Make the paperwork time in the afternoon if you can, so that you can accommodate people who call with requests late in the day (unless your creative time is afternoon, in which case do administrative tasks in the morning).

Some creative people find it hard to work in long stretches. They get their optimum creativity from working in two- and three-hour blocks of time, then clearing their minds, then working for another two- or three-hour block of time. If this is the case for you, follow your natural instincts. Work on important creative or moneymaking projects for two or three hours. Then spend a half hour doing some of the mindless busy work that's cluttering up your desk. Then go back to your creative work. The important thing here is not to get bogged down with artificial deadlines, such as "I have to finish recording all these receipts before I go back to my main project."There's no reason why all your receipts have to be recorded this minute. Some of them can wait until this afternoon or tomorrow. The important thing is to work with your natural and creative rhythms. Once you feel yourself getting restless to get back to your creative work, set aside your paper-work and get to it.

The benefit of this approach is that if anyone wants something from you, you can easily oblige on the day of the request. You just have to make sure you accept the request, write it down so you don't forget it, then get back to your project. If you work this way, you may want to let the answering machine pick up phone calls while you're doing your important projects (assuming that this will work in your business). Also, you must limit the amount of time you spend on administrative tasks. It's easy for that half-hour break to turn into an entire afternoon. Some people set timers to let them know when their half hour has passed; then they'll stretch, walk around the office for a minute, and then return to their important projects.

You may not be able to follow a plan like this, depending on your personality and your business, but you can modify it. Remember, someone else's urgency doesn't necessarily have to be yours. How much is doing the task worth? (To you, I mean, not to the other person.) This is a difficult question for creative people to ask, but you need to start asking it in order to get control of your time. If an editor who plans to pay you $50 for a book review wants it this afternoon, which was when you planned to finish the proposal for a longtime client that might result in a $5,000 sale, tell the editor you're sorry about the book review, the best you can do is tomorrow. The editor will probably accept that. If not, you may have lost $50. Terrible. But it's not worth it to make the $50 sale and lose the $5,000 sale. The value of your time and the relative importance of the different demands on your time should guide your thinking as you respond to requests from clients.

If you don't scatter all your energy going back and forth between important tasks and mindless ones, you will find yourself completing your work with time to spare while still sending out invoices on a routine basis. You will be setting priorities and attending to the important work first instead of getting mired in trivia. Yes, there will still be the occasional day when everything gets completely out of control and you accomplish absolutely nothing, but those days will be fewer and fewer as you organize your efforts.

Banish Interruptions

In addition to setting aside a specific time for paperwork, try not to allow interruptions except during those paperwork times. If your business won't suffer, let the answering machine pick up the phone, especially when you're pressed for time. If you must answer your phone for business reasons, you may get many non-business calls while you're trying to work. When friends or family members call to chat, politely but firmly tell them you're working and you'll call them back. Even if it will take "just a second," tell them you do not have time. Let them know that if it's an emergency (i.e., your cousin needs your left kidney before three o'clock this afternoon), you want to know about it right away, but other than that it needs to be addressed outside of business hours. If telemarketers call, you do not need to be polite. In fact, being polite encourages them. Just hang up the phone and get back to work.

Set clear rules for others so that they don't barge in demanding the car keys when you're trying to close an important account. Specify your work times for your family, and don't allow

---

Figure 35

Banish Interruptions

Set aside specific times for paperwork and administrative tasks. Don't interrupt your important work to do these activities.

Let the answering machine pick up the phone.

Politely but firmly tell friends and family that you'll call back after work hours.

Hang up on telemarketers.

Set clear rules for others, such as family members, who interrupt you.

Specify your work times.

Don't check the mail and your e-mail sixteen times a day. Once for the regular mail and twice for e-mail is sufficient.

---

them to interrupt with questions like, "Where's my blue blouse?" Use signals like leaving your office door ajar when interruptions are okay and shutting it when interruptions are not okay. If necessary, hire a babysitter while you're working, even if you think your children are old enough to fend for themselves.

You also have to avoid interrupting yourself. This takes focus and discipline but is well rewarded in increased efficiency and better, more creative work. Don't check the regular mail and e-mail all the time. Get the mail from your mailbox at a time when you know it will be there. Don't run back and forth to look, even if you're expecting a big check. When you retrieve the mail, file relevant pieces where they belong and toss the rest. Go back to work. Don't decide to make that phone call or answer that letter since it will only take a second (it won't). Check your e-mail once in the morning and once before you're done for the day. That's it. Keep working. (An exception might be if you're working on a project that requires multiple question-and-answer e-mails throughout the day, but keep this under control.) It takes time to log on to the Internet, check your mail, then log off. Limit the time you allow for interruptions.

Controlled Chaos

At the end of the day, clean up your workspace so that you can find what you need for the next morning, but don't put everything away. Nothing can make you procrastinate more than the clean-desk theory. If you're in the middle of a complicated project, there is nothing wrong with leaving it spread out on your desk so that you can pick up where you left off. Just take care of the things that are essential, like washing out your coffee cup before a mold colony grows in it. Of course, you don't want the disorder to get out of hand. Anything not related to the project you're working on should be put away, filed, or thrown out. Otherwise you'll be found buried under an avalanche of paper in your office because you never spent time to keep your organization on track. Spending a few minutes at the end of your workday to clean up will also help you make the adjustment from work back to personal life, and it will help you identify the important tasks for the next day so that you don't have to spend time wondering where to start.

To keep control of your time, you must understand what you have to do and decide which of the things you have to do are the most important. If you're like most creative people, you have little sticky notes littering the house, each one reminding you of a task to finish, an idea to work on, an office supply to purchase. These sticky notes may work when you're an amateur, but not when you're a professional. The CEO of General Motors does not leave sticky notes all over the house. Bill Gates does not leave sticky notes all over the house. (Okay, so you don't want to be an unrepentant capitalist warmonger exploiting the lives and hopes of the undernourished masses. That is irrelevant. You don't have to *be* a soulless robber baron to succeed at business, you just have to emulate some of his habits.)

I have seen people actually compile neat stacks of sticky notes, as if this were an improvement over leaving them strewn about the house. When a task is done, they peel the corresponding sticky note off the pile and throw it away. The inventiveness of creative people when they don't want to do things in a normal, sane way, while impressive, can be counterproductive.

Daily Planning

In order to stay on top of projects and your administrative tasks, you will need two things: a "to do" list and a daily planner. If you have a sticky-note habit, you must break the addiction immediately. Invest instead in a daily planner, which is a healthier habit. You do not need to get the deluxe, gold-embossed, calfskin-bound, executive-size daily planner. You simply need a place to note down appointments, which require you to be at a certain place at a certain time on a certain day. Relying on your memory to warn you of an upcoming appointment is foolhardy at best.

Some people use computer programs like contact managers and calendars to keep track of appointments. As they make different arrangements, they input them and then print out the daily record. This is fine if you like computers and you really will enter appointments electronically instead of writing them down on sticky notes and then putting them on your computer. If using the computer program is too cumbersome, don't use it. Use a daily planner.

How you configure your daily planner is up to you. I always recommend purchasing a planner that allows you to add and subtract pages instead of a spiral-bound planner that you throw away at the end of the year. Being able to add and remove pages gives you more flexibility, and you can use the pages to organize almost anything. Daily planners can hold a checkbook, credit cards, and even receipt envelopes, so that every time you make a business purchase you just pop the receipt into the envelope. When the envelope is full, or when it's Monday and time to do paperwork, just empty it out. You can also devote a section of the planner to notes. If you take your planner with you when you leave the office, it's always there when you're struck with a brilliant idea for a book or devise a new marketing scheme while waiting in line at the doughnut shop. Notes can go in the back of the planner, where they remain safe until you return to the office and put them wherever they belong. You can also keep the names and addresses of your clients in your planner (especially helpful for people who are out of the office a lot), directions to people's homes and businesses, or any information of use to you.

The calendar pages themselves should simply list the appointments you have. If you have only one or two appointments a day, you can use weekly planner pages, which show your week at a glance. If you have more appointments than that, use daily planner pages that show only one or two days at a time. Keep all your business and personal appointments in the same daily planner. Otherwise you will lose your mind. Some people, especially those who have an assistant who makes appointments for them, have separate planners for office and travel. This is extremely dangerous unless you and your assistant keep the schedules well-coordinated.

Most organization experts recommend using just one planner or calendar. The only exception might be to have a wall calendar for reference when you're on the phone and trying to figure out what day of the week a date two weeks from now will be. Don't write anything on this second calendar or you'll just complicate matters.

Your daily planner should always travel with you. It may seem annoying at first, but it will save you many headaches. Instead of saying, "I'll call you to set up an appointment," just whip out your handy planner and make the appointment. Not only does this save you time, but it makes your clients commit to you, which any salesperson will tell you is very important. If you have your planner with you, you always have a place to put a business card you're offered, write down the name of a book a friend recommends, and figure out the tip on a $12 meal. Just make sure any information in your daily planner gets transferred to the appropriate place in your office. The business card goes in the Rolodex, the book title goes on your "to buy" list, and the tip calculations go in the wastebasket.

The "To Do" List

One calendar or planner; therefore, one "to do" list. Some people make "to do" lists that rival the invasion of Normandy for complexity and ambition. They have long-term goals, short-term goals, business and personal goals, and monthly and yearly goals, and then for some reason they get frustrated when nothing gets done. A goal is not a "to do" item. A goal is a goal. You may want to make thirty grand this year. That would be a goal. Sending out five marketing packets every day in order to reach that goal is a "to do" item. You may want to become a best-selling novelist. Becoming a best-selling novelist is a goal, not a "to do" item. *Writing* the best-selling novel is a "to do" item.

Goals

This is not to discount the importance of goals. It is merely to distinguish between goals and the steps you have to take to reach them. Goal-making is something every business owner needs to do. At the start of your business and at the beginning of each year after that, you should compile a list of important long- and short-term goals. You can be as farfetched as you wish when you're putting the list together, but then you need to decide which of these goals is worth trying to reach. Select one or two of the most important goals and decide on the steps required to achieve them. Perhaps you want to find an artist's representative or agent for your work. What must you do to make that possible? You'll need to devise a strong portfolio. If you're a writer, you'll need a manuscript or at least a proposal for a nonfiction book. You'll need to research the best way to find representation in your field. You may have to send letters, make phone calls, or attend professional lunches in order to network. All these concrete tasks are "to do" items and belong on your "to do" list.

In addition to reviewing your long-term goals every year, you should look at your short-term goals once a month. Are you getting closer to meeting them? Are they still important to you? Have new short-term goals come up? By analyzing your goals on a regular basis, you'll keep them in mind and mold your performance to achieve them.

Of course, business and personal goals are often linked. Gaining fluency in another language may be a personal goal that helps you in your business goal of having clients all over the globe. Therefore, you should consider business and personal goals together, especially since, as a creative person, your work and your life are so closely intertwined.

Deciding What's Important

One of the best ways to clarify your goals is to make a list of everything that is important in your life, such as your friends, your family, your work, your pets, and your softball games. Put everything on the list. Then rank the importance of each item. The top three are what you should spend your time on. When you have spare time, attend to other things. It may seem brutal to cut activities and people out of your life, but you have only one life, and you might as well live it in a fulfilling and rewarding way. This is not to say that you shouldn't meet accepted duties and obligations, such as voting on Election Day and helping elderly people cross the street. It simply means that you set priorities and then stick with them.

After hearing about a famous writer who made such a list, I wrote down everything from the dogs I love to the shows I like to attend. I decided that the most important things in my life were family, creative work, and martial arts. Everything else, including friends and theater-going, was less important. I then ranked the top three priorities in order of importance. My husband and child are the most important of my family relationships. Dogs, though I love them fiercely, are less important than the human members of my family. In my creative work, doing what I want is more important than taking jobs that pay well (although my goal is to have a balance of both). And my martial arts activities are sometimes more and sometimes less important. In extremely busy weeks, I don't work out every day. But I do commit to teaching two classes a week to maintain my connection. Identifying my priorities allows me to constantly rededicate myself to the important things in my life, instead of getting sidetracked by the mountain of laundry piled by the washroom door.

When I can fit in coffee with old friends and former students, I do so. But when the choice is between my daughter and my old office mate, my daughter takes precedence. If you don't make these types of choices, the demands on your time will grow intolerable, especially after you've gone into business and everyone thinks you're free to take them to lunch. Keep your top three priorities on a bulletin board in your office. Then ask yourself if what you're doing right now is related to any of the top three priorities. If not, quit doing it. When a friend phones to chat while you're working, politely but firmly tell him or her you can't talk and you'll try to call back later. When a neighbor asks you to watch the kids while she runs to the grocery store, politely but firmly turn her down (unless she wants to pay your going rate).

Before accepting any request for your time and involvement in any activity, ask yourself if it furthers one of your top three priorities. If your kid's school asks you to be a teacher's assistant one afternoon a week since you stay at home (arghh!), think about your priorities before you decide. Would it mean a lot to your son if you were a teacher's assistant? He might hate it, so you're off the hook. On the other hand, he might think it was the most wonderful thing a parent could do and, after all, it's only two hours a week. Don't worry about what the teacher, school administrator, or neighbors will think. They are not on your priority list. Your son is. Whether it matters to him and how much time you have to spare should be your only considerations. On the other hand, if the neighborhood watch committee asks you to run the program, you can quickly decline, since it has nothing to do with your top three priorities (you can always promise to keep your eye out for thieves lurking in the bushes). Yes, I know, civic involvement is an important thing. But there are people with time on their hands, and they should have the opportunity to run the neighborhood watch program. Communities are full of thousands of organizations that need your time, money, and expertise, and you cannot help all or even very many of them. If civic involvement is one of your top three priorities, have at it. If not, you can occasionally

Figure 36

Goal Setting

Once, when very frustrated with all the demands on my time, I listed everything that needed my attention in order of importance. Then I decided that I would devote my time and energy to the top three priorities on the list. Now I always ask if what I'm doing right now contributes to any of the top three items. If not, I question the value of doing it. Below is the list I came up with.

1. Family. Husband, baby, dogs, parents, sibs.
2. Writing, especially fiction.
3. Martial arts.
4. Reading.
5. Speaking engagements to raise awareness of tuberous sclerosis.
6. Friends.
7. Keeping up with academic matters.
8. Former students and work colleagues.
9. Donating time and money to charitable organizations.
10. Hobbies: cooking, needlework.

include activities such as helping out at a food bank when you have time or if it is part of a larger issue, such as teaching your children the importance of charity. But avoid committing yourself to recurring activities, such as hosting the high school's booster club meetings every other Monday. If you don't pay attention to your own business, family, and priorities, you will lose the things that are important to you. All the civic and social involvement in the world won't fix that.

Getting Work Done

Once you've established priorities and goals and have a plan for reviewing them on a regular basis, you can turn your attention to getting your business done. This is where the "to do" list comes in. Your "to do" list should include everything you have to get

---

Figure 37

Setting Goals

Determining Your Priorities

Take a few minutes to brainstorm a list of all the demands
on your time. Be sure to include relationships, activities
you enjoy, your job, anything that requires your attention.
Once you've brainstormed the list, arrange the items in order of importance to you.

_____

_____

_____

_____

_____

_____

_____

_____

_____

_____

What are your top three priorities? Is creative work among
them? If not, you should reconsider starting a creative
small business.

---

done. If you have certain chores that you must accomplish each
week and you don't want to forget them, make a permanent
weekly chores list that you can print out or photocopy. Add your
other "to do" items to this list as they come up. Include everything from returning phone calls to writing letters to sending e-
mail documents to writing books. Then organize the list according
to importance. If you have big projects, you might just list the
name of the project ("presentation for the Jensen account") and
then keep a more specific project list, along with the project
materials, in a project folder or the client's file. When you open
the Jensen project folder, the itemized project list, stapled to the
inside cover, is there waiting for you to cross items off. As certain
aspects of the Jensen account become pressing, like "call Jensen

about presentation," put that specific item on your "to do" list so you don't forget. If you handle only one or two big projects at a time, you can put all the components of the project on your list; if you have more than a few projects, doing this will seem overwhelming since you'll end up with pages of work to do. Try to keep your list to a reasonable length, perhaps one or two pages. As you finish an item, cross it off. Make a new list whenever the old one gets ratty and hard to read. Don't waste time making a new "to do" list every day. That's only for corporate types and obsessive-compulsives. (If you *are* an obsessive-compulsive, by all means go ahead and make a new "to do" list every morning.)

At the top of the list should be items that make money (or that you find creatively fulfilling). They should be written down in order of importance. Then include paperwork and administrative items (the things you do that support making money), and rank those in order of importance. If you have a lot of one type of task, such as making phone calls or writing letters, you might just group them together instead of trying to determine their order of importance. Then, when you sit down to write letters, just write them all. Or make all your phone calls at once instead of doing the priority phone calls in the morning and the less important ones in the afternoon. The only caution is not to spend too much time on these tasks. If an unimportant letter starts taking up more than five minutes of your time, abandon it and move on. Finally, at the very bottom of the list, include things that do not pertain to making money or satisfying your creativity. For me, this includes writing articles for low-paying markets. If I get around to it, I can make a little extra cash and get more exposure for my books, but if I don't, it doesn't make that much difference. It also includes things like magazines and catalogs that I might like to read but should wait until I have time. A good time to do these less important tasks is when you're waiting for appointments. I can't work on an important project in the orthopedist's waiting room, but I can read a business or trade magazine, noting down ideas that I might use, tearing out useful articles, and throwing the rest away.

As you generate more "to do" activities, either over the phone, through regular mail or e-mail, or because you just thought "Eureka! If I send out a press release to the local media, I might

Figure 38

Jennifer's TO DO list

As of 12/10

Small-Business Ownership book (due December 1)
Internet Safety guide (due December 15)
Revise Chapter 14 for art textbook (ASAP)
Edit NTC manuscript (due by 1/16)
Mock up log for Human Kinetics Press (by 1/31)
Finish medieval encyclopedia for '01
Do proposal about book on tuberous sclerosis complex
Query magazine articles about TSC to gauge interest
Invoice Mr. James
Update writing résumé
Letters to Channel 9 reporter and producer, thanks for
        segment, get copy of tape?
My goals for next year

PERSONAL:
Organize personal records file
Finish Christmas shopping (due by 12/25)
Send flowers to Joe and Martha

get some more business," add these to the list. Don't rewrite it, just stick them in there next to tasks of similar importance. Keeping a "to do" list should not be a difficult, time-consuming task. It should be a simple, effective method of keeping track of what you have to do.

As with the calendar, you should have only one "to do" list for both personal and business activities. Just keep your personal activities listed under "Personal." Then, when you're making phone calls for business reasons, you can slip that personal phone call in there too, as long as it doesn't take up too much time and as long as it's something you need to do during business hours. Keep your calendar and your "to do" list near each other, because they're linked. You'll need your "to do" list to determine whether it's feasible for you to take the job a client is offering you, and you'll need your calendar to make an appointment to meet with that person.

Handling Incoming Paperwork

Handling all the paper that comes across one's desk throughout the week seems to be the most difficult task people have. "Experts" give plenty of advice on how to solve this problem, much of it useless. I keep reading about how to "handle a piece of paper only once," and I can't believe people still try to manage their time this way. This is not very useful for most small-business owners.

Why? Well, to some degree, touching a piece of paper once—acting on it right away, filing it, sending it on to someone else or throwing it away—is in the short term an efficient method of getting rid of paper. But your goal isn't to get rid of paper. Your goal is to do your important work and then get paid for it. Following the advice of handling a piece of paper only once means that you give everything the same priority, and that's ridiculous. Although you want to be efficient, your goal isn't to be efficient for the sake of efficiency. Your goal is to be efficient so that you can finish your creative work—to get your work done, not to act on every single stimulus that comes your way. If I get three letters in the mail, one of them a bill, one of them a letter that needs a thoughtful response, and one of them an editor's outline for an article I'm writing, what am I supposed to do? Stop whatever I'm doing right now and complete the article, then write a check to cover the bill and put it in the mail, and then compose a thoughtful response to the client's letter? Of course not. The key to taking control of business is to *act*, not react. If I let the mail dictate what I'm doing, I'm reacting; I'm letting the whim of the letter carrier determine what's important.

However, although it is idiotic to handle a piece of paper only once, it is not idiotic to be efficient when you handle paper. After you open the bill, put it in your accounts payable file. The letter that needs a response should be noted on your "to do" list and filed in the appropriate place. The editor's suggestions should be put with the project folder for the article. Advertising circulars and other junk mail should be tossed, and personal mail should be set aside for after business hours.

Electronic mail should be handled the same way as regular mail. Although e-mail programs allow you to keep the correspondence forever, most people don't like to have some correspondence on the computer and some on paper in a folder. If they're talking to a client on the phone, they want all of the relevant information in a folder in front of them. You can always print out client e-mails, then handle them as appropriate—file them, note them on the "to do" list, or take whatever action is necessary. (So much for a paperless society.)

To handle phone conversations effectively, you need immediate access to any information the client might refer to. For this reason, client files are indispensible and should be kept within reach of your desk. (Try reaching your files while sitting in your chair with the phone to your ear. If you can't reach the files, put them closer.)

Make a record of every phone conversation you have and put the notes in the appropriate client file, first noting any "to do" actions on your "to do" list. Make sure you include the date of the conversation (as well as the year). This will help you document what was discussed. When Mr. Jones calls and says, "Let's cancel that thing we talked about on Tuesday," you'll have a glimmer of an idea of what he is referring to.

Some people prefer computer programs such as contact managers that let them look up information about past interactions with a client. The only drawback—and this may be a minor one, depending on your personality and your business—is that you still need a client folder for relevant paper documents. For the contact manager to work properly, you must note every contact you have with a client. So when you receive a letter thanking you for your work, you must note it on the computer and also file it in the client's folder. Even if you're scrupulous about recording everything, you'll still need the folder to look up specific information about a client or to look at the letter he or she is referring to. If you have dozens of clients, this dual system might work, because you can easily pull up the contact manager information on your computer instead of digging through file cabinets; then, if you need additional information, you can start digging. But you will have to accept some duplication of effort. For people who deal with a handful of clients at a time, simply keeping up-to-date client folders is probably sufficient.

Another option is to fully automate your office. When you receive a letter, scan it into the computer, file the computer document in the appropriate directory, and either toss the letter or store it in an inactive file. Then, when you need to refer to something about a particular project or client, everything is in your computer. You can fax from the computer and easily attach documents to e-mail messages. Such systems work with varying degrees of success, depending on how good your equipment is (a scanner that doesn't accurately reproduce certain fonts isn't going to help you much) and how dedicated you are. Also, this kind of setup must appeal to you, because it requires some work to get started and extra effort to keep it going.

Whether your office is fully automated or not, keep your computer's hard drive organized. Use directories and subdirectories for projects or clients. File individual letters and documents pertaining to the project or client under the appropriate directory or subdirectory. Don't just let everything sit in the undesignated dump site so that you're forced to scan through 200 file names to find what you want. Keep computer disks labeled, and update the label every time the contents change.

Client Files

Organize client files so that the most recent letters and other materials are up front. This way you can more easily find what you're looking for. Expandable folders can be used for clients you have worked with for a long time or with whom you exchange a lot of material. Letters and materials that are more than six months old can be purged and placed in a backup file cabinet or box in the basement or under the bed. Label this container "inactive," and keep it readily accessible and well-organized. You won't need it very often, but when you do, you don't want to waste time looking for it.

Managing Phone Conversations

Keep phone conversations short and businesslike. When people call, be polite but ask, "What can I do for you?" to get them on track. When they make a request or a comment, summarize what they've asked or said to be certain you understood correctly, then give your response. ("You would like me to photograph your daughter's wedding on Saturday, May 7th. My calendar is clear for that day, so I would be more than happy to. Would you like to set up an appointment to meet, so we can go over the different plans that are available?") Then finish the conversation nicely but firmly. ("Fine. I look forward to meeting you on Friday. Goodbye.") Put the appointment on your calendar and add any necessary notes to your "to do" list.

If you're initiating the phone call, you have more control. When you reach the client, a polite "How are you?" is in order, but not a lot of small talk about the weather and the playoff possibilities. If you know the client very well, you may want to spend a minute or two talking on a personal level, but there's no need to belabor it. Some creative people seem uncomfortable dealing with others on a purely business level and feel that they must act as if they have a personal interest in the client. Nice as this is, it can be annoying to the client ("Why is she wasting my time with this? Who cares about my golf game?"). There is nothing wrong with politely but clearly getting down to business right away. ("Mr. Smith, this is Janet Jones. Hope you're doing okay today. Glad to hear it. I'm calling because I have that proposal you asked for and wanted to set up an appointment to go over it with you.")

Sometimes people are uncomfortable asking for work or trying to set up appointments. They feel like a salesperson, which they're sure they could never be, and they get nervous and put off calling. Then, when they do call, they talk on and on without getting to the point, because to get to the point they would have to ask for the client's business, or request a larger payment than is being offered, or do whatever task creative people feel least equipped to do.

If this is you, try making a clear outline of what you want to say before you call your client. (But be sure to listen and respond to your client, not your outline. Your outline just helps you say what you need to say.) For instance, you want to set up an appointment to go over a proposal with a client, which will basically be a sales meeting. You're afraid the client will tell you just to send the proposal, and then you'll never get the job because the proposal will sit on his desk for a month. Make your list of points: The proposal is ready. I'd like to meet with you and go over it. What does your schedule for this week look like? Then call the client and get down to business. If you have difficulty with this step and you can't hire a salesperson because you're it, consider taking a class in public speaking, or attend a salesperson motivation seminar. They can be incredibly silly, but they'll give you more confidence when you approach clients.

Acquiring Office Skills

In addition to learning the appropriate phone skills, you may need to learn other office skills. If you're a writer and you're still using the old hunt-and-peck method of typing, you should take a typing or keyboarding class. If computer tutorials are more your style, invest in one. Learning to type is the easiest, least expensive way you'll have of saving time. If you can't figure out how to keep a general ledger, enroll in a basic bookkeeping course on the subject, either through a continuing education program or a local community college, or even online. If you simply cannot organize your office, hire a professional consultant who will show you how to get and stay organized. Improving office skills increases your productivity and allows you to work more efficiently.

Consolidate Tasks

Also, learn to consolidate tasks. If you're printing out a long document to proofread before you send it to the client, make a phone call or two while you're waiting. If you're calling a client and you're on eternal hold, enter a couple of receipts in your

Figure 39
Time Diary

Monday 12/7/98

Time	*What I did*	*Worthwhile?*
7:30–8:30	Showered, dressed, fed Jessica, made tea, ate a granola bar, played fetch with dogs, got slobbered on, toweled off.	Yes
8:30–11:00	Taught Tae Kwon Do class and worked out afterwards, took another shower. I need to quit duplicating the shower every morning.	Yes
11:00–12:00	Jess took nap. Started to work on book due last week, editor from different publishing company called, wanted manuscript revisions now, negotiated later deadline.	No
12:00–2:00	Jess' babysitter came, has new work schedule, can watch Jess more, yippee! Worked on revisions instead of book, got interviewed by radio show host, sounded stupid. Same editor called back, why didn't I send original art a month ago? (I did.)	No

(continued on next page)

2:00–3:30	If editor is going to be that way, she can wait for revisions. Started back to work on book.	Yes
3:30–4:00	Guilt set in. Back to revisions. Got the mail, publisher sent check for wrong amount, called editor (not there), called accounts payable department (not there). Frustrated because I need the money (the right amount of money).	No
4:00–6:00	Disgusted with wishy-washy behavior, started work again on book. May actually get it done before next year.	Yes
6:00–8:00	Melissa had to leave but fortunately husband got home in time to watch Jess. Work on book is going well, don't stop now!	Yes
8:00–11:00	Ate dinner, watched movie with husband. Jess sent to bed at 8:30, no fussing, good kid.	Yes
11:00–1:00	Worked on book some more, wish the project was going faster, wish I didn't have so much work piled up, would like to have a life again.	Yes

daily ledger. If you send the same six pieces of information to potential clients who want to know more about your business, assemble marketing kits to slip in the mail instead of having to hunt down everything you want to include.

Don't do the same task over and over if you don't have to. Instead of writing a check to your Internet service provider every month, have the fee deducted from your checking account. All you have to do is note it on your general ledger every month. If you use standard contracts or releases, keep a template on the computer. Keep a template of your invoice and other letters or forms you frequently use. Then just fill in the blanks and print out the document, and you've saved yourself tons of time.

Work Schedules

Keep a work schedule and stick to it. If you don't have a schedule, either you'll work all day and half the night (and that's no way to run a life) or you'll work when you feel like it (and that's no way to run a business). While it's true that small-business owners work longer hours than employees, some of that time is wasted and could be put to better use. If you always arrive at and leave the office at the same time, not only will you acquire the discipline needed to run the business, but soon you'll be accustomed to it. At eight every Monday morning you'll be ready to get to work rather than sitting at the kitchen table thinking, "Well, if I wanted I could start work at ten and keep working until seven."

Of course, there's no need to work eight-to-five or nine-to-five or any of the standard business hours, since flexibility is one of the benefits of owning a small business. Some of your business hours should be during the typical business day so that you can reach others and they can reach you. But who's to say you can't work from three in the afternoon to midnight if that suits your rhythms? That's one of the reasons you're in business for yourself.

Along with keeping a set schedule, you should plan to be in your office every day. You can designate some days as vacation or sick days, but for the most part, you should forgo skipping work if you want to keep food on the table. The joy of working for yourself is taking a Wednesday off to take the kids to the park for absolutely no other reason than that it's spring, but by the same token, if you take every Wednesday off, not only will it lose its allure but your business will suffer.

Keep a Time Diary

If you still feel pressed for time, try keeping a diary in which you note how you spend your time throughout the day. If you feel constantly pressed for time in your personal life too, you can keep a diary for after-work hours as well. This will show you how you spend your time. Maybe some of the most time-consuming chores can be made easier through the use of computer software or by hiring an assistant to work ten hours a week. Maybe you need to rethink your processes and ways of doing things. Maybe you need to make more money per project and take on fewer projects. Keeping a time diary will help you make decisions wisely, based on facts rather than inaccurate guesses.

Taking the time to organize your office and administrative tasks will help you keep on top of business. Maintaining organized records and schedules does not have to be an intimidating, time-consuming task, but it does have to be a habit. Make it your habit, and you'll see immediate rewards.

11

Keeping Track of Customers

IF YOU'VE organized your office and streamlined your work routine so that you're operating efficiently, you may nonetheless need a plan for keeping track of customers/clients. If you've followed my advice, you have a calendar or daily planner to track appointments, plus a "to do" list to track activities. Still, the two by themselves don't necessarily lead to happy, satisfied clients.

Of course, every creative person's dream is to have enough clients to keep track of. But keeping track of clients is essential to successful small-business ownership. This includes potential as well as current clients.

You should have file folders with clients or potential clients listed on them so that when someone calls or you receive a letter or e-mail message, you can pull the file, update yourself on the client, and respond appropriately. It is important to set up these files and keep them active. Make sure they're within easy reach of your desk. Always file the most recent action in the front of the folder so that you have events in chronological order. Include notes of telephone conversations, letters, and copies of e-mail messages. Any document that requires action should not be put in the folder without first being noted on the "to do" list.

The problem with this system is that it relies too much on input from the client to spark any action. There's no way to follow up on things. And follow-up is the difference between maintaining a client list and losing it.

Suppose Marianne, a graphic design specialist, gets a call from a potential client who requests a packet of information. On Monday Marianne sends the packet and creates a potential client folder, including the client's name and address plus a note of the material she sent. She files the folder, then starts work on another project. The potential client never responds to the packet of information. Maybe it ended up in Detroit rather than Pittsburgh. Maybe it ended up on the janitor's desk instead of the CEO's. Maybe the potential client got the packet, read it, thought Marianne could help the company, but got caught up with his next project and forgot about it. If Marianne has no method for following up, that's it for a potentially lucrative relationship.

When Marianne sent the packet of information, she could have made a note on her "to do" list to follow up with a call in two weeks. But putting future activities on a current "to do" list is annoying and confusing, since you can't do anything about them until a certain date. Instead of putting a future activity down on her current "to do" list, Marianne could have made a note on her calendar, even though the calendar is for noting appointments, not activities to do. The drawback is that she might overlook the "to do" item on her calendar, since it's not an appointment. Neither solution seems to be very helpful.

Following Up

Depending on how many clients and projects you have, follow-up can be a tricky thing, although it is the key to attracting and keeping clients. A calendar is great for appointments, and a "to do" list is perfect for keeping track of what you have to do right now, but what about things you need to do in the future? Where do they go? The answer is, that depends.

For essential pieces in a project, you need to develop a method for making sure that one action triggers the next. You should become familiar enough with the stages of your projects to know that before you finish the rough draft of that 300-page annual report, you should make sure you have enough paper and printer cartridges on hand to print it out. If not, you should automatically make a note on your "to do" list. Supplies that you need can be noted in the back of your daily planner on a "to purchase" page. The note on your "to do" list can simply say, "Purchase supplies." This way, if you're out running errands and you're near a supply source, you can pick up exactly what you need, because you always take your planner with you, right? At first you may need to list every single step on a project list, but over time you may develop a routine so that you no longer need to do so. When one action logically triggers another, your entire business will run more smoothly.

The project list should describe the steps you need to do, in chronological order, for the project. A photo shoot might require renting a hall and hiring models, plus purchasing supplies, then developing and printing the film. A corporate history might require research in the company's archives, plus interviews of the company's founders. Every component of the project should be listed, such as "corporate history with table of contents, introduction, preface, glossary, and index." Each part, from the table of contents to the index, is a separate piece of the whole and requires specific attention. Forgetting to do the index because it was not on the project list is a failure to complete the project successfully.

Often, contracts will specify elements that must be present, such as a certain length of a manuscript or the number of photos to be submitted and in what form. Note these parameters and limitations on the project list as well.

As parts of the project come due, note them on your "to do" list. For instance, after you've hired the models and rented the hall, make a note to purchase supplies before the shoot on Saturday. This way, as you work through your "to do" list you won't overlook pressing items on any of your projects.

As you maintain your project lists and transfer items to your "to do" list as they become relevant, you may discover that you need to do some future follow-up to continue with the project. Suppose the next step in writing the corporate history is to interview the company's founder, but he's in Hawaii until next Friday. You already know what happens when you try to note future "to

Figure 40

Project List—Internet Safety Guide

Due: 12/15/00

What it is: 40 pages (9,000–10,000 words) describing how to surf the Internet safely. Junior high reading level. Features illustrations, table of contents, glossary, resources, web sites of interest, index. Beth Williams, editor. Publisher has tight deadline.

Finish research (due by 11/1/00)
Revise outline (11/4/00)
Get editor's approval of new outline (?)
Organize research notes (while waiting for editor)
Draft the book (11/15/00)
Determine what could be illustrated with charts, graphs,
    etc. (11/23/00)
Revise manuscript (11/30/00)
Do illustrations (12/5/00)
Write glossary (12/6/00)
Select resources (12/7/00)
Find web sites of interest to kids (ask nieces and nephews
    for recommendations) (12/9/00)
Compile index heads (no page numbers needed yet)
    (12/10/00)
Update table of contents (12/11/00)
Have niece read manuscript (may not have time for this
    step)
Revise, if needed
Send to editor (12/15/00)
Clear schedule for revisions she'll suggest (probably Feb.)
Make suggested changes (Feb.)
Wait for royalties to roll in (in the future)

do" activities on your current "to do" list or on your calendar. So what should you do?

You have a number of choices. If you use a contact manager program on your computer, you can tell it to remind you next

Friday that you need to arrange the interview. You can go ahead and list the task on your calendar and hope for the best. (If you never have very many appointments and you don't have that many follow-ups to do in any given week, this might work.) You can purchase a divided file with all the days of the month listed on individual pockets. Then you can file future "to do" activities in the divided file. All you have to do is check the file each morning to see if there's any follow-up task that you need to put on your "to do" list. The drawback is that you can file follow-up information for only one month at a time. What if the company's founder is playing golf in Texas until August? You can always buy another divided file that has a pocket for each month and use it in addition to the file that has a pocket for each day. At the beginning of the month, you'll fish out all the follow-ups for the month and distribute them between your "to do" list and your daily divided file. (This sounds like more work than it is.)

Instead of keeping all your project lists with the projects themselves, you could keep them in a three-ring binder. You would continue to mark off various parts of the projects as you finished them, but you could also simply consult the binder once a week and leaf through every project to update yourself. At that time, you could note any immediate follow-up tasks on your "to do" list.

You can create a master "projects in progress" plan. This would include relevant information about all your current projects. You can use a spreadsheet program, a ledger book, a notebook, or some butcher paper. It doesn't matter. For each project, list the project name ("corporate history for MJM Studios"), the status of the project ("need interview"), and the follow-up that is necessary ("check with founder on Friday, May 18"). You can modify this however you want and even keep track of the hours you work on each project, depending on your needs. At least once a week, simply check the master plan for follow-up activity and to make sure anything that needs to be done is noted on your "to do" list. If you use a master plan such as this, you need to note status changes in your projects as they occur. Thus, as soon as you interview the company's founder, not only do you have to mark this off the "to do" list but you also have to mark it off the

---

Figure 41

Projects in Progress Master Plan

Project Name	Status	Follow Up	Dates to Remember
Small Bus. Book	revision	needs glossary, TOC, and illustrations	Due 12/1/00
Internet Safety Guide	draft	—	Due 12/15/00
Art textbook	revision	revise Chapter 14	ASAP
Edit NTC ms.	proofread	—	Due 1/16/01
Mock up log	not started	get started!	Due 1/31/01
Finish medieval encyclopedia	revision	add suggested readings to entries, write introduction	get it done sometime in the next century
Tuberous sclerosis proposal	draft	ask Mayo if they'll endorse the book	—
Query magazines re: TSC	not started	ask Shelly who she'd approach	—

---

individual project list, then update the master plan to show the next step in the process. If you feel better the more organized you are, this will work well for you. If you're apt to be lazy about updating lists, don't bother starting a master plan. It won't be helpful in your follow-ups and it'll just clutter up the office.

You can adapt any of these possibilities to your own needs. Or you can create your own follow-up system. Sit down and think up something completely unique. Unless you have a detail-oriented, organized mind, you should keep it as simple as possible. The less duplication of effort that follow-up involves, the better.

Customer Service

By providing appropriate follow-up, you provide excellent customer service, and excellent customer service keeps clients returning to you on a regular basis. We all know the basics of good customer service because we've all been customers. A rude clerk can make you vow never to return to a certain department store. Nothing can get you steamed quite so quickly as a receptionist finishing a ten-minute personal phone call before asking you whom you wish to see. Long lines at a checkout can be irritating, especially if a store manager is wandering around "supervising" instead of helping out. Contractors who promise to have the plumbing fixed by Friday but don't bother showing up until a week from Tuesday can try the patience of the gentlest souls.

We know what good customer service is: being waited on pleasantly and promptly; having someone listen courteously to a complaint; showing up when promised; and meeting deadlines that have been set. But when you're the business owner, it can sometimes be difficult to know whether you're providing good customer service. Certainly you treat your clients professionally and politely. Sure, you make every effort to meet deadlines. Yes, you keep the lines of communication open so that your clients always know the status of their projects.

Balancing Good Business With Good Service

But sometimes things get a little difficult when good business and good customer service directly oppose each other. For example, you may have a small nonprofit organization as a client. You've recently raised your fees owing to an increase in the cost of supplies. But the nonprofit can't afford your new rates. What do you do? Good customer service would say go ahead and keep your rates the same for the nonprofit and take a smaller profit on the project, but good business says you won't stay in business long if you make concessions like that.

Sometimes the needs of two clients can compete. Perhaps one client calls and asks for a project to be done by Monday. If you work all weekend, you'll be able to do it, and the company is offering a premium, so you agree. But that afternoon your oldest client calls and asks you to revise some work you did. Since it will only take a few hours, surely you can have it done by Monday, right? Good customer service says you should take care of your best customers, but if you do, you may not be able to finish the project for the client who called first, and then what will you do?

Good customer service is never as easy as the customer service manuals like to pretend. You have to balance what's good for your business (going out of business doesn't help anyone) while seeing to your clients. In the two cases just presented, no answer is clearly right or wrong. The best thing is to be honest. Let the small nonprofit organization know how much you've appreciated their patronage in the past, but say that because of the increased cost of supplies, you cannot continue doing business at your old rates. Perhaps you can offer a compromise, such as a slight discount on the new fee schedule. Or perhaps the company might be willing to take a lower priority on your schedule in order to qualify for a lower rate.

In the second case, once you've made a promise, you should not make additional promises that interfere with it. Of course, this is easier said than done. You never know when everyone will want you to fulfill your promises at the same time. The best approach, again, is to be honest. Tell your oldest client that you're very sorry but you have made another commitment. Promise to deliver the revision by Tuesday morning, and explain that you'll try to get it done before then. If the customer is unhappy with this arrangement, you have two options. You can invoke your emergency work fee, which is the extra amount you charge for rush jobs, and stay up all Sunday night to finish the revision. Or you can offer the customer a slight discount for the inconvenience. You will probably find that most clients will be able to accept a reasonable explanation and that you won't need to try these additional tactics.

In order to provide the best customer service, don't try to make across-the-board promises and guarantees, especially since the needs and demands of each client will differ. Instead of promising same-day delivery on photos, promise a quick turnaround time. When a client asks what this means, give them a range, such as one to three days, depending on how large the project is and how busy you are. Rarely will this fail to satisfy a client. (People would rather hear a general range than be given a specific promise that you can't keep.) Or you could ask when they'd like to have the photos back and see if you can meet their needs. (Some clients will, in all innocence, say something like, "Well, I was hoping to have them in time for my mother's birthday a week from Thursday," in which case simply nod and say, "I don't think that will be a problem.") Only if you're absolutely confident that you can *always* provide same-day service should you advertise or guarantee it.

Identifying Customer Service Problems

If you have clients who turn down your proposals or never hire you again after a first job, you should investigate what you're doing wrong. Although acquiring many clients can be a good idea—in general, you don't want one client making up more than 25 percent of your business—you also want to hang on to the clients you have.

The clients you lose can tell you a lot about how you run your company and how you can improve it. Asking satisfied customers to rate your customer service skills ranks among the more useless undertakings. You don't necessarily need to know why you have clients; you need to know why you don't. What makes a customer quit working with you or refuse to work with you to begin with? All you have to do is call. (Sending a letter probably won't work; if you irritated the client in the first place, why should he or she bother responding to you now?) Ask the client to be honest about why your services didn't meet his or her needs. Perhaps the client feels that you don't fit with a certain image— maybe you don't seem professional to this client. Perhaps your materials seem unpolished or amateurish. Perhaps you don't work quickly enough or don't make your promised deadlines. Perhaps your rates are too high or the client suddenly developed an aversion to six-foot blondes.

This is not to say that you need to change the way you operate your business on the basis of one dissatisfied client's comments.

Maybe a company felt your rates were too high. This doesn't mean that you should start charging less. It simply means that your rates were too high for that company. If this complaint is echoed by other dissatisfied clients or if you have trouble acquiring clients, however, you may need to pay more serious attention to the question of rates. By the same token, the client might say that a word in your brochure was misspelled, which called your credibility as an editor into question. This is something that you can and should fix right away, whether anyone else ever comments on it or not.

Sometimes the answer will have nothing to do with you. Perhaps a company began doing all their public relations work in-house. There isn't much you can do about that except occasionally remind the client that you'd be happy to help them out should they need extra assistance on a special project. When you're not to blame, the reasons for your clients' defections often seem unfair. I once had a contract with a publishing company to write a book that fit their interests. I worked feverishly to get the complicated, lengthy manuscript done by deadline, missing sleep, barely getting to spend time with my new baby, and putting hundreds of dollars into child care and secretarial services to get me through the job. Shortly after I met the deadline, the acquisitions editor told me that the new managing editor wanted to take the publishing company in a different direction. My book did not fit with that direction, so they were breaking the contract. It was nothing I had done. Nothing was wrong with the book. They simply were no longer interested in publishing it. Even though we had a contract, there was nothing I could do about this except vow never to lose that much sleep over another project again in my life. I also immediately began to market the project to other editors in the field.

On another occasion, a publishing company was sold right in the middle of my making good on two book contracts. It took forever to get paid my advance. I asked the new editor about several other book ideas that the former editor and I had agreed to do (although no written contracts had been signed), including the second edition of an earlier book. The new editor said he would have to wait a year for sales figures and then get back to me. A year!

I immediately identified *that* as a brushoff. Nonetheless, I tried to make certain that I acted promptly and professionally while the new company took over production of my two newly written books. It took them months longer under the new owner to get anything done. Although the people I interacted with were perfectly congenial, it was clear that they couldn't wait to work with their "own" writers. I decided to cut my losses. I took my book ideas to another publisher and established a good relationship there.

In essence: You don't always have control over what happens to your work or to your business, but you always have control over how you respond. If you try to find out what went wrong, you'll be a better, more professional business owner. If you maintain good relations with people who don't deserve it, you may find yourself rewarded in the future (although I wouldn't spend a lot of time on undeserving people). If you remain cheerful and optimistic about finding other clients, chances are that you will. By remaining organized and by developing systems to keep track of projects and clients, you'll be able to keep your clients happy and your business profitable.

Setting Fees and Making the Most from Every Sale

THE MOST common question small-business owners ask—especially those in creative fields—is "How much should I charge?" The answer—"it depends"—is never very satisfying. Setting fees appropriately makes the difference between running a profitable business and one that barely breaks even. It's the difference between acquiring clients and alienating them. The delicate task of setting fees is part art, part science.

But you can take several steps that will help you determine what to charge. You can contact others in a similar business to find out what they charge for their services. The only difficulty here is that others, sensing competition, may not want to be open with you. You can also consult market rate lists put out by professional organizations. *Writer's Market* lists a range of rates for a number of different writing and editing services. The rates vary depending on region of the country, your experience, and other factors, but they can serve as a rough guideline. Other guides list market rates for different professions.

By the Hour or by the Project?

You can charge either by the hour or by the project. There are pros and cons to each approach. If you charge by the hour, you're certain to be reimbursed for the amount of time you actually spend on the project. But if you're a quick worker, you wind up being penalized for your skill. If you charge by the project and you miscalculate the number of hours it takes to complete a project, you can lose money. But if you're an accomplished worker, you can increase the profit you take home for each project.

Some companies do not like to pay outside contractors by the hour. They may be concerned about the IRS reclassifying you as an employee instead of an independent contractor. This concern is especially relevant if you do a lot of work for one company. Being paid by the project helps prevent reclassification. In addition, a company may be concerned that they have no control over the amount of time you spend on a project. You have no incentive to work quickly. In fact, the slower you go, the greater your reward. The client also doesn't know that you're actually working the hours you claim to be working (although if the client distrusts you this much, you may need to work on your customer service skills). For these and other reasons, a client may prefer to pay you by the project.

On the other hand, paying by the hour gives a company some flexibility. I once worked for a publishing company as a freelance editor on a book project. After I started, the publisher asked if I could write several chapters in the book, which I agreed to do. This required an additional project fee negotiation and a new contract. Then the publisher asked me to provide additional materials that could be used by students and teachers. What the publisher wanted was to come to me with various requests relating to the book, knowing that I would see to them. In order to prevent having to negotiate a separate fee for each request, we agreed on an hourly wage and set an outer limit on how much the company would pay in total for my work. This made it very easy for various people involved in the project to solicit my help as they needed it. The only drawback was that for the duration of the project I was essentially on call. Still, I made a lot of money on work that the company wouldn't have sent my way if they'd had to negotiate payment for each piece. Charging by the hour can be beneficial to both the client and the independent contractor.

Whether you charge by the hour or by the project, you'll need to determine what your time is worth, how much a project will cost for you to do, and how much time it will take. All these factors weigh into the pricing decision. If you don't take them into consideration, you can undercharge and have difficulty making a profit.

Using the Full-Time Equivalency Guideline

To determine what your time is worth, most creative small-business owners use the full-time equivalency guideline. This simply shows how much it would cost for a full-time employee to do the task, with adjustments to account for the differences between freelancers and employees.

If you're asked to edit a book, simply determine your hourly rate based on what a full-time editor at a publishing house would cost. Suppose that someone with your experience in your region of the country makes about $40,000 per year editing. Assuming that editors work just forty hours a week (they don't, but then neither do you), that works out to about $20 an hour. But wait. The editor probably has some minimal benefits, such as paid vacation and sick days, and health insurance. The editor's employer also contributes matching funds to the Social Security Administration. The freelancer must pay this herself. The employee takes up office space and uses supplies and utilities that the freelancer must provide herself. This overhead can add up to a considerable expense. In addition, the employee doesn't have to drum up business. If there isn't a lot to edit, she still gets paid. (Of course, if there isn't a lot to edit for a long time, she gets fired and perhaps becomes a small-business owner herself, but that's another story.) To the original figure of $20 an hour, add at least 100 percent more to cover these costs. This comes to $40 an hour, but this is not the price you should quote your clients. There are other costs that you'll need to consider as well.

Project Costs

Once you calculate the basic worth of your time, you will need to add in any extraordinary expenses (beyond the cost of overhead, which is included in the basic hourly rate), such as photo developing and film, any travel you may have to do, or special

purchases. A photo shoot may require a special lens or filter to produce the effect a client asks for. Although you may be able to use the
lens in other work, you will need to include at least part of the cost
in the project, or else you'll never recoup your investment. Add
these costs to your rate. Then add at least 20 percent more to account for unexpected delays and unanticipated expenses.

If you're charging by the hour, use a sliding scale to account
for variable project costs. For projects that will have little additional project costs, assume 10 to 20 percent for incidentals such
as overnight delivery of documents. So if your basic hourly rate is
$40, once you've accounted for various project costs you'll arrive
at $50 an hour. This is the low end of your range. For projects that
will require travel, expensive supplies, or the like, add 100 percent of your hourly wage. The higher end of your range will then
be $100 an hour. This range ($50 to $100 an hour) is the minimum
you should be willing to accept for your work.

Calculating Time

In order to quote a per-project fee, you'll need to calculate time
as well as hourly rates and project costs. Even if you work by
the hour, your clients will want an idea of how long a project
will take. Determining how much time to assign to a project is
the trickiest part of setting fees, and it takes experience. If the
client agrees to pay $8,000 for something that takes you two
weeks to do, you're in luck, but what usually happens is you
get paid $800 for something that takes two months to do, which
is no way to earn a living.

As you discuss the project or put together a proposal for it,
ask yourself questions such as: How much research is involved?
How much organizing will you have to do? Do you have to hire
people for the project? How and where will you find them?
What kind of support will the client offer—access to archives,
a person who can obtain rights so you don't have to? How
many revisions will the project include? What if you have to
reshoot the photos?

Once you have an idea of what is involved in the project,
figure out how much time it will take based on past experience

---

Figure 42

Example of Setting Fees

Project: Martial Arts How-to Book
Description: about 60,00 words with 150 black-and-white
      photos.

Full-time equivalency guideline:
Assume writers make $35,000 a year with two weeks of
      vacation
40-hour week = $17.50 an hour
Add overhead (100%) = $35.00 an hour

Additional project costs:
Film and photo developing: $500.00
Filter for fluorescent lighting: $25.00
Dinner for everyone who agrees to model for the photo
      shoot: $150.00
Gift for owner of studio where photo shoot will be held:
      $50.00
Subtotal: $725.00
Add 20 percent for unexpected delays and expenses:
      $145.00
Total additional project costs: $870.00

Calculating Time:
Hours writing manuscript: 6 weeks × 40 hours per week =
      240 hours
Hours shooting photos: 20 hours (evenings and weekends)
Subtotal: 260 hours
Add 25 percent to cover unexpected delays: 65 hours
Total: 325 hours
325 hours × $35 per hour + aditional costs = $12,245
      (minimum charge for project)

---

and informed guesses (the presentation you did for your boss last year, the term paper you wrote as a senior in college). Then add at least 25 percent more to cover unforeseen delays and difficulties. Finally, multiply the hours by your basic hourly fee and add in any extra project costs.

Figure 43

Setting Fees

To calculate an hourly rate:
> Divide the additional project costs by the number of hours the project will take: $870/325 = $2.68. Rounded up, this would add an additional $2.75 to the hourly wage of $35.00. The new hourly wage is $37.50.

To calculate a project rate:
> Multiply the full-time equivalency hourly rate ($35.00) by the number of hours the project will take: $35.00 × 325 = $11,375.00. Add the additional project costs to this total: $11,375.00 + $870.00 = $12,245.00.

The amount you charge per hour or per project can be revised upward or downward, depending on factors such as your experience (the new kid on the block will probably have to charge less than the old hand), the amount of support the client will provide, how urgent the work is (charge more if you have to drop everything), and what, if any, expenses will be reimbursed by the client. Expect to negotiate fees, even if you set them in advance. (Negotiation is discussed in detail later.)

Using these methods to calculate fees gives you a starting point—a basic minimum fee to charge. There's absolutely no reason you can't charge five grand for the vase that took you two hours and $6 to make (if you can find a willing buyer), but the truth is that most people set their fees too low and end up not covering their costs. You can always adjust your fees downward to attract more clients, but it's much harder to adjust them upward and not lose business.

Setting Rates in Advance

Setting your rates in advance has several benefits. It sends the message that you charge a certain amount for your work, which means clients will be less inclined to negotiate. Further, most people want to know right away how much a project will cost. In fact, they may be pleasantly surprised and hire you on the spot. Setting an hourly or project rate also helps you resist outside distractions when you should be working. Is it really worth $65 an hour to put in a load of laundry? Probably not. Save that for when you're not on the clock.

To come up with rates in advance, consider how you plan to market yourself. Will you write newsletters for people? What variations can a newsletter have, and how will that affect your fee schedule? A newsletter that consists of one 8½- by 11-inch sheet of paper with only text on both sides will require a lot less time to produce than an eight-page newsletter with graphics. If you plan to charge by the hour, what will you charge by the day? What about giving a slight discount of 5 to 10 percent for longer-term or bigger projects?

Instead of determining that it costs $42 an hour to write a newsletter no matter what, you can give a range. Most clients understand that fees vary according to the complexity of a project; they simply want a ballpark idea of what they can expect to spend. Be sure your range doesn't vary too widely (such as $35 to $425 an hour), and give your clients the information they need to determine which end of the range they fall under. If you charge more for consultations when the moon is full, say so. If you give seminars for 10 to 10,000 people, let clients know whether they'll be charged a flat fee or a per-student fee, and tell them if they're entitled to a discount for enrolling large numbers of students. (Clients love discounts.)

Knowing how much to charge is meaningless if you don't stick to your rates. If the client accepts your quotation, fine. If not, you can consider changing what you will charge, but only if the client compromises as well.

Negotiations

Although your clients probably wouldn't think about negotiating with the electrician for installing new lighting in the conference room, they'll want to negotiate with you. Suppose you say, "I charge $40 an hour. For the job you've described, I anticipate it would take ten hours." When the client says, "Ten hours?" you should say firmly, "Yes, ten hours." You're the expert, not the client. Remain firm. When the client says, "At $40 an hour?" and appears to be thinking about doing it himself or herself, you should say, "Yes, $40 an hour." If the client says, "That's too much," do not—I repeat, *do not*—say, "Okay, how about $30 an hour?" I don't care how much you want the job. I don't care if you would do the job for free. You are a businessperson. You must act like a businessperson.

In this situation you have two choices. You can say, "Thank you for your time. I hope you will consider me when you find yourself unable to produce a decent newsletter on your own." (Well, okay, you won't say that last part, but you will thank the client for his or her interest and move on to the next project.) The other choice you can make is to negotiate. Negotiating does not mean that you drop your rate. It means that the client gives up something and you give up something. It's that simple. You can say, "If you would like to sign up for twelve months of news-letters ahead of time, I would be willing to give you a 10 percent discount." Or you can say, "I can provide the text but not the formatting in about seven hours instead of ten." Or you can even say, "If you pay up front I can offer a 5 percent discount." Do not offer all of the possibilities at one time, of course. Let the client respond. Often, just the fact that he or she doesn't have to pay the first price quoted will satisfy the client.

Although it is difficult to talk about money, especially when you're doing something you love, think of yourself as akin to an electrician or other skilled tradesperson. An electrician isn't going to be embarrassed to charge $65 an hour if that is the market rate. If he has experience and satisfied customers, that's what he's going to charge. He may be willing to negotiate, like you, on big projects or in order to get paid quickly, but he's pretty much convinced that he's worth $65 an hour. You should be too.

Client-Set Fees

On the other hand, some markets simply do not let you set the pay. A magazine sets a certain fee for articles of a certain length. A newspaper buys photographs for a specific amount of money. A book publishing contract sets a standard royalty. However, as firm as these fees seem to be, there is still room for negotiation. Again, remember that you're a talented person and it's worth asking. Know your minimum price. If a market pays a lower amount than this, do not submit to that market. You may not know the market's average fee the first time you work with it (check market guides before you submit), but you will the next time.

On the recommendation of one of my book editors, I once sent an article to a magazine editor, who promptly accepted it and paid me in complimentary copies of the magazine. This was after I had spent years and much sweat and blood establishing a reputation as a writer (I had written fourteen books by then). Poets get complimentary copies. Fledgling writers get complimentary copies. Professional writers do *not* get complimentary copies. But it was my own fault for not finding out what the market paid. At any rate, don't submit to low-paying markets. If you mistakenly do, don't submit to that market again, at least not until the policy changes.

Payment on Publication

Writers and photographers should also be wary of markets that pay on publication. An editor can agree to purchase your work, but that doesn't mean it's going to get published any time soon. An editor can hold on to the piece until next June, by which time it's outdated, and then send it back to you, maybe with a $25 kill fee, saying she's sorry but she won't be able to use the piece after all. At the beginning of your creative life you will occasionally have to do this sort of thing in order to get published, but once you have clips, stop it. The only exception might be for a magazine editor you work with frequently who can be trusted to publish the piece within a month or two. If you do have work accepted for publication, send a follow-up letter every now and then as you await publication. If more than three months after acceptance have passed and the piece still has not been published and the editor has not set an issue date for it, politely but firmly withdraw the piece and send it to another magazine. You don't have to let your work sit in limbo forever.

The only time you should stray from your rules regarding minimum pay and payment on acceptance (rather than on publication) is when the work serves some ulterior motive, such as publicizing a book you have written.

Negotiating Set Rates

If a market with set rates accepts your work, you do not need to take the first figure the client quotes. There's usually a pay range, and the first figure quoted will be on the low end of the range. Ask for 20 to 30 percent more—even if the client offers a decent amount. You'll probably get something. You can also negotiate other conditions. Perhaps you'd accept the lower fee if you also got extra complimentary copies of the magazine, or if the editor agreed to run another article you're working on. Remember that you can always withdraw your work from a market (unless a contract has been signed) if you and a client cannot agree on a fee. You may have better luck elsewhere.

Negotiating Rights

Copyright assignments are also negotiable, so even if you cannot increase your pay for a particular piece, you can limit the rights you sell. If an editor quotes a low price and can't increase it, consider selling the less valuable one-time rights to the piece rather than the more valuable first serial rights. If you sell all rights to a work (which you should do only in very rare cases), you should get significantly more than if you sell one-time rights; exclusive rights are worth more than reprint rights. Be sure you know what you're selling and how much more or less you would expect for a different arrangement. (See Chapter 7 for more information on copyrights.)

Negotiating Royalties

Book publishers, song publishers, and others offer royalties for using creative work. A royalty is a payment to the author for each copy of a work sold. It's usually a percentage of the selling price of the work, although it can be calculated in other ways, such as a percentage of profit after production costs are paid. Normally, the percentage of royalty increases as sales do. Although some experts would advise you to get an agent if you must negotiate a royalty agreement, that makes sense only if you're dealing with an especially large publisher. It's not worth giving up 15 percent of your income to pay an agent when you can expect to make only a few thousand dollars. (The agent won't be too thrilled either.)

Book publishers offer royalties on either the retail or the wholesale price of the book. Although the percentage offered on the retail price is usually lower than on the wholesale price, the retail price-based royalty is usually a better deal. You know what the retail price of the book is, but you only know that the wholesale price will be a deeply discounted version of the retail price. Some books are wholesaled—sold to bookstores and distributors—for less than 40 percent of the retail price. In fact, publishers occasionally negotiate even deeper discounts than that, in which case the writer might be lucky to earn a nickel per book.

If a publisher offers a contract, there are several routes you can take. Although the publisher (or a representative) will tell you that they're sending the standard royalty contract, there is no such animal. Everything is always negotiable. If the publisher offers a royalty on the wholesale price, ask for your royalty to be based on the retail price. (You'll probably have to take a smaller percentage of the retail price, but you don't have to say this up front.) You can ask for a larger percentage royalty. You can ask that the sliding scale be changed. On one of my first books, I agreed to a royalty based on the wholesale price of the book. For the first 10,000 copies, my royalty was to be 10 percent; for the next 10,000 copies, 12½ percent; and for anything above that amount, 15 percent. On the next book with the same publisher, I asked whether the royalty could be based on the retail price, but the editor said no. However, she offered a 15 percent royalty on the wholesale price across the board, so that I would make more money on the first books sold. This being better than nothing, I agreed.

Negotiating an Advance

You can also negotiate an advance. An advance comes out of your royalties but is paid to you before any royalties are earned. Usually half is given when you sign the contract and the other half when you deliver the manuscript. By negotiating an advance, you protect yourself from a contract cancelation. Publishers still cancel contracts even if you've negotiated an advance, but unless the cancelation was your fault (you didn't deliver the manuscript on time, or you can't write worth a darn), you generally get to keep the advance. It works like a kill fee; it's the publisher's penalty for backing out. It gives you a little something for the time and effort that went into creating the book, for which you will now have to find a new publisher. At the same time, an advance shows the publisher's commitment to the book. A publisher isn't going to pay you an advance against royalties and then not bother to promote the book. They want to recoup the money they've laid out, including what they've given you. Finally, having an advance helps you defray the cost of putting the book together, especially if it will require travel or expensive illustrations or rights fees.

Before negotiating an advance, determine an appropriate range. Many small publishing companies do not have the working capital to give an advance. That's acceptable. Just be sure other terms of the contract are advantageous. University and scholarly presses are rarely able to give advances. Medium-sized publishing companies routinely offer between $1,000 and $5,000. The big publishing houses can offer anything from a few thousand dollars to six-figure advances, so you'll probably want an agent or at least an experienced attorney to help you with that.

Market guides also provide typical advances offered by various publishers. Always ask for an advance on the higher end of the range. Also, if you've worked with a publisher before, ask for a larger advance. Be prepared to back up your demands ("Since my last book sold so well...." or "Paying for permission to use those quotes will be expensive...." or "Given my experience and unique perspective....)" This way, the publisher has a concrete reason for agreeing to your request.

Essentials of Negotiation

When dealing with markets that pay set rates, remember that the editors almost always have some discretion in the amount they pay. Always counter the first offer with a higher figure. You can always agree to the first figure. It's not as if the editor or client is going to withdraw the offer. (Repeat to yourself, "This is my job, this is how I earn a living, I deserve to earn a decent wage.") To be realistic in your negotiations, get to know the pay rates of various markets. These can be found in guides and trade magazines.

Always be polite and courteous. You don't need to buckle at the first sound of hesitation, but you don't need to destroy a potentially lucrative relationship, either. Counter the first offer, consider the counteroffer if there is one, and make a decision. Be polite but firm regardless of what you decide.

Increase Your Markets

One of the best ways to increase your income involves making a particular piece of work pay more than once. If you've written a general travel piece about Hawaii for a travel magazine, you can sell the reprint rights to the article (assuming that you kept them) to a regional publication. You can also reslant the piece for a parenting magazine and focus it on taking children to Hawaii. You can rewrite the piece for a bridal magazine, giving it a honeymoon slant. Your initial research can pay off in a variety of ways if you put your mind to it. If, however, you simply write the general travel piece and then go on to the next thing, you aren't capitalizing on your time and resources. You've already done the research. You've already written a general article that can serve as an outline. It wouldn't take that much time and effort to sell additional work.

Adding Income to Projects

You can increase the value of each project by adding on to it. Be creative—there are any number of ways you can do this. You can try to obtain several projects at once from a client. Instead of doing the newsletter for a company this month, try to negotiate a contract for the entire year's worth of newsletters now. If you're writing a company's annual report, pitch them the idea of writing a corporate history. If a client wants photos of her retirement party, try to get her to purchase an album and additional prints to send to relatives who couldn't be there. Offer discounts for piggybacked sales. At least *pretend* to offer discounts. Say something like, "I normally charge $2,000 for writing a corporate history, but because I will have to do much of the research for the annual report anyway, I could discount that by 10 percent. You'd need to agree to it now before I get too many other projects lined up." If you've been hired to arrange a direct mail campaign, offer to direct the follow-up campaign for a certain amount more. If you can't get more from one sale, at least get a referral to other people the client knows who could use your services, plus recommendations so that you can target additional clients.

Specialist or Generalist?

Although most creative people specialize in a certain niche—the photographer who shoots weddings, the writer who writes about relationship issues—potential clients need to be aware of your flexibility. It helps attract clients if you can say, "Yes, I've shot over 200 weddings," but it also helps if you can say, "Yes, I do mostly weddings, but I can also do magazine layouts. In fact, my work was recently featured in *Cosmopolitan* magazine." Being known as the best business writer in the city is great, but if you can also write a feature story your newspaper editor will become your biggest fan.

You may need to brush up on some skills to do this, but it's worth the effort. Not only does it give you access to various potentially lucrative markets, it helps prevent you from getting bored by doing the same thing over and over. It also helps you explore different areas that you might like to specialize in. I write primarily about sports—history of and how to. But I've also written on other subjects. After writing a book on popular culture and one on travel, I decided that those were not subjects I was interested in pursuing. The first doesn't attract a lot of readers except academic types, and the second is such a crowded market that it's difficult for any one book to do well; there are so many freelancers in the field that I'd probably starve to death. Does that mean I'm stuck writing about sports until I'm dead? Not at all. I've recently begun writing more personal-experience pieces, which I enjoy and for which there is a market, and I plan to spend some time writing about business, especially as it affects freelancers and creative people (this book is an example of that).

You can also think of different ways to use the same skills. For instance, if you write marketing materials like direct mail copy and brochures, how difficult would it be to also write scripts for radio and television ads, especially for the local market? If you photograph kids, how much more difficult would it be to also photograph pets?

Acquiring Complementary Skills

In addition to using your skills more generally, it doesn't hurt to acquire complementary skills. I learned this when writing my second book, which required photos. I had blithely assumed that the publisher would pay for these until I read the contract all the way through. It appeared that I had a problem. The publisher wasn't going to pay for the illustrations, but the book needed them. I had two options: Pay for them myself or renegotiate the contract. The editor, however, preferred the contract just the way it was. This left me with one option (well, I could have refused to sign the contract, but that seemed like such a defeatist attitude). I had to pay a photographer myself. So I interviewed several, each of whom wanted more to shoot the photos than I was likely to earn from the entire project. So I learned to take photos myself. Now, I would never market myself as a photographer, but I can certainly come up with a photo to illustrate anything I write. I would never have developed this skill if I hadn't been forced to, but it's been a great help over the years.

If you have drawing as well as writing talent, you could increase the value of your writing. If you have some writing skill along with your photographic talent, you could increase the value of your photographs by occasionally writing an article to accompany them. This way you can get some of your creative (nonwedding) photos to pay for themselves. If you shoot videos, how difficult would it be to write the scripts for them? Local car dealers would love you.

You can acquire additional skills in many different ways. Some people are self-taught. Others find a mentor who can show them the ropes. Others take classes through continuing education programs or community colleges. Computer software, videos, or online education can help you acquire additional skills.

By planning how to increase the value of each sale and make each project worth more, you will be able to increase your income without having to spend a lot of extra time trying to market your services to potential customers. By brushing up on old skills and developing new ones, you can offer your clients the benefits of versatility while remaining focused on a specific area of professional competence.

13

Marketing Your Services

As a small-business owner, you have to market your own services. But considering the creative nature of your business, it's likely that the most productive marketing methods will be neither obvious nor straightforward. Buying space in the local paper to advertise your ability to write business plans isn't necessarily going to get you any clients. But what will? And how do you market your services if you're inexperienced? How can you call yourself a wedding photographer if you've never shot a wedding?

Some creative people must market their services in very specific ways. In general, writers approach editors by sending a query letter detailing an article or book idea. Then, if requested, they follow up with a proposal or manuscript. But even if there are specific ways of marketing, how can you improve your approach? If you're a writer who wants to generate more responses from editors, how will you do so? By sending more letters to more editors?

Determine What You Have to Offer

Relax. First things first. In order to sell your services you need to show that you have something valuable to offer. This is true no matter what your business. If you're a creative person, you need samples of your work. An artist needs a portfolio; a writer needs published clips; a musician needs a demo tape. Discover what you need to showcase your talent and then be sure you get it. How can you know? Read trade magazines and books. Check out small-business articles. If you dig, you'll discover important pieces of information and indispensable insights.

Networking

To understand the best ways to market your business, network with others in similar positions. If you're a writer, make contact with other writers, regardless of your field. One extremely busy technical writer constantly fends off requests for different types of business writing from the companies she works for. The few writers she knows personally get referrals from her all the time. The technical writer is happy that she can help her companies out; the companies are happy because they can hire talented writers; and the writers are happy because they can get assignments without having to pound the pavement. The more people you know in your field, the better you'll be able to sell your services. Networking is an essential but frequently overlooked part of small-business success.

You can also network with people in your target client group. Planning to go after the lucrative business writing market? Join your local chamber of commerce. Get to know what businesspeople need. Meet the business leaders in your community.

Don't just network with the obvious people. Expand your horizons. If you plan to write scripts for local television ads, you can let business owners know you're available. Better yet, get to know the people at the cable office who shoot the ads. They'll refer clients to you, and best of all, you don't have to pay them to do it. They'll just be glad they have someone to recommend when clients ask.

Network with people associated with your service. If you photograph weddings, get to know the caterers in town. If you specialize in corporate events, join the chamber of commerce; for pets, get to know groomers and vets. Leave brochures, discount coupons, or other marketing materials with these professionals to drum up referrals.

Join professional and trade associations to keep in contact with people in similar fields and to learn from their experiences. Make a note of such membership on your marketing materials. Nothing makes you appear quite so professional as professional affiliations.

Gaining Experience

If you're just starting out and have little relevant experience, don't invent it. Business owners build relationships based on trust. No matter how talented you are, if you betray that trust, your clients will drop you. They might even sue you for misrepresentation, so it's definitely not worth stretching the truth.

Consider what experience you do have. If you haven't quit your day job, make a point of getting relevant experience before you head out on your own. If you're a salesperson for an insurance company and you want to be a photographer, offer to photograph the company picnic, and contribute the photos to the local newspaper for use in the "About Town" or "Business" section. If you can, have yourself designated "official company photographer." Such experience goes directly on your résumé as a photography job. Although it may not seem possible at first glance, your current employer may be your best bet for gaining relevant experience before you start working full-time at your business.

Start small. Offer to shoot your friends' weddings for the cost of film and developing. Write a business plan for your next-door neighbor in exchange for a lube and oil change on your car. Learn how to barter your services so that you can develop references and a track record.

Some experts discourage people from working for friends and family. They have a valid point. You end up doing work for free when you should be getting paid. You end up frustrated, and your father-in-law ends up unhappy with your work. However, in the beginning, when you have no business and precious little experience, you must start somewhere. Still, you should always think of yourself in professional terms. Professionals do not do anything for free, unless it's a charitable contribution. Doing something for free just because you want the experience devalues your work.

It's the reason why ten years from now your neighbor will still expect you to write his business plans for free. Instead, offer your writing services in exchange for something else, though not necessarily money. You can create a brochure for your hairdresser in exchange for a cut and color. You can create a logo for a friend's new business in exchange for a bushel of apples. The idea is that you're creating something of value, but that you can't yet sell it to people who don't know you.

If you're a writer, you can start with small markets that are low-paying or pay only in complimentary copies, but as soon as you have some published clips you need to move on to professional paying markets.

Take Advantage of Experience

Once you have relevant experience, create a brief bio sheet about yourself and your company. The bio sheet will be something you can present to potential clients who want to know more about you. When you have an important accomplishment, add it to your bio sheet. If appropriate, create additional marketing materials, such as a brochure outlining your services. Make sure you have business cards to hand out to everyone you meet. Keep your marketing materials up to date. If your fees change, your rate sheet should reflect that. If you get a business phone line, have new business cards printed instead of writing in the new number.

Advertising Your Services

You can drum up business in plenty of ways. For certain businesses, such as photography, the first step is to take out an ad in the phone book. Even your home listing should show that you're a photographer. Many potential clients start with the phone book when they're looking for services.

In addition, photographers often use the local newspaper to advertise. But instead of running an ad every week, evaluate what your main services are—portrait photography, wedding photography, Zen photography. Zero in on the times when people need those types of photography. June is the month for weddings, but most people plan many months beforehand. Your ad should be in the paper in December or January (earlier if you're in a very large city where weddings must be arranged well in advance). Simply let people know that you're now booking for June weddings. Keep other times in mind. What about corporate holiday parties? Why not send out a mailing or put an ad in the paper in October or November indicating that you are accepting bookings for the holiday? You might also note that you specialize in corporate events.

If you plan to use newspaper and other print advertising, you need to make sure you're getting value for your money. Print advertising rarely works for writers, but it can be important for photographers and other creative types, depending on their clients. Keep your ads simple and to the point. State what you do, mention any special reason a client should call you now (Christmas is coming up, you're offering 10 percent off family portraits), and indicate a way to contact you. If you want to run a large ad to catch attention, don't stuff it full of words. Create some good graphics and keep it simple.

Be cautious about advertising on radio, television, and online. Although radio and television advertising might be helpful for some creative small businesses, for the most part you will not find them worth the money. Online, you can set up a web page for a fairly reasonable cost. But a good-quality web site has its own domain name, which costs a certain amount of money, and it usually requires a server rental fee of at least $50 a month. That may not seem like a lot given the potential number of customers you reach, but you need to be sure you're generating much more than $50 a month in revenue or else the site isn't worth the time it takes to establish, maintain, and operate it.

Marketing Consultants

If your advertising doesn't seem to be working, or if you're following standard marketing procedures for your profession and you're still not selling anything, you'll need to develop a marketing plan for your business. This plan will change over time as you discover what works and what doesn't.

If you're in a traditional business, such as photographing weddings, outside consultants can help you with marketing. But be sure that the people you consult *do* understand the business. One consultant advised a new writer to approach people at writers' conferences and ask for the names of their agents. The writer felt hurt and frustrated when people ignored her question or gave her the brush-off. A consultant with experience in the publishing industry would have known that two things were wrong with this advice: First, most writers attending conferences don't have agents, and second, of those who do, most would be very uncomfortable giving their agent's name (with its implied consent to act as a reference) to an aspiring writer whose work they did not know. Instead, the writer should have been advised to ask other writers how they broke into print and how they got their first agent. A consultant who knew the publishing industry would know that a writer invited to talk about herself in such a way can rarely shut up. The difference between the two pieces of advice ("ask the name of their agent," and "ask how they got their agent") seems minor but is extremely important. And that's what you pay advisors and consultants for—to know the nuances, the ins and outs, the customs and culture of the profession you need advice about and the clients you wish to reach.

Develop a Marketing Plan

Like a business plan that helps you decide how you want to run your business, a marketing plan helps you stay on track with your advertising. It's important to create advertising and marketing materials with a certain theme or unity of design so that people will begin to associate you with a specific approach or style. Maybe you want to take an understated approach. Your marketing materials should be on elegant, good-quality materials with unobtrusive logos and simple text. Or maybe you prefer something a little more eye-catching, in which case you might try bold colors and bright designs plus snappy text. Develop a sense of what you want people to think when they see advertisements or marketing materials for your business.

Your marketing materials should be geared toward helping your customers solve problems instead of just offering them a product or service. Consider the client's wants or needs as a problem, then provide a solution (your product or service). Look at it this way: Your target client needs to purchase holiday gifts. How is this a problem? Your target client doesn't know what to give his parents for Christmas. How do you solve that problem? Offer a family holiday portrait package with a choice of three different backgrounds. You can probably already imagine how you might write this ad or how it might look.

Your marketing plan should include specific goals plus ideas about how to achieve them. Ultimately, your goal is to generate increased revenue, but to start with, perhaps you want to increase the number of people who ask for your marketing materials. Or perhaps you want to improve the number of editors who respond favorably to your query letters. By setting specific goals, you can then create specific plans. To improve the number of editors who respond favorably to your query letters, you can consider several solutions. If every month you send out 100 query letters and five meet with favorable responses, you can start sending out 200 query letters every month, assuming that the same percentage will receive positive responses. This way you'll double the number of favorable responses from five to ten. However, this approach has its limits: the number of markets you can query without bombarding the same editor every month; and the number of good ideas you can generate in a given month (the number of bad ideas a person can come up with is pretty much endless, but good ideas are an altogether different matter). And what happens when you're ready to increase the response rate again? Are you going to send out 300 letters a month? You could try. But that gets expensive as well as time-consuming. The better choice would be to target your audience or clients more appropriately. If you were able to meet your potential editors' needs better, you would improve the number of positive responses you received every month. To achieve your goal, then, you could do a better job of researching your markets and the editors who acquire material for them.

Business owners often assume that more is better—more advertising equals more clients—but this isn't necessarily the case. Targeting your marketing efforts more specifically can often produce better results. If you provide consulting services to human resource directors, you could put an ad in the local business newspaper once a week, or you could narrow your target by putting an ad in an appropriate trade magazine or a professional organization's news-letter. Targeting your audience can be wiser than blanketing the world indiscriminately with your marketing materials.

You may also want to try a combination of approaches, such as increasing the amount of exposure (sending out more query letters) and targeting your market better (sending letters only to editors who have demonstrated interest in work like yours).

In the same vein, some businesses do quite well with direct marketing campaigns, in which you send a letter or catalog of promotional material to individuals who have expressed an interest in similar businesses before. Targeted mailing lists can be purchased from suppliers for one-time or multiple-time use. You specify the criteria your potential clients should meet (live within certain zip codes, have certain hobbies or interests), and a mailing list service will try to match you with an appropriate list. This can be an expensive approach, but it is often more effective than other print advertising for many types of businesses.

Low-Cost Marketing

You can also improve your marketing by making add-on sales, as discussed in the previous chapter (selling an album to go with the photos), increasing your areas of expertise (so that you can provide photos with your article, for an extra fee), using the same basic research materials and ideas to generate a number of sales without having to put the same amount of effort into each sale, and negotiating fees more favorably. In these ways you can increase revenue without having to spend much more time marketing. Other low-cost methods of marketing your services follow, but use your imagination and think creatively to come up with your own unique ideas.

Conduct Classes

You can market your services without spending a lot of money by conducting seminars or teaching classes. Such classes can be offered either at the college level or in a continuing education program. Classes on creative writing and other artistic pursuits are often well-received, and frequently you don't need an advanced degree to teach them. While you can't spend the entire class period singing your own praises, you can let people know what you do for a living and give them access to your marketing materials and business cards. You can also arrange your own seminars by renting a hotel conference room, distributing fliers, and charging seminar students a fee for listening to advice about your area of expertise. Teaching a class or seminar makes a good addition to your bio sheet.

Help-Wanted Ads

Some small-business owners have good success responding to help-wanted newspaper ads. They send their marketing materials to companies advertising for help in their field of business, and they let the companies know that they can do the work freelance. Often a company will choose to go this route instead of gambling on hiring a full-time person who might not work out. A company can always "fire" a business that doesn't work out, but it's harder to do the same with an employee. If the business doesn't have to be "trained" the same way an employee would, so much the better. When the labor market is tight, creative snall businesses provide an excellent alternative to letting a position remain unfilled for months on end.

Check the Sunday classifieds and relevant trade magazines for ads that seek help you can provide on a freelance basis. You can do the same for online job listings. Visit the web sites of companies for which you might be able to freelance; check out their employment listings and send them your relevant marketing information. You can also visit special web sites that list jobs by position or region. (Try *www.careerpath.com* and *www.careermosaic.com,* among others.)

Press Releases

Each time you accomplish something of interest, such as publishing a book, send a press release to the local media with information on what your business does and how people can contact you. I was once featured on the front page of a local newspaper (slow news day) simply because I alerted the features editor that I had a book coming out. You can also tie press releases to seasonal events to give them a sense of timeliness. For example, you can remind people that Christmas is coming up and offer them some hints for purchasing gifts, then mention your one-of-a-kind ceramics studio where people can purchase unique gifts for under $50. Or issue a press release at graduation time offering ideas for taking snapshots of May graduates, then mention your own portrait special. This is one of the cheapest, easiest ways to generate favorable local attention.

You can send press releases to news publications throughout the country, but it will be harder to get their attention. (Local citizens tend to be of interest to local newspapers.) If you're going to send materials beyond your little corner of the universe, make sure you target the specific editor who will be interested in your subject. Find out that person's name instead of just sending your materials to "Features Editor."

Press releases can also go to your alumni magazine or newsletter, a hometown newspaper, and trade magazines. Professional and trade associations that you belong to can also be notified; they often list members' achievements in their promotional materials. You can also notify local radio stations. Target those that have interviews or talk-show segments. A number of print media accept press releases via fax and e-mail, saving you the cost of mailing the pieces (unless you're faxing materials long-distance).

Write Articles

You can also generate inexpensive publicity by writing articles in your field of business. You don't have to be a professional writer to do this, particularly if you're writing for trade publications; they're interested in knowledge and information more than writing style. But be sure to have the piece looked over by a professional or at least a good amateur before you submit it. If your article is published, you can add a tag stating who you are and what you do. (You might even get paid!)

Tell the World

On your answering machine message, mention your most recent book or article. Or list your special on portrait packages, or give information on how to enroll in your new class on ceramics glazing. Make every contact with the outside world an occasion to market your services. Send thank-you notes to potential customers who bother to listen to you; create a bimonthly newsletter to send to target clients; and use whatever creativity and inventiveness you can.

Remember that you're "selling" all the time. This is one of the hardest tasks for creative people, who tend not to be sales- or business-oriented. Whenever you meet new people, be cordial and polite, and remember names (or ask for business cards). If the person is a potential customer, mentally file the meeting away and later send a note or call to remind the person where you met and what you might be able to do for him or her. If the person doesn't appear to be a potential client, you should still talk about what you do for a living. That person might be married to a potential client or be close friends with one. Understand the impression you make on people at all times.

Once I needed a photographer to shoot several hundred photographs for a couple of books. I attended a wedding and watched a photographer. Being impressed with his work, I approached him after the reception to see if he would want the job. He was abrupt and rude, treating me very dismissively, before I even had a chance to explain what I wanted. If he had been aware of the impression he was making—or aware that everyone you meet (especially when you're on the job) is a potential client—he probably would have been polite to me, and he'd have made a very nice sale. Instead, I found someone else who was delighted to take my money.

Agents and Representatives

Creative people sometimes use agents for marketing. Agents, artistic representatives, or managers can be very useful in acquiring big clients and negotiating deals. How do you know if you need an agent? The work you do must fall within the scope of an agent's abilities. A musician might hire a manager to book shows and arrange travel, but if the musician is planning just to work the local circuit, he or she probably doesn't need to share income with a manager. A photographer might use a stock agency to sell photos, but only if his or her work meets the general needs of businesses that use stock photos. Artistic or unconventional work might not fit this model. (In this case the photographer might need to find a gallery to show the work.) Fine artists occasionally use agents, although mostly they try to arrange gallery showings, which is a different approach altogether. Only writers who work in book-length formats use agents. Article writers, short-story writers, and poets do not use agents, although they may have an agent if they also write books.

Trying to break into the national scene, whether as a musician, a photographer, or a writer, may require an agent. The bigger publishing houses generally require that writers be represented by agents, although a writer could happily make a living selling to small and medium-sized houses without ever knowing the name of an agent.

If you've determined that an agent is the marketing tool you need, you must find out how to acquire one. Although you will be hiring the agent to work for you, agents are usually very selective in accepting clients. They must feel that they have a reasonable chance of selling the client's work. How you contact agents for potential representation varies, depending on the business and the agent. You can make contact by letter or phone, although most agents prefer a letter if they do not know the potential client. Literary agents and their contact information can be found in various trade directories, such as *Guide to Literary Agents* (Writer's Digest Books) and *Literary Market Place* (R.R. Bowker).

A better way to find an agent is through networking. You can attend trade and professional conferences or association meetings. Often agents will be in attendance either as guests or in order to find clients. If possible, you should get a referral to an agent from one of the agent's current clients. This at least ensures that your work will be considered.

Sometimes an agent will find you. If your work has been published and an agent willing to take on new clients is impressed by what you've done, he or she might track you down and offer to represent you. This happened to me once when a former editor (who had never bought a single idea from me) became an agent and asked to represent me. Flattered, I agreed, but nothing came of her efforts (mostly because I'm too impatient to let others do my marketing for me).

An agent will want to see representative samples of your work, so prepare these before you make any initial contact. Find out as much as you can about potential agents before you start asking whether they'll take you on. Anyone can call himself or herself an agent. There aren't any special licenses or exams to pass, although the better ones will be affiliated with special trade or professional groups, such as the Association of Authors' Representatives. Read trade publications such as *Publishers Weekly* to find out which agents and agencies are selling what types of work. Network with creative people who are willing to share their experiences. Your agent will in some respects be managing your career, so you don't necessarily want to accept the first one you meet. And just because an agent is interested in your work doesn't mean he or she will be able to sell it. If you have trouble selling your work, having an agent doesn't necessarily solve your problems.

If you enjoy having control over your work, you may not need an agent. If you do many different kinds of projects that don't fit in one niche, an agent would have trouble keeping up with you (or might not be familiar with the different markets). If you understand contracts and can negotiate on your own, you may not need to share your income with an agent. If you're happy doing projects for small clients, you might have trouble attracting an agent (his or her share of money wouldn't be that great). If any of these circumstances apply to you, it might be wise for you to continue marketing your own work.

If you decide to hire an agent, get to know the industry standards. Is a 15 percent commission reasonable, or do most agents charge 10 percent? Should the agent bill you for office expenses such as phone calls made on your behalf? Should the

---

Figure 44

Low-Cost Marketing Methods

Add-on sales by offering an incentive to purchase more service or product.
Increase your areas of expertise.
Acquire complementary skills.
Conduct classes and seminars.
Respond to help-wanted ads in your field with marketing materials.
Send press releases to local media, trade/professional, and alumni organizations.
Write articles for trade or professional magazines, journals, or newsletters.
Record a message on your answering machine telling about your latest service.
Acquire an agent or representative.
Remember, you're selling all the time!

---

agent charge a fee to look at your work before taking you on as a client? You should also consider your own preferences. Do you want an agent who operates on written contracts or on a handshake? Would you rather sign a contract for a one-year or a per-project agreement?

Once you have an agent, don't relax and assume that your agent will handle everything for you. Insist on remaining informed about the status of projects or clients. Read and understand contracts before you allow your agent to accept them on your behalf. Listen to your agent's advice, but make your own decisions.

Marketing Essentials

By understanding and taking advantage of marketing opportunities, you can build your business without investing heavily in advertising your services. Get to know how others in similar businesses or professions market themselves. Always keep your eyes and ears open. Be receptive to new ideas. Above all, don't just let marketing take care of itself (it won't). Marketing doesn't have to be expensive or time-consuming if you identify your goals and plan how to achieve them.

14

Hiring Professionals and Entering Partnerships

O N OCCASION, a creative person will need to hire other professionals to do something he or she cannot do or would prefer not to do, such as eliminating the ant colony under the desk. Although most creative people know what to do about the ant colony (cherish it as an example of nature's divine variety, vacuum it up, or look under "E" in the phone book for exterminators), we often feel at a loss when it's time to hire accountants and lawyers. We wonder what unholy fixation with numbers or rules would cause one to become an accountant or a lawyer, what strange and warped minds would find delight in balance sheets and the finer details of *habeas corpus.*

But hiring these professionals doesn't have to be an intimidating or frustrating experience. In fact, if you set aside your preconceived notions you'll realize that accountants and lawyers are regular people, just like us only more rigid. You can then appreciate them as an example of nature's divine variety and realize that they too serve an important purpose, which is to file your income tax returns and explain contracts to you.

Creative small-business owners also need to find other creative people. It can be much more difficult to hire a good graphic artist for a project than it is to retain a lawyer to look over a work-for-hire agreement. How to find other professionals, evaluate their work, reach an agreement with them, and ensure a successful working relationship is the focus of this chapter.

Identifying Concerns

Before thumbing through the phone book for the name of the accountant nearest you, stop and consider your expectations. What exactly do you want the person you're about to hire to provide for you? If you need guidance about marketing issues, hiring an accountant isn't going to solve your problems. Make a list of problem areas and then determine the urgency of each issue. Perhaps you're having trouble getting a refund from the newspaper for a misprinted ad it ran. Perhaps you're having trouble coming up with a new ad campaign. And perhaps you're having trouble with collections. Which of these problems needs your attention first? Well, the newspaper refund isn't worth too much time and effort on your part. The ad campaign might be important for acquiring new clients. But if you're having trouble with collections, you probably don't have a good cash flow, which means you can't pay your suppliers, which means you can't do your job, which means your business shuts down. This, then, is a problem that requires immediate attention.

Once you've established priorities, consider who can help you. A problem with accounts receivable could certainly be addressed by an accountant, but do you simply need to hire a collections agency? Or do you need to change your billing system? Do you need to start running credit checks on clients before doing work for them? Hiring a collections agency is one thing, whereas changing your billing system requires a different type of professional advice. Running credit checks requires a third approach entirely. Maybe you need to do all three of these things to improve your collections.

Keep brainstorming, because you may discover related areas that will lead you to problem-solving solutions you might not otherwise consider. If you have problems with collections, do you have related problems, such as difficulty keeping your general ledger updated? If you have this problem, do you also have trouble sending out invoices on a routine basis? If this is the case, you're going to need more than an accountant to get you back on track. Maybe you need to set up a better system for taking care of administrative and recordkeeping tasks. Maybe you just have too much work and need to hire an assistant.

Solving Problems on Your Own

As you consider your concerns, also think about how to address them. We often believe that having experts tell us what to do will solve our problems. But maybe you simply need to educate yourself. Maybe you need to take some classes in small-business ownership or in the use of a new computer program. Maybe you need to network with long-time business owners who can offer suggestions for the problems you're having.

Can you read a book or watch a video on the subject? Can you find a computer program that would do the job you need to have done? Once you've educated yourself and identified your problems and needs, you will be much more likely to hire the right professional and achieve satisfying results.

Hiring Help

For secretarial and bookkeeping services, small-business owners often turn to temporary agencies to provide them with employees who can work by the project or for specific periods of time. Although there are many advantages to this approach—the temp is employed by the agency, which handles most of the paperwork and IRS concerns—there are also drawbacks. Many temp agencies will not provide employees to home-based businesses. They have their reasons, among them concerns of liability and employee safety, but for the most part temp agencies simply haven't caught up with the times. Of those that will send employees to your home, you'll find that the expense is much greater than if you hired someone yourself (although the convenience may be worth the additional expense).

You can also find office help through employment brokers and agencies, which specialize in certain fields. You may have to pay a fee, and your employee may have to pay a percentage of his or her salary to the agency or broker. Help can also be found through the traditional methods of placing ads in papers and recruiting on college campuses.

If you need this type of assistance, read up on employment regulations. Learn how to interview and hire good workers. There's plenty of information available detailing how to hire and keep employees. But if you plan to have part- or full-time employees, you must be prepared to act as a manager as well as a business owner. Sometimes creative people despise this aspect of business ownership and dislike ordering people about. Although some tough-guy business manuals will tell you to get over it, such an approach will usually leave you feeling vaguely unhappy and disgusted with yourself. Instead, reconsider hiring employees. Use temporary contract help when you're swamped. Cut back on the amount of business you do by increasing your rates. Be absolutely positive that you can and will want to devote the necessary time and energy to hiring, training, and managing employees.

Contract Help

You can avoid many of the hassles of hiring assistants if you use an independent contractor or secretarial service. If you dislike typing your own manuscripts, you don't have to hire a secretary to type them for you. You can send your manuscripts to a typing service, which can type and format the text in whatever way you prefer and include copies on floppy disk if needed. Instead of hiring a receptionist to answer the phone, use an answering service.

Services tend to cost more than employees do, but you can use them at your whim. If money's tight this month, you can type your own documents, but when your cash flow is a little better next month, you can use the secretarial service.

Take advantage of service-oriented businesses such as copy centers. Instead of doing all the copying, collating, and faxing yourself, drop some of your work off at the local Kinko's or Copy Co. and pick up the finished work later in the day. Many copy centers offer computer-related services so that you don't have to scan photos into your computer all day long. They charge extra for these services, but not having to purchase expensive equipment, hire an assistant, or devote your time to mundane tasks that can be farmed out to another company (in other words, outsourcing) can save you money.

Professional Assistance

Professionals such as accountants and attorneys can be hired as independent contractors for specific projects on an as-needed basis. Don't worry about paying a retainer. Most professionals will be happy to learn about your business and will let you call for an appointment any time you need to address business-related concerns or problems. Let these professionals know if you're planning to use their services during traditionally hectic times. For instance, you should let your accountant know before April 15 that you're planning to have her do your taxes.

Although it's a good idea to use the same professional for similar needs, it's no disaster if you have to use a different accountant or attorney from time to time. You just shouldn't make a habit of it. The more a professional works with you on a consistent basis, the more he or she can understand your needs and help you run your business, which is why you hired a professional in the first place.

Although businesspeople most commonly need assistance from lawyers and accountants, you may need other professional advice, such as determining a computer setup that's right for your needs. While you could ask the guy at the discount electronics store what he thinks, you can also hire a consultant by the hour to assist you with these matters. Many cities have computer problem-solving services through which a trained technician comes to your home to instruct you or troubleshoot. Such a service saves you the headache of carting your computer back to the computer store. Consultants can work with you to determine the type of computer system that meets your needs. If you don't have time to enroll in a class or training session to learn a software program, computer consultants can show you how to run it immediately.

Getting Recommendations

Before you hire a professional, make certain he or she comes well recommended. Ask around. You never know who has used a lawyer or knows one. As you ask people for referrals and recommendations, use your judgment. A person who complains that he was charged for every paper clip the attorney used may simply have been unaware of how attorneys bill their clients. By the same token, don't dismiss a complaint just because someone complains about everything. There may be some substance behind it. Investigate a professional's record by checking with the associations and organizations that govern the practice. (Is the accountant a CPA? Do you need a CPA?) You can also check with the local chamber of commerce and the Better Business Bureau.

Finding the right professional takes time, so think about it *before* you urgently need that tax statement filed. Take stock of your business. What areas need the attention of a professional? Do you need a lawyer to put together a standard contract but just haven't gotten around to it? If you find the time to search for a lawyer now, you'll be more confident should you need one for more pressing matters later.

Of course, just because an attorney can write up a standard contract for you doesn't mean he or she should represent you in a professional liability case. But he or she could recommend someone. Anyone you hire should have experience in the specific task at hand. Creative people often hire lawyers who are experienced in entertainment law, since that experience is more specialized and more valuable to them than just general contract law. Make sure your potential accountant understands your type of business, the way you earn money, and the expenses you have. Someone who is familiar with home-based small businesses will likely know of advantageous ways for you to use tax laws.

Understanding Fees

When hiring a professional, understand all the fees and expenses involved. Accountants and attorneys generally charge by the hour, particularly for the type of work small-business owners typically ask them to do. Many charge for long-distance calls, copying costs, and other expenses they incur while working on your behalf. Although some will answer brief questions over the phone, others will charge you for a phone consultation. Neither way is right or wrong—just be aware of how you're charged. Instead of calling your accountant eight times with six different questions each time, put all your concerns together and meet once with the accountant to discuss them. This saves everyone time and money.

Creative Professionals

You may need to hire a photographer or graphic artist for a project. How do you go about this? Some businesses provide creative professionals on a per-project basis. A design firm would be happy to provide graphics for your marketing materials. But this can be a very expensive route, and since you won't be a very big account, you may not get the personal service and attention you need. You can hire a photographer from the portrait studio across the street, but he or she may not have the experience you need to shoot the action photos that will accompany your article for *Sports Illustrated.* Many creative individuals work as independent contractors; they are sometimes listed in the phone book. You can interview these candidates, ask to see samples of their work, and get recommendations from satisfied customers.

None of these approaches may seem very helpful, so before you start leafing through the phone book, think about whom you know. Consider your family. Maybe your brother-in-law can provide high-quality photos or the name of a buddy who can provide them. Rule out rank amateurs, but remember that a serious amateur can often provide the work you need at a fraction of the cost of hiring a professional. Also think about friends, former co-workers, your next-door neighbor. They might be able to help you or provide you with leads. A friend who works in the art department of an advertising company might do some freelance work for you (instead of your hiring the advertising company). The friend may have to turn you down so as not to interfere with a noncompete agreement, but it doesn't hurt to ask; she might know freelancers who work with her company on a regular basis, or she might arrange a discount at the advertising agency.

Hiring friends or family members has drawbacks. It's hard to criticize the work of friends or enforce deadlines. If you allow the person plenty of time to do the work (especially if they're a serious amateur with a day job) and clearly specify what you need and when you need it, you can keep the relationship intact while getting the creative services you need. If you do decide to use a friend, a family member, or a serious amateur, work with the person on one small project first before committing to a larger one.

Bartering for Services

If you need to find a professional service but do not have a lot of money to spend, you can consider bartering for services. Many small-business owners use this approach, especially at the beginning. Bartering can help you build your business by giving you experience, recommendations, and referrals. It can also help you get the services you need for little or no money. Any services you receive as the result of a barter are taxed as if they were income, and any expenses you incur while holding up your end of a barter can be written off your taxes. Keep good records and know the market value of the different services you barter.

Some communities have bartering co-ops, networks, or brokers that allow members to pool their resources instead of directly exchanging services. You might photograph a musician's wedding, and the musician might play at the graduation party for an accountant's daughter, and the accountant might set up a bookkeeping system for you. Your skills are assigned a monetary value, so when you give two hours of your time to the barter co-op you get a credit that you can exchange for an equivalent service. (You might spend part of your credit on getting your lawn mowed and part on getting your roof fixed.)

Any barter co-op or broker you use should be a thriving business. If the only two people who belong are a landscape contractor and a pet groomer and you live in an apartment and own a bird, the setup isn't advantageous for you. The network itself (unless it's a community-run co-op) will charge you for the service, so be sure you'll get a good value for your time and money.

If joining a barter network doesn't appeal to you, you can arrange barter transactions by yourself. Don't barter for something just because you can. Barter for products and services that you want or need and would otherwise pay cash for. Although it's possible to barter for products, it's almost always easier to barter for services, since the exchange doesn't require the investment of cash on one person's part. A writer could write marketing materials for a beauty salon in exchange for a couple of free haircuts, but if she wanted a perm or hair color (which requires the salon owner to purchase products) she would probably meet with less success. Before bartering, make sure the service or product is worthwhile. A disastrous haircut isn't worth writing a brochure for. A handmade sweater that falls apart the first time you wear it isn't worth the retirement party you spent five hours photographing.

You can approach almost any business owner to offer an exchange, but if the idea seems intimidating to you, start with people you know. Or begin with smaller businesses, where the owner or manager won't turn you down flat just because they don't have the authority to make a purchasing decision. Think of the businesses you frequent and consider bartering with those owners. My martial arts instructor often barters free lessons for services. I've written letters, newsletters, even a business plan for him in exchange for lessons, which I would otherwise pay for. Such writing work doesn't take me much time, and having another person in class doesn't demand an extra effort on his time or resources, so the exchange works well for both of us.

If a business owner has a service or product that you want, but doesn't need your services, offer a combination of barter and cash. You may need an extensive consultation with an attorney that will cost about $800. The attorney you approach with a barter offer doesn't really need your services. You talk him into letting you design his letterhead and business cards, for which you normally charge $400. You can add $400 in cash to the barter and make the exchange.

You don't want to wind up doing all your business in trade (you do need cash for some things), but bartering is an excellent way to establish your business. Make sure that you (or the network you use) put the terms of the exchange down in writing. Everyone should know the expectations of each party. That way, if something is wrong with the service or product you've bartered for, you'll have a recourse.

Partnering

Bartering for services and hiring professionals sometimes makes creative business owners realize that they could increase their potential by taking on a partner. A writer who hires a photographer or barters for photographic services may realize that the partnership enhances his or her business. The photographer and writer might decide to enter a partnership. Instead of one person hiring the other all the time, both commit to marketing their services together and sharing the resulting revenues.

Partnerships come in different varieties. Some are short-term and project-oriented, others long-term and business-oriented. Partnerships, either casual or formal, can include more than two people, but the more people are involved, the greater the likelihood that a misunderstanding or lack of control will result.

One-time, one-project partnerships are the simplest type. They don't require much risk because you're not committing your entire career or business to the partnership. But because they're so simple, they tend to be casual and informal, which can lead to misunderstandings. Be certain that each partner's responsibilities are carefully laid out and that all partners communicate regularly with each other.

More complex partnerships are business-oriented, not project-oriented. You and another person with similar or complementary skills decide to go into business together, or you decide to take someone into business with you. Clearly define your partnership up front. If you want to remain in control but need an assistant, you really want a good employee, not a partner (and there's nothing wrong with that). Recognize what you want and what you're willing to give up for it. If you and another person intend to have equal say in the running of the partnership or if you both plan to be part owners of the business, you need to enter into a legal agreement that specifies what each of you provides and receives. Be clear about this from the beginning to avoid problems later on.

Collaborations among creative people have a fine, lengthy tradition. But creative work by committee isn't necessarily all that successful. Still, certain teams do quite well. Some writer-photographer teams have created masterpieces, as have writer-illustrator teams. But those partnerships consist of two people with different talents combining them to make something neither could have made alone. Partnerships work best if this is the case. One of you is the creative person, the other the salesperson. One of you is the idea person; the other has the funds to finance the ideas. Complementary partnerships can be very successful.

If you're considering a partnership, spend some time with the potential partner first. If the potential partner is a friend, be especially careful: Is it worth losing the friend if the partnership doesn't work out? If you're thinking about partnering with a friend (which isn't necessarily a bad idea, since you know all about their habits and whatever baggage they travel with), be sure to spend time talking about business before getting down to it.

Some time ago I intended to start a partnership with a friend who is also a writer. She had the contacts, and I had the business and administrative skills. Both of us liked the other person's writing style. Certain that we had a complementary partnership in the works, we arranged to meet with the local representative of the Small Business Administration to clear up a few questions. The representative briefly mentioned liability as a potential concern in a general partnership, along with some other points. Later my business partner-to-be expressed some doubts. She said, "I could just see you driving like a maniac to get to the printer's and hitting a kid and then our company getting sued and my husband's salary used to pay the settlement." Although I was startled by her vehemence (I'm a pretty good driver), I tried to address her concerns. After all, liability is not something to dismiss out of hand. But she kept stressing the risk she and her husband would be taking, as if my husband and I lived in a shed and had six dollars to call our own. In fact, my husband and his father owned a business that generated nearly a million dollars in revenue that year (not that we got to keep much of it). If my partner and I were going to get sued, that business was what the lawyers would go after, not the salary of her office administrator husband, splendid as it might have been. It simply never occurred to her that I would be taking a risk, too. All she could see was her risk. Later she demanded that I agree not to use her list of contacts to further my own selfish ends (I guess she thought I'd ask all her friends to buy my books). Her comments showed that she clearly didn't trust me. In the end, we never started the partnership. The friendship did not survive either. As hurt as I was by her selfishness and distrust, I was fortunate to discover her reservations before committing to a disastrous business arrangement with her.

As this experience shows, it's essential to spend time talking about the business, weighing concerns, and researching and investigating the start-up before actually committing to a partnership. Imagine if I'd learned about my friend's fears and distrust *after* I'd invested significant time and money in the partnership!

Partnership arrangements should be carefully thought out beforehand. Who will be in control? What if the partners disagree on the direction the company is taking? What if the personal circumstances of one partner change and the partner is no longer able or willing to continue operating in the same capacity? Circumstances that can dramatically change the nature of a partnership include one of the partners divorcing, having a child, or becoming ill or injured. What would you do if something like this occurred? Have you considered how to dissolve, sell, or terminate the partnership?

Discuss the purpose of your business and the role of each partner. Work out arrangements in detail. Before entering into a legal partnership, try working on one project together to see how it goes. When you participate in this trial run, don't remain on your best behavior. Try to see how you and your partner handle stress, division of responsibility, and deadlines. Although a lawyer can alert you to potential pitfalls in your plans, you should be the ones making the plans. The attorney should merely formalize the partnership agreement.

At the same time, examine your temperament and honestly assess your personality. Would you make a good partner? Most of the partnership problems I've encountered are my own fault. I like to be in control. Not only do I want to be in control creatively, I also want to be in control of the business end. That being the case, what do I really need a partner for? Certainly, being in business for myself is scary, and if I bring in others I can share the risks and burdens. But being scared is not a good enough reason to enter a partnership. If you're planning to enter a partnership, make sure you have the personality to make it work and that you're partnering with someone else for the right reasons.

Before partnering with or hiring other professionals, be sure you understand your needs and expectations. Do your homework ahead of time to avoid costly mistakes. With careful planning, you'll be able to enlist the right people at the right time to make your business a success.

Taking Your Business Seriously

Y<small>OU'RE ALL</small> set to launch your business. You've got clients, an office, and the final paycheck from your day job. First thing Monday morning, you're sitting at your desk, pencils sharpened. Your best friend calls. "So how's retirement?" she asks, then proceeds to tell you about what a lousy day she's having and how lucky you are not to be as busy as she is.

You can respond by (a) hanging up the phone; (b) reminding your friend that you have a new job, one that is much more demanding than your old one; or (c) letting it pass. My invariable response to provocation like this used to be (a). But for some reason, my hanging up the phone did not stop people from asking me if I enjoyed retirement. So I decided I needed to educate people. I began patiently explaining to my friends and family exactly what I did all day. Since most people think you ought to be able to write a book in six days if you put your mind to it, that didn't help. So I decided to accept the fact that salaried employees will never understand what it's like to run your own business. Although I'm tempted to invite them over to watch me during a typical day, I've decided to learn to live with their ignorance and remarks.

Darrel, a musician, gave up a teaching job to become a carpenter. One of his friends kept asking how he was enjoying his extended vacation, even though Darrel was working longer hours than he ever had when teaching. Darrel graciously handled the comments by smiling and telling a funny story or two about his day. Eventually his friend quit teasing him. I myself do not have Darrel's kind disposition, the ability to cultivate serenity not being among my attributes, but it certainly prevents him from wasting time getting frustrated with people who'll never understand.

The truth is, self-employed people are targets of envy, admiration, and suspicion. The envy is that you seem to be able to get up when you please, wear what you want to work, and take a day off if you wish. The admiration is that you have the self-discipline to actually go to your desk when you could take the day off. The suspicion is that they'd never be able to pull it off themselves.

They're right. It takes a lot of effort to be a small-business owner, especially one in a creative profession. You know that. But no one else does. So what can you do? You need to decide how much energy it's worth to get others to take you seriously. Clients should take you seriously. Friends and acquaintances? What's the point? It's a waste of energy. I do give close friends copies of my books as they come out so that said friends can see that I work for a living, as opposed to getting paid for just being me (which is what they appear to believe). But I've learned to disregard their comments.

As for my family, they take my work more seriously if I talk about what I do on a regular basis. Although I dislike discussing work, especially when I am in the delicate early stages of conceiving and creating, I have found that everyone is happier if I do talk about it. If I tell my husband which editors called today and what they wanted me to do, he gets a sense of what I do and feels connected to me. If I talk about frustrations as well as rewards, he knows my work is like any other job (only better).

It can be hard for others to understand the joys and challenges of creative small-business ownership. That's what professional and association groups are for—to meet other people who understand what it's like. Being a self-employed creative person can be enormously lonely and isolating. You can go an entire day without hearing another human voice. You can miss the teamwork of being an

employee. Or you might miss sitting in colleagues' offices drink-
ing coffee and discussing managers.

By joining professional or trade groups, you can meet like-
minded individuals, which makes you feel less isolated. You can
subscribe to newsletters or trade journals in your area of expertise
to help you feel connected and learn better ways to run your business. You can meet with people in similar situations.

Unfortunately, many aspiring writers and artists spend more
time talking to each other about writing or painting than they
actually spend doing it. Become a writer or painter first and then
find a support group for it!

Taking Your Work Seriously

But the key to having others take your work seriously is to take it
seriously yourself. During the day, I work at my business. That's
all I do. I don't do the dishes. I don't do the laundry. I don't take
the dogs to the vet. I work. When I've finished working, I do the
dishes and the laundry. One of the reasons I own a small business is to have the flexibility I could never get from an employer.
I love taking a few minutes now and then to play with my little
daughter—it's one of the rewards of doing what I do—but at the
same time, I employ a babysitter so that I can work uninterrupted
by my daughter's demands. Although I'm flexible, my work comes
first during working hours.

In my first year or two of freelancing, I had trouble with this.
I took my business seriously, but I didn't understand that that
meant not balancing the checkbook when I should be researching an article. Friends would call up to chat, and I would com-
plain to my husband that they never seemed to understand that I
was working. People constantly asked me for favors without doing anything in return. They assumed that I could babysit or run
errands or do whatever they needed because they were at work
and I wasn't. At first I put up with it, although I complained.
Then I realized that I needed to act like I was an employee. If I
had been in my office at the university, none of my friends would
have called up just to chat. I decided to start treating my home
office the same way. To let friends down gently, I began saying I

was in the middle of a project and would talk to them after they got home from work. Or I'd say I was expecting a phone call and had to hang up. This gave friends a chance to tell me if they needed something important, and also preserved our friendships. Now I rarely get a phone call from a friend or family member during the day unless it is business-related. I have gently but firmly insisted that people treat my time seriously.

On the other hand, interruptions such as salespeople at the door and telemarketers on the phone don't even deserve a civilized explanation. Just say "no," and hang up. If you were raised to be polite, say "No, thank you," and hang up. You don't need to say you're satisfied with AT&T. You don't need to say you never purchase products over the phone. You don't need to do anything but hang up the phone (or close the door). People do not have a right to interrupt you and demand your time when you have not invited them to do so. Don't expend effort or energy on these operations.

Saying No

Like other self-employed business owners, I found it hard to say no to people who wanted me to participate in different activities or events. Since your schedule is flexible, you'll be asked to become Girl Scout leader or handle the school fundraising drive. You may agree to these things because it's much easier to waste your time on PTA meetings than it is to actually sit down and create something worthwhile. But you have to decide what's important to you and get rid of everything else. You must think of yourself as a business owner with a limited number of hours in a given day, to be divided among your work, your family and personal life, and other important people and activities. So why are you baking cookies for the bake sale? If you absolutely had to contribute something, you could have bought some from the grocery store or designated your kid to do it. There are plenty of reasons we do these things (guilt, the desire to have a reason not to succeed), but the best way to handle these reasons is to quit buying into them. Just act like you don't feel guilty about saying "no," and pretty soon you won't. (Trust me, it works.)

Projecting a Professional Image

In order to convince others (i.e., clients) to take your business seriously, you must present a professional image. This doesn't mean that you need to wear Dior to meet with clients or dress in a business suit to sit at your phone and make sales calls. It simply means that your contacts with people must be handled in a professional manner and your work must show that you're a dedicated professional instead of an enthusiastic amateur.

Because almost all of my work happens at a desk with no witnesses, I don't have to worry about my appearance. I generally schlep around in jeans and a t-shirt. I never wear shoes. I frequently have muddy paw prints on my legs and often sport oatmeal on my shirt (courtesy of the toddler who shares my home). But when I answer the phone, I do so in a professional way. (Not, "Yeah?") I do not allow babysitters to answer the phone. I do not allow babies to answer the phone. If I have a daughter on my lap, I do not answer the phone just so she can screech into it and embarrass me. I don't necessarily make said daughter get off my lap, but I don't try to conduct business when the situation is not conducive to it.

If I don't answer the phone, the answering machine picks up. The answering machine also projects a professional message. People know I work from home (as most writers do), so there's no need to pretend otherwise, but by projecting the image of professionalism, I convince people to hire me and keep on hiring me.

Industry Standards

Every creative field has certain professional or industry standards. For writers, the standard industry practice is to query editors with letters. In general, writers don't e-mail or phone editors unless invited to. And editors aren't expected to defend their editorial decisions even if writers don't agree with them. Such details often seem minor, especially to outsiders. ("What does it hurt to call that editor to make sure she got my letter?") And that's why you need to know your profession or industry in order to succeed. That's why it's important to remember that whenever you make contact with potential clients, you should consider how you are perceived or judged. If you're a writer, you should do your best to produce error-free, well-written work no matter what the piece of writing concerns. This is how your professionalism is judged. Even if you're dashing off an e-mail, you have to remember that you're a writer. Therefore, no misspellings or sloppy sentence construction. It wouldn't matter that much if you were in a different business, but if you're describing yourself as a writer, every piece of writing is a walking advertisement.

One writer, describing a novel he was working on, told me that concern with grammar and "English stuff" was nonsense. His story was so good any editor would grab it. It would be easy for the editor to fix the grammar. I don't know what century this particular writer was living in (I can guarantee he's still unpublished if he hasn't mended his habits), but it's not the editor's job to fix the grammar. That's the writer's job. That's what a writer does. (Well, a writer does many other things, but a writer ought to know the language well enough to use it to write.)

Other creative business owners need to consider their image as well. A photographer must meet certain professional standards. When a bride-to-be arranges for a photographer to shoot her wedding, she expects the photographer to show up on time and have the necessary equipment and knowledge to take the photos with a minimum of fuss and disruption. If the wedding is a formal one, she expects the photographer to wear clothes that make him or her blend in. But a surprising number of photographers fail to follow these standards and therefore don't receive referral business.

In order to present a professional image, you need to understand the basic industry or business standards for the work you perform. If you're a writer, you need to know the appropriate ways to contact editors and negotiate pay. You need to meet deadlines that you've agreed to and turn in well-written, error-free manuscripts. That's the bare minimum. Meeting the industry standard doesn't make you good or excellent at what you do. It's the bare minimum. To be outstanding, you have to go beyond that.

In order to understand your business or industry, you must read trade journals and newsletters, meet professionals in the field (other amateurs are just guessing), and network with people you would like to have as your clients. That way you can understand firsthand what your clients need. You should also know the "language" of your industry. What do editors and writers negotiate besides pay? What is a writer really selling? A copyright. If you don't understand copyrights, you have no business selling yours. If you don't understand copyrights, you can't promise not to infringe on them, so you're no good to an editor.

At the same time, you have to be wary of misleading information. Wherever there are aspiring creative people, there are those who are willing to exploit them. The classified sections of writer's magazines are full of ads that read "Manuscripts Wanted." A reputable, royalty-paying publishing company doesn't need to advertise this way. Its name and contact information may appear in *Literary Market Place, Writer's Market,* or another such guide, since that is the purpose of those guides. Beyond that, steer clear of promises aimed at your dearest dreams, such as unscrupulous agents who promise to consider a manuscript if you pay hundreds of dollars in critiquing fees. Most people realize that Random House doesn't need to advertise for writers and that agents don't charge Stephen King hundreds of dollars to consider accepting his work, and they should realize that these are not opportunities. But in their desperation to get published, they'll take the chance.

If you consider yourself a professional, you'll avoid these traps. Remind yourself that professionals don't get desperate. If you want to find a publishing company that may be interested in your material, consult a market guide and submit to markets that accept unsolicited manuscripts. Or attend writer's conferences to make contact with the editors who are guests there. If you think your manuscript may need work before it's salable, seek help. But don't just blindly send a check off to someone who claims to have published sixteen books. (Believe me, just because I've published a couple of books doesn't make me qualified to advise you on your writing. You need to find an editor with experience in your field of writing.) Check first with local writing groups or the writing teacher at a local college. Get referrals and recommendations before seeking the help of a so-called book doctor. That's what professionals do.

Ignore the advice of people who don't know the business. One business magazine recently said that editorial services is a big field for people who work at home. The piece advised readers to take local publishers and newspaper editors out to lunch, ask what assignments they have, and find out how they select the writers whose work they publish. I laughed for ten minutes. I don't know a single editor who could be dragged to lunch with an unknown writer, even if the writer was buying. Newspaper editors have reporters, the AP wire, and plenty of press releases if they need written material. You have to prove to them that you're worth their time, and wasting it doesn't improve your chances. Editors give assignments to writers they trust; all others produce work purely on speculation. This means they write articles or features without the promise of publication or pay. Writers aren't chosen to be published, their work is chosen to be published. And it needs to be interesting, well-written, and somehow remarkable for an editor to choose it. If you can meet local editors and publishers by networking, by all means do so. But your writing is going to have to speak for itself.

The key to projecting a professional image is to educate yourself, consider the source of information (it should come from trusted professional and trade groups or established business owners), and focus on creating and maintaining a professional image.

Broadening Your Horizons

When creative people dream of what they want to do with their talent, they usually have a specific vision in mind. Perhaps they want to write poetry or photograph wildlife. This vision guides them as they make decisions throughout their lives. They might take classes to learn skills that are integral to pursuing the dream. They might gravitate toward other creative people. Then, when they decide to commit themselves to earning a living by their creativity, they get stubborn. If they want to be a poet, by golly, they're going to be a poet and nothing else. As anyone who has ever been a poet knows, this is a good way to starve.

At the same time, creative people often feel that if they worry about the money their work brings in, it will turn them into hacks or soulless automatons. It is this attitude that makes artistic work the poorest paid in the universe. It's as if being paid for your talent were shameful or unworthy of attention.

This of course is nonsense. Ask a basketball player. Talent is well-rewarded in every field of endeavor except for creative fields. If you have talent, you ought to use it. And if you've got talent and you're willing to use it, you're a rare enough person already, so you can expect people to pay you for it. Although most creative people are reluctant to talk about price ("how can you put a price on a little piece of your soul?" one marvels), the problem is that if you don't, someone else will set the price for you and it will be to their advantage, not yours. If you don't feel that you can negotiate with people about your talent, then you shouldn't attempt to make a living with your art. You should keep it as a fulfilling hobby.

But to get back to the case of the writer who is going to be a poet if it kills him. It is good to have determination and dedication. But being a poet is not an occupation that achieves material success. You will be lucky to get published. You will be luckier still to earn a dime for your efforts, let alone pay the rent. Although it might offend one's sensibilities to consider it, you might think about writing to fill a specific need. If you're a poet, you have a talent with the language. You're accustomed to creating an atmosphere with just a few words. You could write greeting cards with that ability. The funny thing is, sometimes when you apply your creativity in new and unusual ways, you find yourself rewarded for the experience. Although I'm not a poet (I would make a terrible poet), I once made $1,600 for a week's worth of work writing greeting card sentiments for a computer software company. With $1,600 I was able to fund an entire summer of writing morbid fiction (a stage I have fortunately outgrown).

It's a trade-off. Some people hold down full-time jobs, promising themselves that they'll pursue their art in their spare time. But after you attend to your job, your personal needs, and your family life, plus minimum amounts of sleeping and eating, it's not as if you have a lot of time left over for creativity. Sure, you can get up earlier in the morning or go to bed later at night. But I don't know very many creative people for whom that's enough, unless they're only a little bit creative. In order to get the time you need to pursue your creative goals, you have to find ways to make your creativity pay. Running a creative business frees you up to be creative. It keeps you in a creative mindset. It helps you make contact with people who can help you further your dreams. So if you're a poet who writes greeting card sentiments, it doesn't make you a sell-out or a lesser poet. It makes you a smart poet. It also frees you from the pressure of either keeping a deadly day job or trying to make your poetry pay, which is probably impossible. It means you don't have to become an academic and teach a bunch of vacant 20-year-olds the definition of iambic pentameter.

By broadening your horizons in this way, you'll be able to take your creativity more seriously and demand that others do the same. One artist describes how her family never took her art seriously and refused to listen to her requests for more time to work on her art—until she landed a freelance assignment that paid for a trip to Florida. Now they practically beg her to go work in her studio. Unfortunately, most people who aren't creative are like this; they don't take creative work seriously unless it's financially rewarding.

But it's true that you and those around you will take your creative work more seriously if you get paid for it. You will feel better about spending your time on creative work when it contributes to the family instead of taking away from it. And although you may not have envisioned writing greeting card sentiments when you penned your first haiku, there's nothing wrong with using your talent in different ways, depending on what a job requires. What's wrong is not using your talent at all.

Allowing Time for Creativity

The main drawback to running a business based on your creative talent is that it can sap your creativity. If you're constantly forced to produce writing or art on demand to meet certain deadlines, you can become drained and burned out. You have to guard against this by being careful not to overcommit yourself and by building time into your schedule for the creative work that you most enjoy but that may not bring in money.

Just as you schedule time to do administrative work in your business, you should set aside time to work on your creative projects as well. Of course, you may not be able to produce masterpieces in the three hours on Wednesday afternoon that you allot for the production of masterpieces, but the point is you must allow time for your own creative pursuits. Most creative people have certain times when they feel more creative than others. They may know that certain conditions are conducive to creativity. Try to duplicate these times and conditions when arranging your work schedule. Some people find that their best creative work is done late at night after everyone is in bed and can make no demands on them. They should allow time for this work by not scheduling appointments early in the morning; otherwise either they'll pass up the creative work in order to get some sleep or they'll be so tired after doing their creative work that their business suffers.

You also must give yourself permission to pursue creative work at unscheduled times. Perhaps you are about to update your general ledger when you notice that the sky is a spectacular color. You would be insane to sit down and work on the general ledger instead of painting.

However, you also need self-discipline to get your paying work done. While you can skip work tasks to pursue creative projects, it's no fair skipping the general ledger because you want to go eat an ice cream cone. The whole point of working in a creative business is to have time to work creatively, so make sure that such work remains a priority.

By broadening your horizons, you can make your creativity pay. By taking your work seriously and demanding that others do so as well, you can make your creative business a success. Investigate professional standards and always do your best to project a professional image when you're dealing with clients or potential clients and you will find yourself quickly building a satisfied clientele. And keep your creative fires burning by allowing time in your schedule for the creative work that's most important to you, whether it pays the bills or not.

16

Part-Time Small-Business Ownership

SOME PEOPLE try to balance small-business ownership with a full-time job. Since this requires even more juggling than full-time business ownership, you'll need some special help. Not only will you have to balance youe full-time and part-time jobs, but you'll also have to balance family, personal life, and other commitments and interests you might have.

There are several important aspects of part-time small-business ownership to consider. If you're simply pursuing a hobby, enjoy yourself and be sure to give yourself time to do it. But if you're pursuing a creative business—you want to publish the short stories you write or shoot photographs for pay—much of what has been described in this book applies to you. If you plan to run your business full-time someday, use your time now to get ready. Acquire clients, pick up the appropriate equipment, put aside a nest egg for those lean times that invariably come. Then pick a date to make the transition from part-time to full-time small-business ownership. It doesn't have to be this month or this year, but it should be a specific date. Not only will selecting the date help you focus and prepare for it, but it will also help prevent you from putting it off for the rest of your life because you're nervous about making it on your own.

Make the decision and then determine the actions necessary for it to happen. Setting a date and then daydreaming about success without doing anything to ensure it ultimately results in failure.

As you work toward your goal of full-time small-business ownership, think of what you can do to ease the transition. Are you at a job where you can negotiate a part-time or shared position so that in the beginning stages of your business ownership you will have some steady income? Is there some way your current employer could become a future client? What would you need to do to ensure that the company would hire you? Be sure to gain the experience you need now, while you have the opportunity.

It won't be easy (nothing worthwhile ever is), but make the most of the chance you have. If you decide you hate running your own business, you haven't lost anything. Let your creative work remain an important hobby, but don't turn it into a business. If you discover that you don't have the dedication to run your business part-time, you won't have the dedication to run it full-time. Be glad you discovered this now, and simply accept that different things work for different people. But if you work at it, you will be able to make the transition to full-time business ownership and use your creativity to make a living.

Some creative people always keep their day jobs. They find their regular work stimulating and interesting. Maybe they're in a creative industry already and don't feel the need to make any changes. Maybe they're a lawyer or a physician, and keeping in touch with what's happening in those worlds inspires them. For whatever reason, they keep their day jobs and work at their part-time business on the side. Both the part-timer who has no interest in becoming a full-time small-business owner and the part-timer who can't wait to quit her day job need some special help.

Finding Time for Creative Work

The most common complaint of the person who wants to work creatively but holds a full-time job is that there's never enough time. The difference between people who remain aspiring artists and people who become artists is that the latter find the time.

It's a simple decision, but it's one that you have to keep making over and'over. Sometimes it's hard to convince ourselves of how simple the decision really is. Here it is: You either commit to your creative work or you don't. If you don't, you'll never know what you might have made or what you might have become. If you do, you never have to have regrets. You may fail (not really a big deal), but you won't have regrets. So make the decision to commit to your creativity and then follow through.

Occasionally people ask me how I manage to do all that I do. (Sometimes these are the same people who think I sit in front of the television eating bonbons and watching soaps all afternoon.) From the time I was 27 to the time I was 32, I earned a PhD in medieval literature, achieved the rank of black belt in Tae Kwon Do, met and married a wonderful man, had a delightful daughter, and published three books, all the while teaching college English. Without a personal trainer, nanny, or executive assistant. The key? I didn't watch television. Television is the biggest time-wasting trap creative people face. You must unplug the beast and get on with life. (Not that I think you need to be productive every second of the day. But if you want to relax, relax. Take a walk. Read a book. Play fetch with the dog. *Don't* sit in front of the television.) Most people watch television a couple of hours a night. If you watch television just one hour a night, you're wasting time that could be used for your business or your creative work. Don't tell me that you have to watch the evening news in order to keep informed. Pick up the morning paper, give it fifteen minutes, and you'll learn all you need to learn. Hop online for five minutes and check out the headlines. For more in-depth information, subscribe to news weeklies like *Time* or *Newsweek,* or thoughtful monthlies like *World Press Review.* Take this reading material with you to a doctor's appointment or read it when you have to stand in line at the motor vehicle registration department. Just don't find excuses for watching television.

Yes, I know that you might need to refer to the nature documentary you're watching in some article you may write someday. Tape it. If you write an article about apes in the jungle, congratulations, you have a piece of research already done. If you want to write scripts for television, tape the shows worth emulating. Then watch them, zapping through the commercials, which will at least save you a couple of minutes. If you're really interested in writing scripts for television, you won't just watch the shows, you'll analyze them, so take notes. Watch the structure of the acts. Watch the punch lines and how they're set up. Don't just think, "I could do that!" Think how you could do better than that. Use your critical skills. Purchase and study scripts. Just don't sit in front of the television eating nachos and tell me you don't have time to be creative.

A few courageous souls out there have already unplugged the television but still don't have time to work creatively. Like many people, you're probably overcommitted. You work all day, so you feel guilty for not being with your kid, so you can't work while she's still awake, and once she's asleep, since you've been neglecting your husband, you need to spend some time with him, and now that you've accomplished that, you have to get the dishes washed and the laundry folded and put away. Then you're exhausted and you have an early meeting in the morning, so you go to bed, wishing you had time for the work that's important to you. Sound familiar?

It doesn't have to be like that. Making a few changes can free up time for you to use creatively. Maybe you can find a job that's closer to home so that your commute's not so long. Pay attention to your husband and kid at the same time, or designate one evening a week "kid night" and one evening a week "husband night," and the rest of the evenings "creative work nights." Sometimes simply rearranging your schedule makes all the difference. Instead of doing the dishes at night, do them in the morning just before you head off to work. Throw a load of laundry in the washer before you leave, and toss it in the dryer as soon as you get back from work. That's your load for the day.

Enlist Help

Enlist others to help you drop things off, pick things up, and recommend better approaches. An essential goal is to get your family, if you have one, involved in your business. Not only can they help by running errands for you, they can help by clearing time for you to write. They can juggle their schedules so that you have more free time to work creatively. They can also be persuaded to make fewer demands on your time. (You may have to insist at first.)

Different people will have different skills that you can put to use. My mother became my best salesperson when my first book was published. She went around to bookstores, checking to see if it was in stock and if not, why not. She told everyone she knew about the book and how good it was. She came to every book signing and made everyone else she knew come too. You probably have friends or coworkers (or a mother) who would be willing to help out as well. You can show your 6-year-old how to affix stamps or alphabetize paperwork. You can ask your next-door neighbor who's home all day to sign for packages. You can teach your dog to pick up dirty socks and drop them in the laundry basket. Be inventive and relax your standards. (If you have to redo everything you ask other people to do, you're not going to get anywhere, are you?)

Giving Up Other Activities

To juggle a part-time business with full-time work, you have to give some things up. When you're doing something that's not creative work, you must ask yourself whether what you're doing is more important than your creative work. If you're helping your child study for a test, maybe that is, for the moment, more important than creative work. After all, when you became a parent you knew there would be sacrifices. But there will be other things. You may have to give up home-cooked meals every night. You may have to quit your bridge group.

Perhaps you enjoy a hobby such as needlework or gardening. Is it more important than your creative work? You may have to give it up. You can't do and be everything, not if you want to commit to your creativity. Hire sitters, house cleaners, lawn-care companies. Become a little slack, a little slothful. Don't vacuum every other day. Vacuum once a week. Or twice a month. Or only when you can no longer tell whether the living room rug is beige or brown. Dust whenever you start sneezing from the mites and not a day before. Teach anyone who can learn how to do chores. The only chores you absolutely have to do are the cumulative ones, the ones that pile up, like laundry and dishes. Even then, *you* don't have to do them. Maybe your spouse can. Maybe you can alternate. Maybe you can trade housecleaning services for marketing materials.

Actively Creating

If you live by your own rules, you can carve time out of your life to dedicate to creating. But you must dedicate that time to your creative work. I recently read an essay by an aspiring writer who constantly felt that she had to choose between her children and her writing. She described how much she wanted to be a writer. She took classes and went to seminars. Then she told her tragic tale of attending a writer's workshop where a real live published author appeared. After the workshop, the real live published author planned to go to the local pub and continue talking about writing. His adoring acolytes were invited to follow. Said aspiring writer called to tell the babysitter she would be late, but her son, sick in bed, begged her to come home. She was torn. How could she be a writer if she had to go home to her sick son? But duty called. She left the real live published author and his acolytes and reluctantly comforted her son, presumably resenting him in the process. What's wrong with this story? Why doesn't it tug at my heartstrings? Why don't I recognize the conflict between being a mother and a writer, since it's one I live with every day? Because this is not about a conflict between being a mother and a writer. It's about a conflict between being a mother and wanting to hang out at a bar. Because, essentially, a writer writes. A writer doesn't go to workshops and talk about writing. A writer doesn't follow other writers around and talk about writing. A writer writes. Only after she is done writing and doesn't have anything better to do does she go to a workshop. There's a reason why the people at workshops are all *aspiring* writers. It's because writers write.

You shouldn't make sacrifices and carve time out of your life just so you can follow some guy in a black turtleneck to a pub and knock back a couple of Budweisers. Sure, there will be times when you need guidance. Sure, you'll need to network and ask people for advice and suggestions on how to market your work. But first of all you have to create something. Then you can think about who you're going to sell it to.

If you're working part-time at your creative work, this is a hard lesson to learn. Because it's easier to think about being creative than it is to actually be creative. After you've worked all day long and you've come home and fed the kids dinner and put the dogs out, you might be able to summon up the energy to go to a coffee shop to talk about writing, but you're probably going to have trouble convincing yourself that you should spend the next four hours trying to create something where there was nothing before. So if you're going to make a go of a part-time creative business, you must focus on the business. Don't expect to come home from work and relax. Expect to come home from work and do more work.

One musician, Dave, works at a gym every weekday beginning at 5 am. By two or three in the afternoon, he's off work. If he has a gig that night, he goes to bed, then wakes up in time to get ready. He plays, hangs out afterward, then goes to his job. He has actually arranged his work schedule so that he's at his freshest when doing his creative work. When he's done with his creative work, that's when he devotes attention to his full-time job.

Integrating Part-Time and Full-Time Work

If you have a full-time job, you'll need to integrate it with your part-time business. You may need to reach potential clients during business hours. What will you do? Can you devote your lunch hour to this? Can you switch your schedule around so that you're off at three and able to interview people for your articles before five, when they leave work? You'll have to save your vacation and sick days for those times when you have essential work to do for your business. (Of course, it's terribly dishonest to use sick days for your freelance work, so make sure you have the sniffles before taking time off to hunt down a quote you need.) Invest in a reference library in your home so that you don't have to figure out how to get the statistics you need between now and tomorrow morning, when you have to fax that article to the newspaper editor.

Make sure your part-time business doesn't cause a conflict of interest with your present employer. (This is a great way to get fired.) If you work full-time for an advertising agency and you're a part-time advertising consultant, you might make a few important people mad, making it difficult for you to acquire and keep clients. Therefore, quietly switch jobs, then hang your shingle out.

Addressing Client Concerns

Potential clients of your part-time business might think you can't perform work as well or as quickly as a full-time business owner could. This perception will be your biggest marketing obstacle. In some fields it's less important and less obvious than in others. You should never lie to a client or a potential client about the fact that you have a day job. They're bound to find out, and then they'll wonder what else you're lying about. (However, no one says you have to bring it up.) Some writers report more success with certain editors after they began working full-time at their businesses. Such clients like being able to call up at ten in the morning and assign something due at five that afternoon. Other clients want to feel that they can have your full attention whenever necessary, not just after you're done with your day job.

To overcome this difficulty, you must convince potential clients that you can do something no one else can because of your experience, talent, or unique perspective. You must also assure them that you're available to meet their needs. If you can't honestly promise your clients this, you may need to rethink the focus or market for your business. You may have to lower your rates or provide other incentives for potential clients to work with you.

Working part-time allows you not to panic if you don't sell anything right away or don't have a client first thing Monday morning. But it's important not to get discouraged. Think of your part-time business as an apprenticeship period, which all creative people must go through. If you have the talent and the dedication, you will succeed. Then you can take your business in any direction you want to grow.

Glossary

Account: The name for an entry in a bookkeeping or accounting record.

Accounts payable: Money owed by a person or business, but not yet paid.

Accounts receivable: Money earned by a person or business, but not yet received.

Accrual basis: A method of accounting that records expenditures when they are committed to and records income when it is earned. The other main accounting method is *cash basis.*

Amortization: Spreading out the cost of equipment and supplies over a lengthy period, usually to meet tax deduction requirements.

Assets: Everything a person or business owns.

Balance sheet: A financial record that shows the assets of a business on one side and liabilities and capital on the other. The totals on each side of the balance sheet are the same (they "balance").

Business license: A permit to operate a business, required of some businesses in some localities.

Capital: Equity or ownership interest in a business. The difference between assets and liabilities.

Cash flow: The amount of cash immediately available to meet business expenses.

Cash basis: A method of accounting that records expenditures when they are paid and records income when it is received. The other main accounting method is *accrual basis.*

Certificate of deposit: A safe investment tool; a depositor agrees to let a bank or other financial institution use his or her money for a set period of time for a specified interest rate.

Copyright: Ownership of a creative work, and the legal right to publish, sell, and distribute such work.

Corporation: A company with a business ownership arrangement that limits the personal liability of the owners.

Cost of sales: The direct cost of making a product to sell, including employees' wages.

Creditor: A person or business to whom payment for goods or services is owed.

Credits: See *Liabilities.*

DBA: "Doing Business As." A term applied to the fictitious name a business owner gives to his or her company.

Debits: See *Assets.*

Deduction: An expense that can be subtracted from earnings to reduce the amount of taxable income of a person or business.

Depreciation: The loss of value of goods that occurs over time, especially with goods such as cars and computers.

Expenses: Costs involved in running a business, including the purchase of goods and services, plus intangibles such as depreciation.

Fiscal year: A twelve-month period of business recordkeeping, usually the same as the calendar year.

General ledger: An accounting record that records income and expenses.

General liability: Potential legal obligation for damages to another person or someone's property.

General partnership: A type of business with two or more equal owners; the personal liability of the owners is not limited.

Gross earnings, income, or profit: Basically all the same thing. The amount received for a product or service in excess of the cost of goods.

Income: Money received in exchange for labor or services.

Income statement: A financial document that shows income and expenses for a specific period of time.

Individual retirement account: An investment fund for retirement needs with special tax advantages.

Insurance: Indemnity or promise of protection against loss offered in exchange for a specified amount of money (a premium).

Invoice: A bill or statement showing how much is owed for a service or product.

Liabilities: Money owed by a person or business.

Liability: A potential legal obligation.

Limited liability corporation: A form of business ownership that protects owners from personal liability but offers tax advantages over traditional corporate status.

Mutual fund: An investment tool consisting of groups of people investing in groups of companies. By spreading the risk, the safety of an individual investor's investment is increased.

Net earnings, income, or profit: Basically all the same thing. The amount of money earned after all expenses have been deducted. The term "net net profit" is sometimes used to indicate the amount of money earned after income taxes have been deducted.

Net worth: The value of a business after its liabilities are subtracted from its assets.

Operating capital: Money used to finance day-to-day business expenses; especially necessary at the start, when income does not meet expenses.

Outsourcing: Contracting with outside providers to deliver needed goods or services essential to the operation of a business.

Payables: See *accounts payable.*

Professional liability: Potential legal obligation for damages incurred while performing one's profession.

Profit-and-loss statement: See *income statement.*

Receivables: See *accounts receivable.*

Replacement value: The cost of purchasing new equipment should a loss occur, rather than the actual worth of a piece of equipment that may have depreciated since being placed in operation.

Revenue: All money generated by a business, including income for services, earnings from interest, or money from one-time sales of assets.

Risk reduction: The act of protecting assets from potential loss.

Royalty: Payment made to the creator of an artistic work each time a copy of the work is used or sold.

Sole proprietorship: The simplest type of business ownership, with a single owner in charge of all operations; the owner's personal liability is not limited.

Tax exemption: Special exclusion from paying certain types of taxes.

Write off: See *deduction.*

Resources

Trade Associations and Professional Groups

American Society of Journalists and Authors
    1501 Broadway, Suite 302
    New York, NY 10036
    (212) 997-0947
    www.asja.org

Authors Guild
    330 West 42nd Street
    New York, NY 10036
    (212) 268-1208
    www.authors-guild.org

Editorial Freelancers Association
    71 West 23rd Street, Suite 1910
    New York, NY 10010
    (212) 929-5400
    www.the-efa.org

Home Office Association of America
909 Third Avenue
New York, NY 10022
(800) 809-4622
www.hoaa.com

National Association of Home Based Businesses
10451 Mills Run Circle, #400
Owing Mills, MD 21117
(410) 363-3698
www.usahomebiz.com

National Association for the Self-Employed
2121 Precinct Line Road
Hurst, TX 76054
(800) 232-6273
www.nase.org

National Writers Union
113 University Place, Sixth Floor
New York, NY 10003
(212) 254-0279
www.nwu.org/nwu

Service Corps of Retired Executives
409 Third Street SW, Fourth Floor
Washington, DC 20416
(800) 634-0245
www.sbaonline.sba.gov

Small Business Administration
409 Third Street, SW
Washington, DC 20416
(800) 827-5722. Check phone book for local office.
www.sba.gov/starting

Writers Guild of America East
    555 West 57th Street
    New York, NY 10019
    (212) 767-7800
    www.wga.org

Writers Guild of America West
    7000 West Third Street
    Los Angeles, CA 90048
    (213) 951-4000
    www.wga.org

Insurance Resources

Independent Insurance Agents of America
    127 South Peyton
    Alexandria, VA 22314
    (800) 261-4422
    www.iiaa.org

Insurance Information Institute
    110 William Street
    New York, NY 10038
    (800) 331-9146 or (212) 669-9200
    www.iii.org

National Insurance Consumer Hotline
    (800) 942-4242

Recommended Reading

General

1001 Ways to Market Your Books. John Kremer (Open Horizons Publishing)
Children's Writer's and Illustrator's Market. (Writer's Digest Books)

Collection Techniques for Small Business. Gini Graham Scott
    and John J. Harrison (Oasis Press)
Complete Idiot's Guide to Finance and Accounting. Michael
    Muckian (Simon and Schuster)
Encyclopedia of Associations. Annual (Gale Publishing)
Fearless Creating. Eric Maisel (Putnam)
Freeing Your Creativity. Marshall Cook (Writer's Digest Books)
Guide to Manuscript Formats (Writer's Digest Books)
How to Get Ideas. Jack Foster (Berrett-Koehler Publishing)
Idea Catcher. Editors of Story Press (Story Press)
Photographer's Market. (Writer's Digest Books)
Songwriter's Market. (Writer's Digest Books)
Writer's Guide to Book Edit…. Jeff Herman (Prima)
Writer's Market. (Writer's Digest Books)

Business Magazines

Entrepreneur Magazine
Independent Business
Working at Home
plus local and regional business magazines, newsletters, and
    newspapers

Advertising Trade Magazines

American Demographics
Art Direction
Marketing Tools
Potentials in Marketing
Signcraft

Art Trade Magazines

Airbrush Magazine
Applied Arts
Art Business News
Arts Management

How
Letter Arts Review

Business Management Trade Magazines

Communication Briefings
Small Business News

Desktop Publishing/Graphics Trade Magazines

Computer Graphics World
Desktop Publishers Journal

Entertainment Trade Magazines

Amusement Business
Backstage West
Boxoffice Magazine
Callboard
Hollywood Reporter
Stage Directions

Journalism/Writing Trade Magazines

Authorship
Editor and Publisher
Freelance
Poets and Writers
Small Press Review
The Writer
Writer's Digest

Marketing Trade Magazines

Art Materials Today
The Crafts Report
Educational Dealer

Events Business News
Sales and Marketing Strategies and News

Music Trade Magazines

Recording
Songwriter's Monthly

Photography Trade Magazines

Commercial Image
News Photographer
Photo Editors Review
Photo Lab Management
Photo Review
Photographic Processing
The Rangefinder

Index